INSTITUTIONAL RESEARCH AND PLANNING IN HIGHER EDUCATION

Globalization, demographic shifts, increases in student enrollments, rapid technological transformation, and market-driven environments are altering the way higher education operates today. *Institutional Research and Planning in Higher Education: Global Context and Themes* explores the impact of these changes on decision support and the nature of institutional research in higher education. Bringing together a diverse set of global contributors, this volume covers contemporary thinking on the practices of academic planning and its impact on key issues such as access, institutional accountability, quality assurance, educational policy priorities, and the development of higher education data systems.

Karen L. Webber is Associate Professor in the Institute of Higher Education at the University of Georgia, USA.

Angel J. Calderon is Principal Advisor of Planning and Research at RMIT University, Australia.

INSTITUTIONAL RESEARCH AND PLANNING IN HIGHER EDUCATION

Global Contexts and Themes

Edited by Karen L. Webber and
Angel J. Calderon

Routledge
Taylor & Francis Group

NEW YORK AND LONDON

First published 2015
by Routledge
711 Third Avenue, New York, NY 10017

and by Routledge
2 Park Square, Milton Park, Abingdon, Oxon, OX14 4RN

Routledge is an imprint of the Taylor & Francis Group, an informa business

Library of Congress Cataloging-in-Publication Data

Webber, Karen L. (Karen Lynne)
    Institutional research and planning in higher education : global contexts and themes / by Karen L. Webber and Angel J. Calderon.
        pages cm
    Includes bibliographical references and index.
    1. Universities and colleges—Planning.   I. Calderon, Angel J.
II. Title.
    LB2805.W34 2015
    378.1′07—dc23
    2014039694

ISBN: 978-1-138-02143-3 (hbk)
ISBN: 978-1-315-77772-6 (ebk)

Typeset in ApexBembo
by Apex CoVantage, LLC

Printed and bound in the United States of America by Publishers Graphics, LLC on sustainably sourced paper.

CONTENTS

Foreword by Randy L. Swing   *viii*

Preface   *xi*

Acknowledgments   *xv*

SECTION I

Institutional Research in Context   **1**

1   Institutional Research, Planning, and Decision Support
in Higher Education Today   3
Angel J. Calderon and Karen L. Webber

2   Institutional and Educational Research in Higher Education:
Common Origins, Diverging Practices   16
Victor M.H. Borden and Karen L. Webber

3   Transnational IR Collaborations   28
Charles Mathies

SECTION II

**National and Regional Context of
Institutional Research**   **41**

4   Institutional Research and Planning in Higher Education
in the United States and Canada   43
Gerald W. McLaughlin, Richard D. Howard, and Sandra Bramblett

5 Institutional Research in Europe: A View from the
European Association for Institutional Research 58
Jeroen Huisman, Peter Hoekstra, and Mantz Yorke

6 Decision Support Issues in Central and Eastern Europe 71
Manja Klemenčič, Ninoslav Šćukanec, and Janja Komljenovič

7 Institutional Research in the UK and Ireland 86
Steve Woodfield

8 Strategic Planning and Institutional Research:
The Case of Australia 101
Marian Mahat and Hamish Coates

9 Institutional Research in South Africa in the Service of
Strategic and Academic Decision Support 115
Jan Botha

10 Institutional Research in Latin America 128
F. Mauricio Saavedra, María Pita-Carranza, and Pablo Opazo

11 Institutional Research in Asia 139
Jang Wan Ko

12 Institutional Research and Planning in the Middle East 147
Diane Nauffal

SECTION III
Themes of Institutional Research Practice **157**

13 Business Intelligence as a Data-Based Decision Support
System and Its Roles in Support of Institutional
Research and Planning 159
Henry Y. Zheng

14 Strategic Planning in a Global University:
Big Challenges and Practical Responses 174
Julie Wells

15 In Light of Globalization, Massification, and Marketization:
    Some Considerations on the Uses of Data in
    Higher Education   186
    Angel J. Calderon

16 Toward a Knowledge Footprint Framework:
    Initial Baby Steps   197
    Anand Kulkarni, Angel J. Calderon, and Amber Douglas

17 The Evolution of Institutional Research: Maturity
    Models of Institutional Research and Decision Support
    and Possible Directions for the Future   213
    John Taylor

18 Eyes to the Future: Challenges Ahead for Institutional
    Research and Planning   229
    Karen L. Webber

Contributors   *238*
Index   *245*

FOREWORD

Like many individuals involved in the study and management of higher education, my learning curve continued a strong upward slope in the years following the completion of my doctoral studies. That was particularly true in developing and valuing a global perspective on postsecondary education. I was fortunate to have a comparative higher education class in graduate school taught by a visiting international professor as part of a program that valued global perspectives. The years after graduate school provided rich opportunities to work in higher education settings around the world—Australia, Scotland, England, United Arab Emirates, Japan, Canada, South Africa, and more. As preface to this volume on the internationalization of institutional research (IR), I wish to share perspectives and hopes for the global future of the field.

As documented in this book, many aspects of institutional research are shared globally. Shifts in demographics, financial constraints, international competition, and new technologies impact higher education worldwide. Such changes—often referred to as "disruptive innovations" because they force higher education professionals to rethink even core organizational functions—occur against a background of greater expectations for colleges, universities, and technical institutions. The demand for informed and skilled workers and citizens has never been greater. As the stakes rise, so does public interest in knowing that these institutions are up to the challenge.

The United States is the birthplace of the field of institutional research. It was created to address the specific structures, management decisions, and needs for data-informed decisions of the American higher education model. Since the mid-1960s it has proven to be indispensable as a management tool and catalyst for the academy in the United States. Key to that success is the close match of IR structures to the management decisions faced by higher education leaders. The caution in this tale is that each country's unique higher education model demands that IR be shaped for that model. It would be a huge mistake to "copy and paste" the American model elsewhere with the assumption of fit. The astute reader will find subtle (and in some cases, glaring) differences in the expectations for IR in the countries spotlighted in this book. Effective IR is intrinsically aligned with the decision-making culture, and unique societal issues, of the institutions it serves. To paraphrase an oft-used quote about politics—"All IR is local." As such, transporting, without translating, IR practices across countries should be avoided.

Still, there is a great deal of common ground and opportunity for sharing and networking that easily crosses national borders. The basic toolkit of IR—longitudinal studies, setting data in context, measures of central tendency, designing controlled research in real-world settings, and the like—can readily be shared among IR practitioners no matter their work locations. The smart development of IR around the world rightfully calls for international sharing of good practices, as highlighted in this book.

Another commonality is the purpose of IR as decision support and the natural tension between basic research and action research that defines the field. In some countries, the roles of institutional researcher and scholarly researcher are differentiated to a larger degree than in other countries. This phenomena is represented by the degree to which associations, conferences, and professional journals have developed to accommodate unique segments of the larger research community. Plainly stated, higher education needs a wide range of research including exploratory, experimental, theoretical, and applied. Viewing research forms as a continuous variable, rather than as dichotomies, offers greater insight about the value, opportunity, and numerous paths that develop when working with raw data and seeing them through to data-informed decisions that improve the academy.

What brings the international IR community together is the focus on institutional improvement. Fortunately, the field has avoided "bottom-line thinking" of improving the academy just for the sake of academics themselves. The international focus on improving the success of students and transfer of value to the sponsoring society is as basic to the field of institutional research as our grounding in the scientific method. The intention of creating public good is a shared foundational principle of IR that easily crosses international borders.

The sense of urgency that permeates the field of institutional research is nearly ubiquitous. The cliché conclusion of journal articles that "more research is needed" (no matter how accurate the statement) underestimates the test for decision support that operates in real-world, real-time settings. While it may be true that few decisions about institutional structures qualify as life or death events, institutional researchers are keenly aware of the positive impact that our work can create. And it is because of that knowledge that we hold ourselves accountable for pushing the boundaries of institutional research as quickly as we can.

The success of IR in meeting our self-imposed highest aspirations for the field is supported by the core idea of this book—sharing knowledge for our mutual success. The field of IR has long been notable for the value placed on networking and sharing of ideas and methods. The Association for Institutional Research, the prominent professional home for IR practitioners, established a network of affiliated organizations that quickly dotted the globe. These affiliated organizations provide crucially important linkages and support as IR develops in countries around the world. And once the field is well established, they become even more important as trusted pathways for networking and knowledge exchange.

The current state of IR, and certainly the future of the field, is best understood as an international collaboration. International engagement through our commonalities and unique responses to international variations makes the IR field stronger. Such engagement is personally satisfying, and advances our profession. But most importantly, it benefits the people we seek to serve—our students and sponsoring societies.

Randy L. Swing
Executive Director,
Association for Institutional Research

PREFACE

The practice of institutional research and planning is an important part of the decision support process in higher education across the globe. In some regions it enjoys a long history, now an established contributor to the institution's planning process, while in other regions it is a relatively new administrative unit that is positioned for continued growth and success. The responsibilities broadly assumed by professionals as institutional research, planning, and/or quality assurance are key to decision makers. In this book, we have assembled a wide range of views from leading practitioners across the globe. These authors reflect on their many years of experience in the field and they shed a light on the past, present, and future as well as institutional research and implications for higher education, generally. We live in an age where rapid increases in student enrollments, technology, knowledge transformation, and globalization have required institutional leaders to consider their role and position in higher education of the future. The collected views expressed in this book will resonate anywhere there is an institution considering the impact of changes occurring in higher education broadly as well as its impact on one's home institution.

For those engaged in higher education planning, one common characteristic that identifies (or even makes us bond together) is the fact that we look inward, but we also look outward to interpret, reflect, and understand what is occurring around us. Reflection has been an important feature of education; hopefully this is a good thing for all—the state, civil society, and market forces.

Purpose of This Book

This is a book to be used as a tool to help practitioners consider their role and how they can transform the nature and practice of institutional research through reflection—as richly manifested by the variety of views and perspectives offered in these pages. This is not a book about the mechanics of IR, but rather a book that seeks to encourage debate on the contribution of IR and planning to higher education. Of late, IR as a field of study within higher education (HE) has been receiving more attention from students, faculty members, and policy makers. In part, this is due to the growing interest in the field as a decision support function within HE, but also because IR *is* about exploring, understanding, and explaining the institution and *for* the institution. This is a point that we seek to emphasize time and again throughout this book. In regions or institutions where IR is relatively new, it may take on important tasks related to data collection, data management, and reporting of basic accountability information to senior leaders. As leaders see the value of the IR practitioners in their ability to transform data into usable information within the context of broader HE issues and specifics of the institution, IR can be transformed to assist in decisions or empower change in a broader and deeper way. As leading practitioners and scholars in their fields, authors in this book have championed the IR cause and their insights are invaluable in shaping the nature and practice of IR; as a consequence, the discussion strengthens IR and individual and institutional capability for sound decision making. As a field of practice, IR consists of a set of applied but defined functions within an institution. IR is also about collaboration and supporting decision and policy makers as they navigate their way through HE. It is also about exploring new frontiers and considering the future of institutions, systems of education, and the forces that shape society and the economy.

Broad Themes and Book Structure

The structure that this book follows is straightforward: section 1 discusses the range of roles and descriptors for IR and offers some broad perspectives and challenges of IR to generate thinking about IR from a global viewpoint. Chapters in section 1 cover what tasks are typically included in the practice of IR, how it relates to educational research, how it can contribute to higher education, and how institutions and systems are collaborating and sharing data across borders in light of globalization. In section 2 we focus on the practice of IR and planning across countries and world regions. Decisions had to be made about coverage and the chapters that are presented herein analyze and reflect on themes and issues that are occurring right now. Authors present general higher education themes, issues, and dilemmas experienced in these countries/regions but, most importantly, they channel these reflections through the lens of IR and planning perspectives. There is richness in each of these chapters, and we encourage the reader to navigate through the chapters as desired. These chapters speak independently, have their own identity, but are woven together through the lens of institutional research as expressed in that country or region. In section 3, we provide some examples in the practice and nature of IR. In addition to considering the past and the present, these chapters explore possibilities for strengthened practice in the future.

Chapters in section 3 focus not only on the main tenets of institutional research, but also seek to provide guidance to practitioners, decision makers, and academics on the future of IR. Anyone who reads the book from beginning to end will not only journey through all world regions but will also navigate through many critical themes and current issues that resonate in the field of higher education policy and management.

Audience of This Book

While this is a book that focuses on the nature and practice of institutional research and planning, it has a significant focus on institutional management within higher education. This is also a book that it speaks to the policy analyst or the observer of developments in education (either in government or in education-related agencies or in any postsecondary institution). There are three primary audiences for this book:

- Higher education officials who work primarily as administrative practitioners in the areas of institutional research, academic assessment/quality assurance, academic planning, and institutional effectiveness.
- Faculty members in the fields of higher education policy and management as well as academic researchers in the fields of educational research (and those affiliated through research centers concerned with the study of higher education and postsecondary education policy in general).
- Students who are enrolled in graduate-level courses in institutional research, strategic planning, and related courses in higher education administration.

A Vision for the Future

We hope that the IR discourse presented in this book speaks to all readers, regardless of geography, system, or institutional characteristics, for furthering and deepening the knowledge base of what we all do to advance institutions and national systems. Above all, we hope that this book contributes to the debate on how IR and planning advances higher education globally.

Higher education has been undergoing a significant transformation over recent decades. Examples of the transformation include the increased numbers of students entering higher education (which now exceed 200 million globally and are projected to exceed 500 million by 2035), the emergence of new institutions and forms of delivery, and the increased recognition of HE to economic development. In reality HE has always been undergoing transformation of one form or another, except that the wave of reform seems to be gathering greater pace in a globalized world.

Some observers argue that HE is in a flux and that many of the world's universities and colleges will disappear as a consequence of online education, emerging technologies, new modes of educational delivery, new and emerging institutions, and government reform. In the 1980s, predictions were made that 10 to 30% of the more than 3,100 higher education institutions (HEI) in the United States would close their doors by 1995 (Keller, 1983). Reality is that the number of HEIs in the United States increased by 29% from 3,559 in 1990–91 to 4,599 in 2010–11 (US Department of Education, 2013). Worldwide, there were more than 22,000 HEIs in 2014 (www.webometrics.info/en). What the future holds for higher education is hard to predict, other than to reinforce the view that change will continue.

We believe in the future of higher education, and we are excited about the positive contribution that IR makes to support institutions and systems of post-secondary education globally. What we have witnessed over the past 50 years has been a democratization in terms of both students having access to HE and an increase in the number of institutions offering postsecondary education programs; even new institution types and delivery modes have emerged and succeeded. In many countries, HE is becoming universal in terms of access—a college or university degree is now a prerequisite for many occupations. We have also witnessed that globalization has gained a stronghold in every facet of human activity. To the extent that change continues to occur in higher education, the field of institutional research and planning as a decision support and as a set of defined functions will continue to evolve.

References

Keller, G. (1983). *Academic strategy: The management revolution in American higher education.* Baltimore, MD: Johns Hopkins University Press.

US Department of Education, National Center for Education Statistics. (2013). *Digest of education statistics, 2012.* Washington, DC: National Center for Education Statistics.

ACKNOWLEDGMENTS

This book was made possible by the enthusiastic interest from Routledge editor Heather Jarrow, who not only embraced but also supported our proposal from the start. We are grateful for her professional guidance and encouragement during this endeavor. We also express our thanks to the production team at Routledge.

To our colleagues around the world who contributed to this volume, we extend our gratitude and thanks. Without you and your experiences in regions far and wide, we could not have amassed the information. Readers of this book will have a fuller understanding of how institutional research has grown in our globalized world of higher education.

We also thank our work colleagues at the University of Georgia and RMIT University, who listened to us during our moments of doubt and encouraged us to march on with this enterprise. We express our particular thanks to Ms. Anne Sidner in the Institute of Higher Education at the University of Georgia for her assistance with manuscript preparation.

We thank our families for allowing us time to devote to this project when attention to their needs may have been preferred. They are patient with us, and they know we love both our families and our work.

SECTION I

Institutional Research in Context

1

INSTITUTIONAL RESEARCH, PLANNING, AND DECISION SUPPORT IN HIGHER EDUCATION TODAY

Angel J. Calderon and Karen L. Webber

Introduction

Tasks related to institutional research (IR) have existed as long as there have been institutions of higher learning. The term IR has only been in vogue since the late 1950s, when IR offices began to be established across institutions in the US (Reichard, 2012). Many of the functions attributed to IR have evolved in parallel to the evolution and transformation of institutions of higher learning across centuries. Every turn of the decision making process at any institution has required some kind of evidence or an argument that brings validity or legitimacy for any proposal under consideration. While it may be spurious to argue that the concept of IR existed in the medieval university, or in the early university of the modern period of the English, German, or French models, it is feasible to argue that the practice and the nature of what is considered IR has been an active part of the modern university, particularly after World War II. The roots of IR reside in the United States, where its practice is clearly identified in terms of its roles, functions, and professional endeavors (Calderon & Mathies, 2013; Saupe, 1990). The term IR has greater salience in the US, Australia, United Kingdom, and in the European countries, but it is increasingly recognized in other regions of the world.

When considering IR, it is also useful to reflect on the term higher education (HE), as it has only been in use in recent decades. While the idea of what a university means is broadly understood, the term higher education is less understood as it encompasses a variety of institutions, and it may have different connotations across borders (Gibbs & Barnett, 2014). Not every higher education institution (HEI) is a university, but every university is a higher education institution. Across jurisdictions and national systems of education there are vast differences in the composition, governance structure, and funding arrangements of HEIs and that makes a single IR typology rather impossible. If there are differing perspectives or understandings of the kind of institutions that educate people at the highest level of education, it is therefore equally fitting to ponder what we mean by institutional research.

In this chapter, we ponder on the notion of IR and the kind of decisions it supports for the advancement of institutions and national higher education systems. We also offer some thoughts on the global practice of IR in light of the rapid technological transformation; the changing societal expectations on higher education; the purposes HE serves for the development of regions, countries, and international relations; and the role that IR plays in supporting these drivers of change.

Seamless Institutional Research

It is not our intent to delve deeply into the discourse of what is IR, as the available literature indicates a broad consensus on its accepted scope (e.g., Howard, McLaughlin, & Knight, 2012; Klemenčič & Brennan, 2013). Further, several chapters in this book illustrate the practice of institutional research and planning from a global perspective. The most widely used definition of IR is that by Joe Saupe (1990), which describes IR "as the sum of all activities directed at empirically describing the full spectrum of functions (educational, administrative, and support) at a college or university, which are used for the purposes of institutional planning, policy development, and decision making" (p. 1). In essence, IR is viewed as a set of functions, activities, and roles that practitioners perform in order to assist decision makers in formulating well-versed or evidence-based decisions. The sorts of decisions that IR supports can range from day to day operational activities or strategic-oriented activities that have a short- or long-lasting impact on an institution or system. IR is the sum of activities that aim to explore the intricacies of an institution—including its origins, where it is and where it is going, and understanding its sets of relations within the wider social, economic, and geographical context in which it operates and has a reach. From an IR perspective, the study and research of institutions is channeled through the various lenses of actors, activities, purpose, and other elements that characterize institutions.

Fincher (1985) described IR as a specialized administrative function and fittingly styled its practitioners as organizational intelligence specialists. In considering the existing literature on the foundations and practice of IR, IR offices are seen as the engine rooms of the university; developers of policy-related research and research-led policy, and catalysts for institutional change. Fincher's work prompted Terenzini (1993) to consider the forms of personal and professional competence, institutional understanding and knowledge needed for effective IR practice. Discussed in other chapters of this book, Terenzini identified three tiers: technical and analytical—*Tier 1*, issues intelligence—*Tier 2,* and contextual intelligence—*Tier 3.* In his latest consideration of the tiers, Terenzini (2013) observes that Tier 1 still applies today in its entirety; Tier 2 remains valid but requires expansion in light of technological advances, knowledge acceleration, globalization, and progresses in every facet of human activity; and Tier 3 requires a broader focus and a heavier emphasis on the importance of awareness and analysis of an institution's state, national, and international environments.

We concur with Terenzini's (2013) broadening of the parameters canvassed under each tier. Other researchers have also advocated such an approach (for example, Calderon, 2011; Klemenčič & Brennan, 2013). Calderon (2011) argues that IR practitioners are now playing an active and visionary role in developing strategy and assessing the long-term positioning for institutions and national systems. We believe that the greater awareness of issues that affect IR are critical to the strength of the profession today. This comes through experience in the field, keeping abreast of the latest scholarly literature, contemplation of the literature, and collaboration with peers on how IR professionals can provide effective decision support at their institution.

So What Then Is IR?

There are a variety of approaches to defining and viewing IR as a whole. As a way of illustration, some approaches as highlighted in existing literature are noted below:

- *Purpose:* Volkwein (1999; 2008) and Serban (2002) define it on the basis of purpose. They identified five functions/faces of IR: largely as information analyst, then as policy analyst, 'spin doctor,' scholar/researcher. These last four functions are deemed secondary to the information analyst function and Huisman (2013) poses the question whether this is problematic for IR in that it appears as being inward-looking.
- *Functions:* Dressel (1981) defines IR as linking what decision makers need to know about an institution and all of what that pertains (objectives, purposes, and processes).
- *Mission:* Thorpe (1999) defines it on the basis of the use of mission statements by IR offices as a communication vehicle to define tasks and functions.
- *Services:* Maasen (1986) defines it on the basis of the services IR provides, which he characterizes in terms of collecting data on institutional performance, collecting data on the institutional environment, analyzing and interpreting data collected, and transforming it into information for decision support in planning and management. Also, Delaney (2009) defined it on the basis of services with IR practitioners serving as higher education industry knowledge analysts, and functioning as knowledge brokers.
- *Role of individuals:* Swing (2009) sees that an expanded role for IR practitioners is to actively engage in the process of managing and leading institutional change.

Invariably, the way IR is performed depends on the environment that prevails within the HEI and within the boundaries where institutions operate. Across the globe, governments have enacted legislation for institutions to provide information about how institutions spend public funds and how HEIs are transforming the lives of those people who benefit. In many ways, the central role of IR has been cemented through these legislated requirements for institutions to provide information on the evidence of effectiveness. Historically, IR and planning offices have been charged with responsibility in extracting, validating, and reporting institutional data. Having access to information, tools, and methods for analysis has underpinned the foundation for IR to undertake a range of studies to better understand institutional performance as well as provide foundation for institutional repositioning and setting strategic directions. These are a few of the many common threads that define the practice of IR and planning whether it is undertaken in an institution based in North America, Europe, Latin America, or Asia.

Some of what we know about institutional research comes from several multistate and national surveys conducted in the 1980s and 1990s, gathering information from members of the international and regional groups for the Association of Institutional Research (Knight, Moore, & Coperthwaite, 1997; Lindquist, 1999; Muffo, 1999; Volkwein, 1990). The most recent survey was conducted in 2008–09 by Volkwein and colleagues, and similar surveys have been completed in Japan, Africa, and the Middle East (Ehara, Volkwein, & Yamada, 2010; El Hassan & Cinali, 2010).

In the US and Canada, survey responses were received from over 1,100 IR offices containing over 3,300 professional staff (Volkwein, 2011). The survey found that 38% of these units in colleges and universities have office names including traditional terminology like "institutional research," "analysis," "information," "reporting," or "studies." A second large group (35%) reported office names including words like "assessment," "accountability," "accreditation," "evaluation," "effectiveness," and "performance." There is a wide array among these units of other names and combinations of names with "planning" and "IR." Institutional researchers and IR functions are also embedded in offices of strategic planning, enrollment management, budget, policy analysis, information technology, and the registrar.

In this chapter and throughout the full book, the terms "institutional research" or "IR" encompass all of these variations. Moreover, whatever is called institutional research is not limited to higher education institutions. We know from these surveys that foundations, government bureaus, state education departments, and research-oriented organizations of many varieties also hire people with training in research and analysis.

Other studies on the practice of IR (e.g., Delaney, 2009; Leimer & Terkla, 2009) highlight that while there may be common aspects that IR practitioners perform (such as institutional reporting, data analysis, and interpretation), the range of activities that IR and planning offices perform may depend on the institutional type (e.g., research intensive, regional-focused, community- or world class-oriented), or whether such HEI is private, for-profit, or public. Ultimately, the purpose, functions, activities, services, roles, and mission of IR is determined by institutional decision makers. IR is what serves best or fits the purpose of institutions and this is what then defines IR within an institution. The intrinsic measures of relevance and success of IR is by its service delivery and capacity in supporting decision making at the institutional level, and its impact within the institution and its operational jurisdiction (either within a region, nation, or across-borders). The above information shows that there is not an easy way to describe what the typical IR office generally does, nor what it is expected to perform. However, there is a blend of tasks, roles, and functions that come together to define institutional research in higher education.

Forces of Change

So much has been said about the forces of change that are rapidly transforming higher education: globalization, demographic shifts, rapid technological transformation are among many drivers. These key drivers are having an impact on every facet of human activity. Technology has increased the accessibility to timely data and the capacity for analysis to support decision making. Globalization in context has exponentially increased the mobility of people and skills, capital, trade flow between countries, borderless diffusion of knowledge, and production chains. Demographic shifts have widened diversity in the student mix. All these changes are influencing the way HEIs are perceived to benefit society.

It is the convergence of the different competing demands from the state, the civil society, and market forces that are determining the future of HE (Dill, 2014; Pusser, 2014). Governments expect that HEIs contribute to their public policy objectives, and their mechanisms to effect these is through the funding arrangements and other instruments at their disposal to ensure compliance with the array of demands placed on HEIs. The space that HEIs occupy in society in general is considered important to economic development, but the alliances between HEIs and a variety of associations and interest groups are dispersed (and these can conflict with the stated mission of HEIs). Further, the adoption of market-driven mechanisms to support and develop HE is shifting the dynamics in how institutions operate, behave, and interact with its various stakeholders and strategic actors.

As a consequence of these competing demands and the increased competition for resources and recognition, there are growing tensions arising about the relevance, viability, and legitimacy for HEIs. This posits the question about the extent to which institutions are able to adapt their strategic mission to fulfill these differing demands. There is a range of views on this matter on the institutional effectiveness of adaptation—exploring these is outside the scope of this chapter. Over the years, universities have adapted to change, reform, and, more importantly, there has been not only a 'democratization' of education in terms of increased number of students but also of institutions of higher learning. All of these drivers and developments are adding a layer of complexity to the nature of work in general, and it has resulted, in our view, in a strengthened role for the practice of IR, planning, and decision support in institutions. In this regard, we see that the role of IR is not only to collaboratively assist decision makers in navigating through these complexities but also for IR practitioners to be agents of change for the advancement of institutions and national systems. The ability for IR practitioners to interpret, adapt, and influence policy makers is vital for their ongoing professional success.

While the need for general knowledge about higher education remains the foundational dimension for the work IR practitioners and planners perform (Terenzini's Tier 1), it is one that can be underestimated by many given the attention to detail and technical expertise that is required. The more information that is collected, the greater the complexities in managing it, and yet it exponentially widens the scope for analysis and it provides an opportunity for exploring new possibilities and for fostering institutional innovation. We are of the view that for this innovation to occur not only requires IR practitioners to have a very good understanding of the data, but also the ability to interpret and draw inferences about a variety of internal and external data sources. Furthermore, it also requires that decision makers provide support, vision, and commitment in resources for the objectives institutions seek to achieve. IR practitioners need to develop and enhance their skills so they are effective in combining qualitative and quantitative approaches in the fulfillment of their professional duties. It also requires them to have a good understanding of public policy, and the forces of change that have an impact on HE.

As discussed above, IR activities are not all confined to the domain of an office of institutional research or planning. IR activities are often undertaken in other administrative or functional areas of institutions (for example, marketing, international recruitment, and academic services). It is often the case that analysis of faculty and staff are undertaken through the office of human resources; or analysis of student retention or student progress are completed through offices that manage learning and teaching activities, student services, or other related areas. The same can be said about analysis of research output and impact that is often undertaken by the grant or research offices. The separation of these activities largely depends on the organizational structure of institutions and cultural influences. For an effective institutional research agenda to advance an institution's strategic direction, it is desirable and is often the case to have regular liaison or coordination of effort between these various functional areas.

Balancing IR Expectations and Tensions

Given the variety of roles and functions performed by IR practitioners, it is not surprising that there are different tensions arising as a result of the varying expectations about what IR does within the institution, and what it does for the education sector overall. Volkwein (1999; 2008) describes the contradictory 'faces' by which IR practitioners can be characterized in terms of their organizational role and culture and the purposes and audiences of IR. These tensions apart from remaining unresolved, given the nature of IR and the evolution of HE across the globe, are also the challenges that are likely to define the IR profession in years to come, regardless of the type of institutions in which IR is practiced or exercised. Other researchers have also discussed the tensions confronting IR (Calderon, 2011; Huisman, 2013). Below are some thoughts on these tensions based on our more than 50 years of combined professional IR experience.

Support to the vice-chancellor or president is the first priority for IR practitioners, followed by supporting or servicing the HEI council or board and the wider university management group. As a result, there is limited scope in adequate servicing beyond these priority groups, if not optimized by having advanced tools or information systems that empower users to access a range of services not entirely reliant on manual intervention. IR is often seen as a centralized function, but it needs to be supported by faculty as well. The ability for IR and planning offices to service those outside priority groups is dependent on the staffing level, resources, infrastructure, and technology at their disposal. This is perhaps one of the most pressing issues that hinders an IR unit's ability to be effective. The extent to which IR offices are able to balance the various management expectations will determine the IR unit's success. As von Prondzynski (2013) says, for a university to be successful in its planning and decision making, it needs to be competent in communication, consultation, clarity, and openness. The part that IR plays is one that enables and fosters these four pivotal areas.

In many countries, traditional models of centralized decision making in HEIs are being progressively replaced by decentralized models. There are instances where decision making occurs at the departmental or functional unit level. In some ways, this progressive shift may hinder the ability of IR and planning offices in being effective in their ability to serve the stakeholders for which they are accountable. IR practitioners may experience competing priorities and feel they are at the mercy of many 'masters.' There is the danger that in decentralized models of decision making, IR may become a scarce activity and result in simply an aggregation of departmental activity. However, in light of globalization and marketization of HE, these shifts should provide a greater incentive for coordinated action and collaborative IR and planning practice across institutions.

Time and project management is another tension that IR practitioners have to contend with on a daily basis. This occurs not only because of the demands on IR practitioners for information, strategic advice, and expert opinions, but also because those requirements are added to ongoing work priorities. The urgency of responding to requests for information and advice can be detrimental to sound and robust analysis. Analyses done too quickly may disadvantage an institution in the long run or haunt the individual providing such advice. Given the proliferation of computing facilities and the emergence of sophisticated analytical tools, there is also the assumption that authoritative information is readily available and digestible, when often enough it requires some form of intervention before it can be used to inform decision making. Furthermore, increased accountability requires IR practitioners to handle a number of competing priorities, ranging from government funding and statistical agencies, quality assurance, and accreditation offices, activities linked to college ranking efforts, and ad-hoc requests. Time and project management tensions are evident across all supporting roles within institutions. The ability to manage a variety of conflicting priorities and time restrictions are often gained as IR practitioners wave their way through years of work along the various tiers of organizational intelligence as described by Terenzini.

As previously discussed, the nature of IR work is that it is *about* the institution and *for* the institution, the system, and the jurisdictions in which it operates. This leads to another tension in that there are elements of IR that can be described as educational research, a domain that is more academically oriented than IR (see chapter 2 for a broader discussion). This tension arises as the institutional context and institutional intelligence settings between IR and educational research sometimes intersect in fulfilling the expectations of the institution (as an academic institution and incubator for knowledge generation) and that of the state, civil society, and market forces in delivering on agreed policy objectives. Given the extent to which there is recognition on the purpose and practical applications of both the IR and educational research endeavors, the two can complement each other through institutional and system-wide studies and their implications, and findings from the two can advance and reinforce each other.

IR practitioners contribute in shaping the future of HE through the analyses they undertake about the parts of the institutions: how these fit within the broader agenda of the role of HE in the state project; the influence and impact on the civil society and market forces. A successful IR practitioner should be: a) able to bring the threads together of the drivers of change within the institution and the confines of the regional and national systems and beyond; b) able to identify and therefore able to conclude on the imperatives for change across and within industries; and c) able to speculate on the future of HE (Calderon, 2011). The ability of IR practitioners to influence institutional or system change hinges on their spatial proximity to decision makers and their hierarchical standing within the institution. The fact that IR practitioners have access to data, information, and knowledge and widely interact with officials throughout the institution means that they are in a unique position to influence decision making.

Broadening IR Practice

Although a few individuals in state and national government systems may perform IR tasks, the broad scope of IR has generally been confined to the boundaries of an institution (Maasen & Sharma, 1985). The focus of IR has been to undertake self-studies for institutional improvement and effectiveness, and to undertake specialized research that supports institutional decision making. However, this broad scope is being redefined as there is a growing number of institutions globally that operate beyond and across multiple national borders. Additionally, institutions are part of national systems of education and respond to varying national policy imperatives and sectoral interests, plus institutions have formal strategic alliances with like institutions (either within a region or within national borders or even internationally).

There is also a growing trend for IR practitioners to undertake studies within and across industry sectors (and in other domains) that require specialized knowledge residing outside IR and planning offices. In this regard, we note that the decision making process at the institutional level is not only multilayered across these various entities (some which may also respond to different legislative, accreditation, and reporting requirements, among many other things), but it is also dispersed across stakeholders and critical actors (within and outside the institution). In turn, this requires that IR practitioners be aware of the wider spectrum of institutional activities, strategic intent, and policy within the education industry and across industries over multiple jurisdictions. Further, traditional models of university governance are progressively being transformed so that universities are becoming not only strategic actors competing in decentralized markets in a comparable manner to private companies, but are also knowledge production actors supporting public policy goals of government, with an ever increased public accountability and scrutiny but with shrinking government financial support (Whitley & Gläser, 2014). These profound reforms in HE are changing the nature and characteristics of institutional management and the way activities are planned, developed, and assessed. These changes are invariably having an impact on the roles, functions, service, and purpose of IR. IR practitioners are not only required to adapt and embrace new forms of modus operandi, but need to respond by broadening and deepening their skills so they can be effective in the emerging workplace models resulting out of ongoing reforms taking place worldwide.

IR practitioners can operate across several functional units and perform various roles within the university, including admissions, marketing, quality, assessment, and strategic planning. While this can be seen as a positive, it can be a negative in that it may hinder professional progress, as it is reliant on knowledge expertise as opposed to management expertise. IR practitioners are not alone on this dilemma of the roles and functions performed by most blended professionals as described by Whitchurch (2009). Blended professionals, like those who perform IR functions, can be characterized by not having a defined identity within the realm of institutions. In some respects, perhaps this loose sense of identity can be advantageous to the practice of IR, as it can be an incentive for innovative work practices and for pursuing exploratory and speculative research to advance the institution's mission and play an active role in shaping HE policy generally.

These tensions that we are able to distill from our combined years of experience in different institutional settings across different nations leads us to the paramount issue with which IR practitioners are confronted. In other words, what is the IR practitioner's identity? IR practitioners wear many hats and generally own none; they are active in shaping strategic directions for the institutions but are usually behind the scenes (some even call it 'back room' workers); they are agents of change but are not involved when the crunch comes to making a decision. While it is an identity issue, it is one that is equally opportunistic in how IR practitioners define their role for the future. IR equips decision makers to making sound and informed decisions. Given the hierarchical structure of institutions, many IR practitioners are, in the formal sense, one, two, or more layers removed from the inner sanctum of institutional decision making. In the informal sense, IR practitioners are closer to the formal decision making or influential in the shaping of policies, but are often seen as simply data providers. The reality is that there are many data gatherers across the institutions but IR practitioners tend to be distillers, weavers, joiners of dots, interpreters, and policy builders.

Concluding Remarks

This discussion has highlighted the broad scope of institutional research and planning activities and its merits to support the development and transformation of HEIs globally. The fundamental contribution of IR is to support institutional decision making and to orient senior institution leaders to exercise sound, diligent, and well-informed judgment in the decision making process. IR practitioners not only contend with the 'data' aspect but they are progressively becoming active actors in the policy discourse.

As the transformative nature of HE reforms continues unabated around the world, government, market forces, and civil society have varying degrees of expectations of the capacity of HE to deliver on the 'social good' and 'private gains' for all of those with vested interest in it. The contribution that IR provides as a set of activities, functions, services, and roles these practitioners perform in supporting decision makers continues to be critical to the overall institutional performance and strategic management. It remains critical because of the increased need to manage vast amounts of information, to process it, and transform it to well-informed and considered decisions that meet the expectations of a variety of strategic actors (i.e., state, civil society, and market forces).

In pondering the practice of IR and planning across various institutional sectors and across different national context and systems, we see common threads that identify professional practice. In part, this is a reflection of the fact that HEIs tend to model themselves on other institutions. While HEIs possess a distinct set of behaviors, mission, and purpose, among many distinct features, institutions often display similar structures (DiMaggio & Powell, 1983; Ramirez & Christensen, 2013). The historical context and legacies of institutions matter to the way HEIs operate, process, and embed decision making. The way those processes are affected at the institutional level reflect the nature of institutional research and planning within institutions. These differences, together with institutional alliances, account for the way institutional management and governance practice affect the form of institutional research and planning across institutions.

Increasingly, IR practitioners in our global world will need to give considered thought to the nature of HE delivering services for the good of students, industry sectors, the country, and the broad range of stakeholders, all of whom have vested interests in higher education. The gradual shift from managing institutional research through the institutional management lens to the broader context of HE, and considering wider implications not only to the institution but to the state, civil society, and market forces will occur over time as HE continues to be transformed in the 21st century.

References

Calderon, A. (2011, June). Challenges and paradigms for institutional research in a globalised higher education system. Keynote address, *Fourth Conference of U.K. and Ireland Institutional Research*. London, England.

Calderon, A., & Mathies, C. (2013). Institutional research in the future: Challenges within higher education and the need for excellence in professional practice. In A. Calderon & K. Webber (Eds.), *Global issues in institutional research, New directions for institutional research*, no. 157, (pp. 77–90). San Francisco, CA: Jossey Bass.

Delaney, A. M. (2009). Institutional researchers' expanding roles: Policy, planning, program evaluation, assessment, and new research methodologies. In C. Leimer (Ed.), *Imagining the future of institutional research, New Directions for Institutional Research*, no. 143, (pp. 29–41). San Francisco, CA: Jossey Bass.

Dill, D. (2014). Public policy design and university reform: Insights into academic change. In C. Musselin & P. N. Teixeira (Eds.), *Reforming higher education: Public policy design and implementation*, (pp. 21–57). Dordrecht, the Netherlands: Springer.

DiMaggio, P., & Powell, W. (1983). The iron cage revisited: Institutional isomorphism and collective rationality in organizational fields. *American Sociological Review, 48*(2), 147–160.

Dressel, P. L. (1981). The shaping of institutional research and planning. *Research in Higher Education, 14*(3), 229–258.

Ehara, A., Volkwein, J. F., & Yamada, R. (2010). Institutional research environment in Japanese institutions: Comparative studies between the United States and Japan using the AIR survey. Paper presented at the AIR Forum, Chicago, IL.

El Hassan, K., & Cinali, G. (2010). MENA-AIR survey results. Paper presented at the AIR Forum, Chicago, IL.

Fincher, C. (1985). The art and science of institutional research. In M. W. Peterson & M. Corcoran (Vol. Eds.), *Institutional research in transition. New Directions for Institutional Research*, no. 46, (pp. 17–37). San Francisco, CA: Jossey-Bass.

Gibbs, P., & Barnett, R. (2014). *Thinking about higher education*. London: Springer.

Howard, R., McLaughlin, G., & Knight, W. (2012). *The handbook of institutional research*. San Francisco, CA: Jossey-Bass.

Huisman, J. (2013, July). Institutional Research in Higher Education: Speaking truth to power . . . and whether it would be wise to do that on your own. Keynote address, *Sixth Conference U.K. and Ireland Institutional Research*. Birmingham, England.

Klemenčič, M., & Brennan, J. (2013). Institutional research in a European context: A forward look. *European Journal of Higher Education, 3*(3), 265–279.

Knight, W. E., Moore, M. E., & Coperthwaite, C. A. (1997). Institutional research: Knowledge, skills, and perceptions of effectiveness. *Research in Higher Education, 38*(4), 419–433.

Leimer, C., & Terkla, D. G. (2009). Laying the foundation: Institutional research office organization, staffing and career development. In C. Leimer (Ed.), *Imagining the future of institutional research. New Directions for Institutional Research*, no. 143. (pp. 43–58). San Francisco, CA: Jossey Bass.

Lindquist, S. B. (1999). A profile of institutional researchers from AIR national membership surveys. In J. F. Volkwein (Ed.), *What is institutional research all about? A critical and comprehensive assessment of the profession. New Directions for Institutional Research*, vol. 104, (pp. 41–50). San Francisco, CA: Jossey-Bass.

Maasen, P.A.M. (1986, September). Institutional research and organizational adaptation. Paper presented at the eighth European Association for Institutional Research, Loughborough, England.

Maasen, P., & Sharma, R. (1985). *What is institutional research? A primer on institutional research in Australasia.* Melbourne: Australasian Association for Institutional Research.

Muffo, J. A. (1999). A comparison of findings from regional studies of institutional research offices. In J. F. Volkwein (Ed.), *What is institutional research all about? A critical and comprehensive assessment of the profession. New Directions for Institutional Research*, vol. 104, (pp. 51–60). San Francisco, CA: Jossey-Bass.

Pusser, B. (2014). Forces in tension: The state, civil society and market in the future of the university. In *Thinking about higher education* (pp. 71–89). Basel, Switzerland: Springer International Publishing.

Ramirez, F., & Christensen, T. (2013). The formalization of the university: Rules, roots, and routes. *Higher Education, 66*(6), 695–708.

Reichard, D. J. (2012). The history of institutional research. In R. D. Howard, G. W. McLaughlin, & W. E. Knight (Eds.), *The handbook of institutional research* (pp. 3–21). San Francisco, CA: Jossey-Bass.

Saupe, J. (1990). *The functions of institutional research* (2nd ed.). Tallahassee, FL: The Association for Institutional Research.

Serban, A. (2002). Knowledge management: The fifth face of institutional research. In J. F. Volkwein (Ed.), *Knowledge management: Building a competitive advantage in higher education. New Directions for Institutional Research*, vol. 113, (pp. 105–112). San Francisco, CA: Jossey-Bass.

Swing, R. L. (2009). Institutional researchers as change agents. In C. Leimer (Ed.), *Imagining the future of institutional research. New Directions for Institutional Research*, no. 143, (pp. 5–16). San Francisco, CA: Jossey Bass.

Terenzini, P. T. (1993). On the nature of institutional research and the knowledge and skills it requires. *Research in Higher Education, 34*, 1–10.

Terenzini, P. T. (2013). "On the Nature of Institutional Research" Revisited: Plus ça Change . . . ? *Research in Higher Education, 54*(2), 137–148.

Thorpe, S. M. (1999, November). The mission of institutional research. Paper presented at the Conference of the North East Association for Institutional Research. Newport, RI. http://files.eric.ed.gov/fulltext/ED439640.pdf.

Volkwein, J. F. (1990). The diversity of institutional research structures and tasks. In J. B. Presley (Ed.), *Organizing effective institutional research offices. New Directions for Institutional Research*, vol. 66, (pp. 7–26). San Francisco, CA: Jossey-Bass.

Volkwein, J. F. (1999). The four faces of institutional research. In J. F. Volkwein (Ed.), *IR: What is it all about? New Directions for Institutional Research*, vol. 104, (pp. 9–19). San Francisco, CA: Jossey Bass.

Volkwein, J. F. (2008). *The foundations and evolution of institutional research*. In D. G. Terkla (Ed.), *Institutional research: More than just data. New Directions for Higher Education*, no. 141, (pp. 5–20). San Francisco, CA: Jossey Bass.

Volkwein, J. F. (2011). *Gaining ground: The role of institutional research in assessing student outcomes and demonstrating institutional effectiveness*. National Institute for Learning Outcomes Assessment, Occasional Paper #11, Champaign, IL.

Von Prondzynski, F. (2013). Decision making in universities should be predictable and clear. *Times Higher Education*, 11 April. www.timeshighereducation.co.uk/comment/opinion/decision-making-in-universities-should-be-predictable-and-clear/2003069.article.

Whitchurch, C. (2009). The rise of the blended professional in higher education: A comparison between the United Kingdom, Australia and the United States. *Higher Education, 58*(3), 407–418.

Whitley, R., & Gläser, J. (2014). The impact of institutional reforms on the nature of universities as organisations. *Research in the Sociology of Organizations, 42*, 19–39.

2

INSTITUTIONAL AND EDUCATIONAL RESEARCH IN HIGHER EDUCATION

Common Origins, Diverging Practices

Victor M. H. Borden and Karen L. Webber

Introduction

In many instances, the issues, activities, and strategic directions for institutional research and educational research share commonalities. However, there are some differences that exist, some subtle and others more substantial. Awareness of the differences can assist in institutional research effectiveness and academic planning across all higher education institutions. The authors of this chapter have in common a career trajectory that began within institutional research operations, culminating in directing institutional research offices at major research universities, then transitioning to academic staff positions (professors) within higher education academic programs. We share this trajectory with a modest number of individuals and have worked with colleagues whose careers have gone in the opposite direction: starting in academic staff positions and then moving into the administrative ranks as institutional research practitioners. Each of us has worked with colleagues who remain in one "camp," as well as those whose careers have swirled among institutional research, higher education research, educational policy research, and related jobs in other sectors, such as in health care organizations, government agencies, and polling organizations. We all have in common skill sets that include applied research design and analysis as well as information management. When we are in either institutional research or higher education research positions, we also have in common the general topical domain and, in many cases, the specific topics that we explore. However we also vary widely in the specific methods and topics that we explore both within camps and between them.

In this chapter we compare and contrast what we will for convenience label institutional research (IR) and higher education research (HER). To do so, we will necessarily over-generalize about each to highlight some of the distinguishing factors. We note up front that these distinctions are at times illusory. In addition, there are several related practices that we will set aside in our discussion, such as higher education policy research, typically conducted by individuals who work within government and other public agencies, and academic program evaluation, typically coordinated by academic administrators with more general portfolios and conducted by staff within academic units, sometimes with support by the staff of formal institutional research offices.

IR Versus HER: The Views of Aspiring Practitioners

In a seminar on institutional research taught by one of the co-authors, doctoral students were asked what they thought most distinguishes IR from HER. Several themes emerged from their answers, including differences in the purpose to which the results of the research are intended, to whom the researcher is accountable, and the generalizable domains of the research. Regarding purpose, students noted that institutional research is intended to serve key decision makers (primarily senior administrative staff) at the university. One student noted that the purpose generally may be viewed as providing the institution competitive advantage in attracting students or academic staff, or to obtain funding from competitive sources (mainly research grants). Another cited purpose for institutional research was to assist in allocating financial and human resources as part of budgeting and management processes. Higher education research, on the other hand, was viewed as intended for a community of peer scholars who also study the subject. Higher education research was also noted to serve decision making and resource allocation purposes, but primarily at higher levels, including regional and national governments. One student noted that both types of research ultimately served improvement purposes: for institutional research, the target of improvement was a specific institution's programs and overall effectiveness; for higher education research, the target of improvement was perceived to be higher education as a sector in its service to the education and development needs of the populace.

Because of these differences in purposes and target audience, several students noted that the format and content of studies would differ. Institutional research studies would more likely be cast in a local context and include information regarding the history of the issue within the institution and the ramifications for decisions related to the results. Moreover, institutional research would likely be cast in relatively simple terms, with a spotlight on practical implications and complex technical aspects of research methodology or statistical analysis downplayed. Higher education research, in contrast, would likely be cast in terms of the lines of theoretical frameworks that guide the inquiry and relevant research previously pursued. The full complexities of research methodology and analysis would be well developed for scrutiny by experts in these techniques and as the ultimate criteria for credibility and judgment of academic value (and publication prospects). There are times when the lines between IR and HER blur, such as when the IR analyst serves as the scholar in Volkwein's (1999) faces of IR. However, in more typical cases, IR analyses are more applied and focused on improvement of a specific institution.

In addition, we note a few instances in US institutions (e.g., University of California Berkeley, Georgia, Michigan, Michigan State, and Pennsylvania State University) where IR originated in conjunction with an academically focused unit, and in these cases, by nature of the close alliance with academic staff, a higher number of scholarly analyses, external funding, and publications resulted. As an example, the University of Georgia's (UGA) Institute of Higher Education (IHE) originated in 1964 to work with the state's higher education institutions to improve instructional strategies, curricula, organization and operation, and to serve as UGA's institutional research facility. UGA's IHE served to fulfill the institutional research needs for about four years before the Office of Institutional Research became a separate unit in 1968 (Midgette, 1990). In the seminar on IR, three students offered alternative metaphors for the relationships between IR and HER. The first suggested a Venn diagram with an area of overlap, representing the kind of research that serves both local and more general purposes, or the application of general higher education research to institutional questions. A second student offered a concentric circle metaphor, with institutional research being a subset of the broader domain covered by higher education research. A third student likened institutional research to the individual pieces of a jigsaw puzzle, with higher education research representing the complete picture when the pieces were in place. Generally, students noted that each metaphor captured an aspect of the relationship but each had limits. In a chapter on "Planning and Executing Studies" within the first handbook on the topic of institutional research, Dressel and associates (1971) build a formal case for distinguishing institutional research from academic educational research on three primary points:

> It [IR] does not share the mantle of academic freedom; it is primarily utilitarian and therefore has a distinctive set of values; and its ultimate success depends less on the research findings than on promotion of action to alleviate functional weakness and to increase the effectiveness of the institution.
>
> *(p. 38)*

The informed views of the doctoral students, and the more formal characterization by Dressel and associates (1971), capture well the essence of the theoretical distinctions between IR and HER. However, as noted in a quotation that has been variously attributed to Albert Einstein and American baseball player Yogi Berra, among others: "in theory, theory and practice are the same, but in practice, they are not." In the remainder of this chapter, we first explore the historical roots that unite and distinguish IR and HER. We then focus on the current practices and practitioners within the IR and HER communities, including the organizations with which they affiliate and the venues through which they disseminate. Finally, we consider some formal definitions and the prospective future relationships and roles of IR and HER in relation to the increasingly globalized market of higher education.

Historical Roots

In a chapter within the recent *Handbook of Institutional Research* on the history of IR, Reichard (2012) cites as one of the earliest series of papers about institutional research *College Self-Study: Lectures on Institutional Research* (Axt & Sprague, 1960), which traces United States institutional research back to a 1701 study of the governing structures of Scottish universities conducted to inform the design of Yale University's initial governing board structure. Reichard provides other scattered examples of institutional research studies from the US in the 18th and 19th centuries but suggests that the rise of Taylorism (scientific management) in the first half of the 20th century increased the distribution and frequency of college self-study. In particular, the survey became a popular tool among institutional researchers. A 1937 report released by the Carnegie Foundation for the Advancement of Teaching identified 240 such surveys (Eells, 1937). During this time period, the study of higher education institutions was perhaps as much or more oriented toward informing scholars (HER) than university administrators (IR). In 1938, Schiller Scroggs (1938) published a study entitled *Systematic Fact-Finding and Research in the Administration of Higher Education* that more closely reflected the development of the functions and purposes of modern institutional research.

In the 1920s, larger institutions of higher education, especially public ones like the University of Minnesota, started organizing academic experts within the university to assist the administration in managing issues related to enrollment growth. These often started out as committees, for example, the Committee on Educational Research appointed at the University of Minnesota in 1924 (Stecklein, 1959), comprised of academic staff and deans, which coordinated a set of studies related to student selection, testing, admissions, class size, teaching methods, and curriculum characteristics. This function eventually (by 1956) evolved into an administrative unit named the Bureau of Institutional Research.

The publications cited by Reichard (2012) trace the origins of institutional research that represent the scholarly work of what we would today characterize as higher education researchers, that is, academics who focus their scholarship on issues related to the development and characteristics of higher education institutions and the postsecondary educational sector more broadly. In this sense, the study of institutional research (as opposed to the ongoing practice) is a topic of higher educational research, as represented in the concentric circle metaphor offered by one of the aforementioned doctoral students in the IR seminar.

Indeed, the work of several notable academic scholars in the 1940s, 1950s, and 1960s, including Burton Clark, Clark Kerr, C. Robert Pace, Kenneth Feldman, and Alexander Astin, was instrumental to the development of institutional research as a professional practice. It is interesting to note that several of these scholars and their colleagues who had disciplinary roots in psychology and sociology were also central to the growth of higher education as a research discipline. The genesis for these units were higher education research centers established within major universities through funding from the Carnegie Corporation in the mid-1950s (Goodchild, 2002), including the University of California Berkeley's Center for Studies of Higher Education (CSHE), which was established in 1956 as the first research institute in the United States devoted to the study of systems, institutions, and processes of higher education (http://cshe.berkeley.edu/brief-history-cshe). Similar centers were established at the University of Michigan and Teachers College of Columbia University.

In a parallel fashion, Dressel and Mayhew (1974) trace the origins of the study of higher education as an academic discipline to classes on the topic first offered by Clark University president G. Stanley Hall in 1893. Similar courses were noted as being offered in education departments (not yet higher education) during the 1920s. Ewing and Stickler (1964) identified 27 formal higher education degree programs that were in place by 1945. As with institutional research, the growing interest in higher education as a field of study was then stimulated by the research centers that were established in the 1950s and 60s at the University of California Berkeley, as well as at the University of Michigan and Teachers College at Columbia University.

Goodchild (1991) provides considerable detail on the nascent higher education classes and eventually degree programs that emerged from 1918 through 1929 at the Ohio State University, Teachers College of Columbia University, the University of Chicago, the University of California Berkeley, and the University of Michigan. Goodchild notes as the impetus for these programs the increasing specialization of higher education institutions and the resultant need for more professional administrators and particularly senior leadership. Growing college enrollments during the 1920s and 1930s expanded the focus to include student personnel and institutional research. Thus institutional research was approached through higher education programs primarily as a professional practice and not as a researcher endeavor.

Although tasks consistent with IR have been carried out in European institutions for many years, formal IR was later to be established, and in some regions, just now forming. In the 1980s, as some EU national governments granted higher education institutions more autonomy in exchange for forms of accountability (Neave & Van Vught, 1991), institutions were prompted to use their internal capacity to generate information and data in order to satisfy the government's demands to oversee the institutions. As Huisman et al. note in chapter 5, EAIR is a leading society for higher education officials that links research, policy, and practice. More so than in the US and Canada, many European policy makers believe that 'research' should be done exclusively in academic departments and institutes, not in the administration. Following discussions by scholars such as Teichler (2000), Tight (2012), and El-Khawas (2000), the silver jubilee book reflecting on 25 years of EAIR (Begg, 2003) examined the dialogue between HER and HE practice.

However, when these authors reflected on higher education research, they specifically meant the academic discipline of higher education, not the application of data, issues of data management, or analytic work that traditionally defines IR. Huisman, Hoekstra, and Yorke (in chapter 5 of this book) further believe the perceptions of differences between IR and ER in the central EU region created a barrier against the interaction between the two worlds of academic work and administration.

Networking and Dissemination in IR and HER

As institutional research expanded as a practice through the 1970s and beyond, scholarly practitioners like Sydney Suslow at the University of California, Berkeley, John Stecklein at the University of Minnesota, Paul Dressel at Michigan State University, F. Craig Johnson at Florida State University, Paul Jedamus and Thomas Mason at the University of Colorado, Cameron Fincher at the University of Georgia, and Joe Saupe at the University of Missouri contributed to the growing literature on institutional research through such volumes as *Institutional Research in the University: A Handbook* (Dressel & Associates, 1971) and the monograph series, *New Directions in Institutional Research*. The Association for Institutional Research (AIR) emerged in the early 1960s through a set of meetings among these colleagues and others, with the association incorporating in 1965.

Recently celebrating its fiftieth anniversary, AIR includes over 4,000 individual members[1]. On its website, AIR declares as its primary purpose (www.airweb.org/AboutUs/Pages/default.aspx) "to support members in the process of collecting, analyzing, and converting data into information that supports decision-making in higher education." Due to the state-based governmental control of public institutions in the US, there is a network of state-level associations affiliated with the national association.

The international spread of institutional research began with a meeting of AIR in Vancouver, Canada, in 1973. Colleagues from other countries discovered "similar but different" interests and ultimately started forming their own affiliated organizations, starting with (mentioned above) EAIR: the European Higher Education Society, which was formed in 1979. The AIR website currently lists 10 international affiliate groups, four of which are multinational professional associations: European (EAIR), Australasian (AAIR), Middle-East North Africa (MENA-AIR), South East Asia (SEAAIR), and Southern African (SAAIR). Several individual countries have also developed IR organizations, some of which are currently affiliated (Canadian and Philippine) and some of which are not (United Kingdom, Chinese, and Dutch).

Reflecting on the growth of institutional research internationally, Taylor, Hanlon and Yorke (2013) note:

> In reality, outside the United States, institutional research is poorly developed in terms of professional or community identity within higher education

institutions. Indeed, in many countries and in many institutions of higher education, the term institutional research is barely recognized, although most of its constituent practices are well recognized (such as student number forecasting, business intelligence reporting, and stakeholder feedback monitoring).

(p. 60)

Many of the individuals and other scholars who deeply influenced the development of both IR and HER maintain ties with academic associations. Sociologists, for example, could affiliate with the education section of the American Sociological Association. Similarly the American Psychological Association includes divisions for Educational Psychology and School Psychology, as well as Evaluation, Measurement, and Statistics. With the growth of academic higher education programs within schools of education, more individuals interested in postsecondary education came to affiliate with the American Educational Research Association, which established a division (J), dedicated to postsecondary education. As with many academic "subspecialties" within the broader field of education, continued growth stimulated the development of an association completely dedicated to the topic. The Association for the Study of Higher Education (ASHE), incorporated in 1976, currently enrolls 2,000 individual members, who, as the ASHE website notes (www.ashe.ws/?page=182), are "dedicated to higher education as a field of study."

As with most professional and academic fields, the membership associations, like AIR and ASHE, sponsor the primary journals for disseminating research and development of the field. As a professional association, AIR lists a range of types of publications as a promoter or sponsor. The journal *Research in Higher Education* is listed as the "official peer-reviewed academic journal" of AIR, although it is independently published by the Springer publishing company. AIR also has a close working relationship with the publisher of the *New Directions for Institutional Research* monograph series, the Jossey-Bass division of Wiley publishing. AIR also self-publishes a monograph series under the *Resources in Institutional Research* series, as well as two article series, the *Professional Files* and *IR Applications*, each of which features a single study in each issue. Similar to AIR, ASHE publishes a monograph series, the *ASHE Readers*, single study reports (*ASHE-Higher Education Report*), and lists as its primary peer-reviewed journal, *Review of Higher Education.* Both AIR and ASHE include among their publications listings the "flagship" peer-reviewed journal, the *Journal of Higher Education*, as well as the popular annual sourcebook, *Higher Education: Handbook of Theory and Practice.*

The primary peer-reviewed journals of higher education—*The Journal of Higher Education, Review of Higher Education,* and *Research in Higher Education*—reflect the common interests of IR and HER, that is, a broad understanding of higher education and the postsecondary institutions through which higher education is manifest. Conversely, the self-published monographs and reports of AIR and ASHE highlight some of the distinguishing aspects of IR and HER. AIR's Professional Files and IR Applications are distinguished from academic journal articles as "they address fundamental aspects of institutional research work and are less focused on theory and theoretical perspectives" (www.airweb.org/EducationAndEvents/Publications/ProfessionalFiles/Pages/default.aspx). The generality of HER is reflected in the *ASHE Higher Education Report*, which provides a "definitive analysis of a tough higher education problem, based on thorough research of pertinent literature and institutional experiences," as well as in the purpose of the ASHE Reader Series, "to keep abreast and informed about issues affecting higher education in the United States and abroad" (www.ashe.ws/?page=69).

Definitional Perspectives

The professional AIR and academic ASHE associations epitomize the similarities and differences between IR and HER in practice. They also support continuing efforts to define and refine the respective practices by providing venues for presentation, discourse, and debate on the topics. As an academic field, HER is primarily debated within academic circles, where the focus is on the topics of research more so than the field as a whole. IR, however, is an institutional practice and, as such, is often debated within administrative circles where more basic definitional issues define the shape, form, and funding prospects for an office or division devoted to its practice.

The most widely cited definition of institutional research, offered by Saupe (1990), is included within the first paragraph of the seminal AIR publication, *"The Functions of Institutional Research"*:

> . . . research conducted within an institution of higher education to provide information which supports institutional planning, policy formation and decision making.

But behind this seemingly straightforward definition is debate regarding the form and purpose that this takes in practice. In the documented characterizations from when the field was emerging as a profession in the 1960s, Suslow (1972) describes the role of the institutional researcher as someone who "serves higher education and, in turn, his institution through critical appraisal and careful investigation of its processes and programs" (Section 1 Par. 1). Similarly, Dressel and associates (1971, p. 23) suggests that the "basic purpose of institutional research is to probe deeply into the workings of an institution for evidence of weaknesses or flaws which interfere with the attainment of its purposes or which utilize an undue amount of resources in so doing." Fincher (1978) offered a more summative description of institutional research as "organizational intelligence." Twenty years later, leading IR scholars were still offering commentary on the definitions of IR, including Terenzini (1999) who noted that the various extant definitions had in common the relationship between the conduct of research and analysis to the practice of administering higher education institutions and programs. In the same volume, Peterson (1999) argued that the role of IR is to serve as an institution of higher education's "postsecondary industry knowledge analyst," which implies a rather high-level consultative role to the senior administration. More recently, Borden and Kezar (2012) argued that decision making in higher education is a collaborative organizational process and not as much an activity among just a few managers as implied through earlier definitions and perspectives of institutional research. As a result, they suggest the need to shift "the purpose of IR from one that informs decisions to one that contributed to organizational learning and thereby facilitates improvements in organizational effectiveness" (p. 86).

In contrast to the formal definitions and elaborate debate about the purpose of IR, there is less introspection as to the meaning and purpose of HER. However, in considering the challenges that face higher education in the future, Teichler (2014) discusses the difference between educational research and institutional research, reminding us that higher education research examines the views, the activities, and the work context of those who study current activities policies, and anticipate the future roles of actions. Higher education researchers can focus on theoretical concepts and relationships, and do not necessarily have to draw practical solutions. However, the analytical work undertaken by institutional researchers is more often linked to decision making, and may emphasize the immediate practical value of higher education research.

As already noted, Goodchild has written extensively on the development of higher education as a field of study (e.g., Goodchild, 1991, 1996, 2002). Although the authors could not find similar formal definitions of higher education research, there are several informative published definitions of research and development that are included within governmental activities. The Organization of Economic Cooperation and Development (OECD) has sponsored since 1963 the publication *Proposed Standard Practice for Surveys on Research and Experimental Development,* more commonly known as the Frascati Manual (OECD, 2002). The core definitions included within the Frascati Manual are employed internationally, including by the US National Science Foundation, the agency through which most federal research funding is distributed. The Frascati Manual basic definition is as follows:

> Research and development (R&D) activities comprise creative work undertaken on a systematic basis in order to increase the stock of knowledge, including knowledge of man, culture and society, and the use of this stock of knowledge to devise new applications.
>
> *(OECD, 2002, p. 30)*

Further distinctions are then made between basic research, applied research, and experimental development:

Basic research is experimental or theoretical work undertaken primarily to acquire new knowledge of the underlying foundation of phenomena and observable facts, without any particular application or use in view. **Applied research** is also original investigation undertaken in order to acquire new knowledge. It is, however, directed primarily toward a specific practical aim or objective. **Experimental development** is systematic work, drawing on existing knowledge gained from research and/or practical experience, which is directed to producing new materials, products or devices, to installing new processes, systems and services, or to improving substantially those already produced or installed.

Both IR and HER can be accommodated within this spectrum, but again with some necessary vagueness. HER is perhaps best placed on the cusp between basic and applied research. As an applied field of study, HER is necessarily geared toward applied research but its standards and practices require theoretical underpinnings and so theory development is part of the realm. IR is better positioned on this spectrum between applied research and experimental development, with a focus on developing new systems and services as opposed to products.

Future Prospects for the Relationship Between IR and HER

The common roots, overlapping topical interests, and common methodological approaches of IR and HER have kept these pursuits closely aligned through their relatively brief histories. The leading scholarly influences on IR are typically individuals who have occupied academic positions, either prior to, concurrently with, or after careers leading institutional research offices. However, there have also been some tensions between these "camps" as institutional researchers sometimes are told that their work is not theoretical enough for publication in the major peer-reviewed journals. Conversely, higher education academics are occasionally puzzled if a proposal to the AIR conference is rejected because it does not have sufficient practical implications.

Such tensions are not unique to IR and HER and exist within each area. There are some tensions, for example, between the US and international affiliate IR organizations due to differences in governance and accountability arrangements. Within both arenas, there are epistemological tensions, for example, between those who favor positivist and typically quantitative inquiries as compared to those who favor constructivist and typically qualitative approaches. The diversity of perspectives that belie these tensions are critical to the enhancement and development of both IR and HER.

Terenzini's (2013) updated musings on the 'Nature of Institutional Research' remind us that knowledge of the scholarly literature is essential to considering how to carry out good institutional research on a daily basis. In addition, and following the path of Terenzini's tiers of intelligence (2013), recent reports such as that prepared by National Association of System Heads (Gagliardi & Wellman, 2014) note the need for more frequent and perhaps more rigorous analytic work to be accomplished by IR professionals. Indeed, "deeper and broader information and analysis, and more compelling narratives are needed to satisfy the growing appetite for knowledge among internal and external stakeholders" (p. 2). This compels us to consider how to focus energy and time in daily work roles in such a way to strengthen IR in higher education institutions. A value in and a need for IR exists in using strategies and techniques to inform and leverage strategic change and organizational learning that can propel change. This is even more important in our global world and the need to consider actions and goals of higher education worldwide. Good organizational intelligence, the type of information that looks both inward and outward, is central to the management of higher education. IR leaders are positioned well to help with these goals.

Note

1. Although AIR was incorporated in 1965, a number of colleagues gathered for annual meetings in the five years prior, thus a celebration was held in 2010 to celebrate 50 years of conferences for IR professionals.

References

Axt, R. G., & Sprague, H. T. (Eds.). (1960). *College self-study: Lectures on institutional research.* Boulder, CO: Western Interstate Commission for Higher Education.

Begg, R. (Ed.). (2003). *The dialogue between higher education research and practice.* Dordrecht, the Netherlands: Kluwer Academic Publishers.

Borden, V.M.H., & Kezar, A. (2012). Institutional research and collaborative organizational learning. In R. D. Howard, G. W. McLaughlin, & W. E. Knight (Eds.), *The handbook of institutional research* (pp. 86–106). San Francisco, CA: Jossey-Bass.

Dressel, P.L., & Associates (1971). *Institutional research in the university: A handbook.* San Francisco, CA: Jossey-Bass.

Dressel, P.L., & Mayhew, L. B. (1974). *Higher education as a field of study: The emergence of a profession.* San Francisco, CA: Jossey-Bass.

Eells, W. C. (1937). *Surveys of American higher education.* New York, NY: Carnegie Foundation for the Advancement of Teaching.

El-Khawas, E. (2000). Research, policy and practice: Assessing their actual and potential linkages. In U. Teichler & J. Sadlak (Eds.), *Higher education research: Its relationship to policy and practice.* Oxford, UK: Pergamon.

Ewing, J. C., & Stickler, W.H. (1964). Progress in the development of higher education as a field of professional graduate study and research. *Journal of Teacher Education, 15,* 397–403.

Fincher, C. (1978). Institutional research as organizational intelligence. *Research in Higher Education, 8*(2), 189–192.

Gagliardi, J., & Wellman, J. (2014). *Meeting demands for improvements in public institutional research.* The NASH Report. Washington, DC: National Association of System Heads.

Goodchild, L. F. (1991). Higher education as a field of study: Its origins, programs, and purposes, 1893–1960. In J. D. Fife & L. F. Goodchild (Eds.), *Administration as a profession. New Directions for Higher Education, No. 76.* (pp. 15–32). San Francisco, CA: Jossey-Bass.

Goodchild, L. F. (1996). G. Stanley Hall and the study of higher education. *Review of Higher Education, 20*(1), 69–99.

Goodchild, L. F. (2002). Higher education as a field of study. In J. J. F. Forest (Ed.), *Higher education in the United States: An encyclopedia (Vol. 1)* (pp. 303–309). Santa Barbara, CA: ABC-Clio.

Midgette, N. (1990). *History of the institute of higher education (1964–1984).* Athens, GA: Institute of Higher Education, University of Georgia.

Neave, G., & Van Vught, F. A. (Eds.). (1991). *Prometheus bound. The changing relationship between government and higher education in Western Europe.* Oxford, UK: Pergamon.

Organization of Economic Co-operation and Development. (2002). *The Frascati manual: Proposed standards for surveys on research and experimental development.* Paris, France: OECD.

Peterson, M. W. (1999). The role of institutional research: From improvement to redesign. In J. F. Volkwein (Ed.), *What is institutional research all about? A critical and comprehensive assessment of the profession. New Directions for Institutional Research, No. 104,* (pp. 21–29). San Francisco, CA: Jossey Bass.

Reichard, D. J. (2012). The history of institutional research. In R. D. Howard, G. W. McLaughlin, & W. E. Knight (Eds.), *The handbook of institutional research* (pp. 3–21). San Francisco, CA: Jossey-Bass.

Saupe, J. L. (1990). *The functions of institutional research (2nd ed.).* Tallahassee, FL: Association for Institutional Research. www.airweb.org/EducationAndEvents/Publications/Pages/FunctionsofIR.aspx.

Scroggs. S. (1938). *Systematic fact-finding and research in the administration of higher education.* (Doctoral dissertation). Yale University. Ann Arbor, MI: Edwards Brothers.

Stecklein, J. E. (1959). The history and development of the Bureau of Institutional Research at the University of Minnesota. Prepared for the Conference on Institutional Research, Stanford University, July 19–25, 1959.

Suslow, S. (1972). *A declaration on institutional research.* Tallahassee, FL: Esso Education Foundation and Association for Institutional Research.

Taylor, J., Hanlon, M., & Yorke, M. (2013). The evolution and practice of institutional research. In A. Calderon & K. L. Webber (Eds.), *Global issues in institutional research. New Directions for Institutional Research, No. 157,* (pp. 59–75). San Francisco, CA: Jossey-Bass.

Teichler, U. (2000). Higher education research and its institutional basis. In S. Schwarz & U. Teichler (Eds.), *The institutional basis of higher educational research,* (pp. 13-24), Dordrecht, the Netherlands: Klewer.

Teichler, U. (2014). Possible futures for higher education: Challenges for higher education research. In J. C. Shin & U. Teichler (Eds.), *The future of the post-massified university at the crossroads: Restructuring systems and functions.* Basel, Switzerland: Springer International Publishing.

Terenzini, P. T. (1999). On the nature of institutional research and the knowledge and skills it requires. In J. F. Volkwein (Ed.), *What is institutional research all about? A critical and comprehensive assessment of the profession. New Directions for Institutional Research, No. 104,* (pp. 21–29). San Francisco, CA: Jossey Bass.

Terenzini, P. T. (2013). "On the nature of institutional research" revisited: Plus ça change . . . ? *Research in Higher Education, 54*(2), 137–148.

Tight, M. (2012). *Researching higher education.* (Society for Research into Higher Education). Maidenhead, UK: Open University Press.

Volkwein, F. (1999). Four faces of IR. In F. Volkwein (Ed.), *What is institutional research all About? A critical and comprehensive assessment of the profession. New Directions for Institutional Research, No. 104,* (pp. 9–19). San Francisco, CA: Jossey Bass.

3

TRANSNATIONAL IR COLLABORATIONS

Charles Mathies

Introduction

As the traditional boundaries of the communities and jurisdictions of higher education institutions (HEIs) evolve, there is a growing impetus for HEIs to embrace a new model in which they collaborate and partner beyond their national borders. HEIs and national higher education systems (Systems) are no longer operating only within their national context as they are finding themselves in a global higher education environment of prestige building and competition. A global hierarchy of HEIs is emerging that is largely defined by the quality of the students attending and researchers employed (Lauder & Brown, 2011).

Simultaneously, this is occurring at a time of decreasing public fiscal support and substantial changes to higher education (HE) funding frameworks (Jongbloed, de Boer, Enders, & File, 2010; Lebeau, Stumpf, Brown, Lucchesi, & Kwiek, 2012; Slaughter & Leslie, 1997; Slaughter & Rhoades, 2004) while an increasing number of students are enrolling (Calderon, 2012). The result is HEIs and Systems are searching beyond their national borders for ways to improve their efficiency and effectiveness of teaching, learning, and research. This chapter looks at the ways HEIs and Systems collaborate across national borders to drive institutional effectiveness, improve institutional policy development, and enrich the information used by campus leaders.

The Global Higher Education Environment

Operating in the relatively new, global HE environment is the main force motivating HEIs and Systems to collaborate across borders. While there is no true singular unified system, HE globally can be viewed as a "complex combination of (1) global flows and networks of words and ideas, knowledge, finance, and inter-institution dealings; with (2) national higher education systems shaped by history, law, policy and funding; and (3) individual institutions operating at the same time locally, nationally and globally" (Marginson, 2006, p. 1). While the effects of global transformations impact HEIs and Systems differently (Marginson, 2006), the pressures of competition, movement toward a standardized system, and increasing financial considerations are fundamentally the same.

The competition in HE globally is essentially over resources. HEIs and Systems compete over physical (facilities and technology), human (students, academic staff, and researchers), and financial resources. In modern HE there is increased "global branding" with more HEIs aiming to be "world class" (Altbach, 2011; Altbach, Reisberg, & Rumbley, 2009; Salmi, 2009). As prestige and reputation rests on research and students (Lauder & Brown, 2011; Marginson, 2006), the amount and quality of these resources possessed directly impacts placement in the hierarchy. A clear example of this can be seen in the competition over international students. There is an assumption that international students are an additional source of revenue while concurrently adding prestige; as such they are highly desired. The Organisation for Economic Co-operation and Development (OECD, 2012) reports that in 2010, more than 4.1 million students enrolled outside their country of citizenship, an increase of more than 10% over the previous year and almost double from ten years earlier (2000 = 2.07 million students; OECD, 2012). However, the distribution of international students globally indicates that in 2010, 77% were enrolled in OECD member countries with over 50% in just six countries (Australia, Canada, France, Germany, United Kingdom, and United States). Additionally, Slaughter and Cantwell (2012) show smaller countries have a more difficult time competing for international students than larger countries. Taken together this indicates a hierarchy and stratification among countries, HEIs, and systems competing over international students.

While competition over a finite amount of resources is occurring, Lauder and Brown (2011) stress there is also, simultaneously, an ongoing global standardization of HE. Pushing this are elements such as the movement of students between HEIs (mobility, particularly internationally), formation of international student and staff markets, introduction of global ranking (league) tables, and the restructuring of the occupations within domestic and global labor markets (Lauder & Brown, 2011). The New Public Management (NPM) model has been at the center of many recent reforms (Bleiklie, Enders, Lepori, & Musselin, 2011; Marginson, 2010) and movement toward a more uniformed global HE system. While there are many critics of NPM and its role in shaping HE, global comparisons of HEIs, through mechanisms such as research metrics and ranking schemas (league tables), are now possible in large part because Systems and HEIs are becoming more alike (Marginson, 2011). It is now not enough to be competitive within one's own country or region; it is about being competitive globally while remaining locally connected (Marginson, 2004, 2011). But doing so requires complete and accurate internal, regional, and international data for analysis and comparisons

(Altbach et al., 2009). Coupled with the increasing complexity in managing HEIs and Systems (Calderon & Mathies, 2013), the need of evidence and information leads back to institutional research (IR) offices, or a similar type unit, to guide and provide internationally relevant information. This suggests IR offices need to identify, find, and collaborate with partners outside their country.

How Data Is Shared Across Borders

Higher education is primarily a collaborative endeavor, from teaching to research, and advances in technology have made it easier to produce data in formats that allow for collaborations among a group of HEIs and Systems (Carpenter-Hubin, Carr, & Hayes, 2012). Shaman and Shapiro (1996) argue that eleven dimensions can be used to differentiate data-sharing paradigms. Four of these (primacy of purpose, control of process, membership criterion, and regularity of activity) are useful in distinguishing transnational IR collaborations from one another. The primacy of purpose examines the principle purpose for collaborating and sharing data; is it the primary or a secondary reason this group works together? The control of process examines whether decisions about the data collection and sharing are made internally by the participants or imposed by an external entity. Membership criteria are whether participation is voluntary (invitational) or compulsory. Lastly, the regularity of activity examines how often (regularly scheduled dates and intervals or on ad-hoc/as needed basis) data are shared.

Benchmarking

Perhaps the most common form of transnational IR collaboration is benchmarking projects. Benchmarking provides a standard of institutional performance comparisons (e.g., based on indicators, metrics, and analytics) among a selected group of comparable organizations (European Centre for the Strategic Management of Universities, 2008, 2010; Watson, 1993). It is a way of discovering what is the best performance being achieved, whether in another HEI or System (Stroud, 2010). In short, benchmarking enables HEIs and Systems to compare themselves to other HEIs and Systems, as "'benchmarks'" (indicators and metrics) are the 'what' and the benchmarking is the 'how'" (Stroud, 2010, p. 1).

Benchmarking fits into Shaman and Shapiro's (1996) typology as the primary reason for sharing data, in which the control of the process is by the project partners, whose participation is voluntary, and is performed on an ad-hoc basis. Benchmarking should be dynamically conceived, during which relevant indicators and benchmarks are clearly defined and where institutional performance can be measured in comparison with multiple peers (European Centre for the Strategic Management of Universities, 2008). The traditional rationale of benchmarking is to provide the management with external and objective standards for measuring the quality, effectiveness, and efficiency of activities and help identify possible areas or opportunities for improvement (McLaughlin & McLaughlin, 2007). A common barrier in HE benchmarking is the belief that each HEI and System is unique and thus not comparable to another HEI or System (Lyddon, McComb, & Mizak, 2012). However, it can be argued that HEIs and Systems globally perform many of the same functions and are thus comparable; they all recruit and enroll students, hire staff to teach and conduct research, and award degrees (Lyddon, McComb, & Mizak, 2012).

Global Rankings

As a second reason for participation under Shaman and Shapiro's (1996) typology, ranking schemas gather data from HEIs around the world in effort to determine and hierarchically order HEIs. While there are currently nine active global, and over fifty national and regional, ranking schemas (Hazelkorn, 2011), there are three global ranking schemes that receive the most attention. These three schemas are the Times Higher Education World University Rankings (THE), the Academic Ranking of World Universities (ARWU), and the QS World University Rankings (QS). The ARWU was the first global ranking schema starting in 2003 (Hazelkorn, 2011) and was designed as a means for Chinese HEIs to benchmark against top international HEIs. The QS and THE started together as a single ranking schema in 2004 and subsequently split in 2010. While they all differ on methodology and emphasis (weighting of variables and categories), each rank HEIs primarily using three categories: the quality of teaching and learning, the quality of staff and researchers, and the quality and amount of outputs from research (publications and citations). The U-Multirank released its first ranking in May 2014 and will likely have a significant impact in transnational IR collaborations in Europe due to its substantial support from the European Commission.

As a second reason for participation, ranking schemas serve to control the process by a third party, whose participation is voluntary (though it can be argued it is becoming compulsory for many), and is performed on regular (yearly) basis. Ranking schemas request HEI officials to submit data as defined by them (a third party) and not by themselves or their governing agency. It asks all participants to follow similar guidelines and definitions when submitting data, regardless of who they are, where they are located, or previously ranked. In essence, these ranking surveys are asking for HEIs globally to collaborate by providing data in the same format. While there are serious and noted critics of the ranking surveys (see Hazelkorn, 2011; Shin, Toutkoushian, & Teichler, 2011 for in-depth discussions on rankings), they allow for comparisons of HEIs across different Systems because they use similarly defined data elements. However, using ranking data for transnational HEI comparisons should be limited to the actual data elements submitted (collected) and not the rankings themselves. This is due to the use of reputational surveys, relative lack of controls over data verifications (whether data was actually entered similarly by each participant), and that not all HEIs participate in each survey.

Consortia and Networks

As an association of two or more participants (HEI/Systems) that participate in a common activity, consortia help participants reach common goals. Often, members of consortiums collaborate through shared data exchanges, joint research ventures, and pooling resources to improve services for specific initiatives such as library holdings or technology purchases. Higher education consortiums are nothing new; they have existed within Systems (national borders) for years. Some notable examples include the Committee on Institutional Cooperation (CIC), the Association of American Universities (AAU), and the Commonwealth Association of Universities (CHEMS). However a number of newer consortiums have been established that include members from multiple countries. For the most part, these newer international consortiums are regional in nature, as some notable examples include the League of European Research Universities (LERU), Association of European Research Libraries (LIBER), and the Asociación de Universidades Grupo Montevideo (AGUM).

The data exchanges within these newer regional consortiums have primarily focused on issues related to student and staff mobility, accessing and disseminating research findings, and quality assurance. Key activities include collection of common data elements, developing standards of data definitions and its management, exchanging best practices, and training of staff. International networks are similar to consortiums but are typically less formal in their structure and smaller in size. Participation in networks typically comes in two forms, based on individuals or among a group. The individual based networks often begin from contact from within a larger professional association (conference) or transnational project. These are situations where individuals, typically with similar positions, from different HEIs come together to exchange data, practices, and ideas for a specific purpose (e.g., recognizing credit from foreign HEIs, managing student mobility, etc.). The networks among HEIs are usually strategic partnerships where HEIs have aligned themselves with another HEI for a specific purpose. Typically, these networks are made at senior management level and are used as ways to meet strategic goals (e.g., building research capacity, developing research, or training in niche areas). The HEIs align with one another to share practices and data, facilitating a working relationship in line with the network's purpose. Participation in a consortium or a network fits into Shaman and Shapiro's (1996) typology as both the primary and secondary reason for sharing data, in which the control of the process is by the project partners, whose participation is voluntary, and is performed on both an ad-hoc and regular basis.

NGOs and Transnational Integration Agreements

Lastly, there are a number of non-governmental organizations (NGOs) and formalized integration agreements among multiple national governments (typically regional in nature) that encourage transnational IR collaborations. Some of the main NGOs involved in higher education globally include OECD, World Bank, and UNESCO. These NGOS focus on collecting and sharing information (data) supporting their views of higher education's purpose, structures, and reforms. Many initiatives are concentrated on connecting research to innovation and economic development, quality assurance, and mobility of students and staff. Perhaps the most robust and formalized transnational government integration agreements impacting higher education are in Europe. Many reforms in European higher education have been shaped by the regional harmonizing efforts (Bologna Process, Lisbon Accords, and their subsequent follow-ups) and are often directly supported (and funded) by the European Commission (EC), the executive body of the European Union (EU), or the education ministries from the countries within the European Higher Education Area (EHEA). One of the larger recent initiatives launched by the EC, and emblematic of how these multinational integration agreements encourage transnational collaborations, is the Erasmus+ initiative that is the EU's umbrella program for all education and training for 2014–2020 (European Commission, 2014). The Erasmus + supports three primary activities promoting transnational cooperation among HEIs and Systems through strategic partnerships, knowledge alliances, and capacity building projects. All three activities require significant collaboration and exchanging of data and practices among partners from different countries.

The transnational integration agreements are not limited to Europe. In North America, the Program for North American Mobility in Higher Education (NAMP) promotes student and credit exchanges among HEIs in Canada, Mexico, and the United States. It was conceived out of the North American Free Trade Agreement (NAFTA) and funds collaborative efforts consisting of at least two HEIs from each country. In Central America, the Central American University Superior Council (CSUCA) promotes regional harmonization (specifically on topics of evaluation, accreditation, and student and credit mobility), joint postgraduate degree programs, and collaborations in research and libraries. The CSUCA is an official member institution of the Central American Integration System (SICA), which is an economic and political integration agreement among eight Central American countries.

The NGOs and multinational integration agreements fit into Shaman and Shapiro's (1996) typology, as sharing data is the secondary reason for these groups to exist, which the control of the process is by a third party whose participation is both voluntary and compulsory, and is performed on regular basis. The majority of the NGOs and transnational integration agreements require data collaborations, typically at the System (national) level, but their influence on the definitions, elements (variables) exchanged, and overall framework of what and how data is collected impacts both Systems and HEIs. Both the NGOs and transnational integration agreements primarily focus on other issues than higher education (usually economic or political). However both groups are very interested in higher education as they see it as an important influence to their primary interests (typically tied to economic development). Increasingly the opinions and reports of these groups are being used to shape educational policy and practice in HEIs and Systems globally. There is clear evidence that policymakers look to these groups for policy guidance and, in turn, are using transnational comparative assessments (Crossley, 2012). This is important to note as their influence in higher education will likely continue to grow as the future governance of HEIs and Systems will likely come from a collection of stakeholders from a variety of jurisdictions, including industry, NGOs, and national and regional governments (Calderon & Mathies, 2013).

Considerations When Sharing Data Transnationally

In any comparison of HEIs or Systems, there are concerns both technical (primarily related to data) and human (or political; Teeter & Brinkman, 2003). These issues should be considered prior to an agreement to work with another HEI or system, as they lead to the fundamental question of 'does what happens within one HEI or system (learning, research, and teaching) compare to another due to differences in histories, cultures, and governance structures'? Additionally, large disparities exist across HEIs and Systems in attitudes and practices related to the openness, definitions, and management of data. The act of comparing data from other HEIs and Systems compounds already existing concerns over the validity, accuracy, and reliability of internal data assessments (Teeter & Brinkman, 2003). While the short answer is yes, in that information (data) can be comparable to another from another country, it is only possible though through careful planning. While transnational IR collaborations are not international comparative research endeavors per se, they should follow many of their basic rules and practices (see Hantrais, 2009; Øyen, 1990 for more on international comparative research). While there are numerous items to consider when comparing HEIs and Systems transnationally (far more than there is space in this chapter to address), there are six issues as key areas to be addressed: equivalence, culture, data definitions, language, scope of data, and data management.

Equivalence

Equivalence has been defined as "the components and their properties being compared are the 'same', or indicate something equivalent" (Teune, 1990, p. 54). This includes understanding the scope of the data (see below for more) collected and shared in collaborations. In short, the information (data) being compared and shared among HEIs or Systems needs to be the same. While no perfect solution exists to address the equivalence issue for all HEIs and Systems (Goedegebuure & van Vught, 1996), there are ways to minimize the impact of the cultures and contexts of each country involved. This necessitates the use of equivalent instruments (which measure the same characteristics/data elements across all partners) and data to measure transnational comparisons (Mills, van de Bunt, & Bruijn, 2006). The necessity of equivalent comparisons requires agreement on data concepts and definitions from basic elements such as gender and degree program to more complex elements like socio-economic class and academic field (Mills et al., 2006).

Culture

However, as Goedegebuure and van Vught (1996) point out, the problem of equivalence is not just whether the shared data are the same, but also whether they are the same in their significance or importance to each partner. This leads to the necessity of understanding the cultures of the HEIs and Systems involved. This is both internal (history, organizational structure, values, etc.) and external (economic, political, funding, etc.) to HEIs and Systems (Tierney, 1988). Tierney (1988) suggests thinking about culture within higher education as a framework consisting of the environment, mission, socializations, information, strategy, and leadership. Each of these six elements exists within each HEI and System but take form and evolve differently. The cultural values, and the importance attached to these values, are different for each HEI and System and acknowledging and addressing these differences among partners is crucial.

Data Definitions

There is a strong need to use clear data definitions in transnational collaborations, as each partner will have differences in how they define their own data elements. This is for basic as well as complex data elements. Even when similar data elements are used, their context of use could differ greatly (Mills et al., 2006). Take for example the concept of what is considered a university degree. As Palfreyman (2008) points out, there are many differences as to what a university degree is, based on how long it takes to earn a degree (credits required), how teaching is delivered, what content is offered, and how academic performance and quality is assessed. Using the same clear definitions by all partners is essential to achieving equivalence and thereby enabling comparisons among HEIs and Systems from different countries.

Language

Tied into developing clear data definitions is the issue of language. This is an issue in terms of not only the language abilities of the staff involved in the collaborations, but also in the data and their definitions. For the staff involved it means finding a common language to use for meetings, data elements shared, and outputs (reports, action items, etc.). While there are many staff members at universities who are multilingual, this could be a significant burden when considering ICT (technology) staff (or other specialized staff) that might not be but are essential members when it comes to data captures, retrieval, and sharing due to their technical skills or topical expertise. So care is needed when picking which staff members to participate in these collaborations.

Scope of Data

There is a need, by all partners, to understand what data is available to share. Quite simply, the scope of the available data dictates what questions can be asked and answered. This includes not only which data elements are or are not available from each partner but also how they are defined (see previous section for more) and captured. This is particularly relevant when considering the level of analysis; is it micro (individuals) or macro (HEIs)? The more complex data that is available to be shared, the more sophisticated the questions that can be answered. In short, if all partners are not matching in their scope of data available, limitations will be encountered in terms of what can ultimately be compared.

Data Management

Lastly, there are large disparities across HEIs and Systems in attitudes and practices related to the management of data. Yanosky (2009, p. 12) defines data management in higher education as the policies and practices by which HEIs and Systems effectively collect, protect, and use digital information to meet academic, business, and governance needs. The five categories of data management, comprising of data integrity and quality, analytics, data stewardship and security, contents and records management, and the management of research, describe how HEIs and Systems manage their data and ways they differ from one another (Yanosky, 2009). The differences among HEIs and Systems in managing their data stem from not only cultural differences, but also legal. It is important to recognize and address differences among partners because left unresolved, it will likely lead to more problems in other areas (e.g., cleanliness of data, accuracy of reports, etc.).

Conclusion

One of the founding fathers of comparative research, Sir Michael Sadler, said "the practical value of studying, in a right spirit and with scholarly accuracy, the working of foreign systems of education is that it will result in our being better fitted to study and understand our own" (1900, in: Higginson, 1979, p. 50). This quote is very applicable to transnational IR collaborations as well. Transnational comparisons enhance the institutional decision-making process as it adds to the existing body of internal information (indicators) of current and previous performance. Instead of an isolated analysis, the expanded perspective provides a greater understanding of the HEI or System and how it fits into the global higher education environment (context; James, 2012). Understanding institutional context is extremely important as questions arise, such as what does it mean when a measure is less than or greater than the mean value of the comparison group: is it positive or negative and why (James, 2012)? In short, comparison information is about improving the knowledge on specific aspects or operations of an HEI or System so action can be taken to improve one's own performance (James, 2012).

As James (2012) argues, the development of institutional comparisons must be developed carefully, purposefully, and with methods acceptable to all partners. One of the main roles of IR offices is to provide decision support services, i.e., providing relevant data and assessments to guide strategic decisions. Many HEIs and Systems are facing increasingly difficult financial situations and collaborating with foreign HEIs or Systems is a relative low cost way to bring in new, but vitally relevant information. With the increasing standardization of higher education (data collections and reforms) coupled with advances in technology, IR offices are finding it easier than ever to look beyond their national borders for collaborative opportunities. The more and richer information that is available can improve institutional decision making, and in turn, provide a competitive advantage in the global HE environment.

References

Altbach, P. (2011). The past, present, and future of the research university. In P. Altbach & J. Salmi (Eds.), *The road to academic excellence: The making of world-class research universities* (pp. 11–32). Washington, DC: World Bank.

Altbach, P., Reisberg, L., & Rumbley, L. (2009). *Trends in global higher education: Tracking an academic revolution*. Report prepared for UNESCO 2009 World Conference on Higher Education. Paris, France: UNESCO.

Bleiklie, I., Enders, J., Lepori, B., & Musselin, C. (2011). New public management, network governance and the university as a changing professional organization. In T. Christensen & P. Laegreid (Eds.), *Ashgate research companion to new public management* (pp. 161–176). Aldershot, UK: Ashgate.

Calderon, A. (2012). Massification continues to transform higher education. *University World News. No. 237.* Retrieved September 2012 from www.universityworldnews.com/article.php?story=20120831155341147.

Calderon, A., & Mathies, C. (2013). Institutional research in the future: Challenges within higher education and the need for excellence in professional practice. In A. Calderon & K. Webber (Eds.), *Global issues in institutional research, New Directions for Institutional Research. No. 157,* (pp. 77–90). San Francisco, CA: Jossey Bass.

Carpenter-Hubin, J., Carr, R., & Hayes, R. (2012). Characteristics, current examples, and developing a new data exchange. In R. Howard, G. McLaughlin, & W. Knight (Eds.), *The handbook of institutional research* (pp. 420–433). Jossey-Bass, CA: San Francisco.

Crossley, M. (2012). Comparative education and research capacity building: Reflections on international transfer and the significance of context. *Journal of International and Comparative Education. 1*(1), 4–12.

European Centre for the Strategic Management of Universities. (2008). *A practical guide: Benchmarking in European higher education*. Brussels, Belgium: European Centre for the Strategic Management of Universities.

European Centre for the Strategic Management of Universities. (2010). *A university bench-marking handbook: Benchmarking in European higher education.* Brussels, Belgium: European Centre for the Strategic Management of Universities.

European Commission. (2014). *Erasmus+: Higher Education—Cooperation between institutions.* Retrieved March 2014 from http://ec.europa.eu/education/opportunities/higher-education/institutions_en.htm.

Goedegebuure, L., & van Vught, F. (1996). Comparative higher education studies: The perspective from the policy sciences. *Higher Education. 32*(4), 371–394.

Hantrais, L. (2009). *International comparative research: Theory, methods, and practice.* Basingstoke, UK: Palgrave Macmillan.

Hazelkorn, E. (2011). *Rankings and the reshaping of higher education: The battle for world-class excellence.* Basingstoke, UK: Palgrave Macmillan.

Higginson, J. (Ed.). (1979). *Selections from Michael Sadler: Studies in world citizenship.* Liverpool, UK: Dejall and Meyorre.

James, G. (2012). Developing institutional comparisons. In R. Howard, G. McLaughlin, & W. Knight (Eds.), *The handbook of institutional research* (pp. 644–655). San Francisco, CA: Jossey-Bass.

Jongbloed, B., de Boer, H., Enders, J., & File, J. (2010). *Progress in higher education reform across Europe: Funding reform.* Vol. 1: Executive summary and main report. Brussels, Belgium: Directorate General for Education and Culture of the European Commission.

Lauder, H., & Brown, P. (2011). The standardization of higher education, positional competition, and the global labor market. In R. King, S. Marginson, & R. Naidoo (Eds.), *Handbook on globalization and higher education* (pp. 485–496). Cheltenham, UK: Edward Elgar.

Lebeau, Y., Stumpf, R., Brown, R., Lucchesi, M.A.S., & Kwiek, M. (2012). Who shall pay for the public good? Comparative trends in the funding crisis of public higher education. *Compare: A Journal of Comparative and International Education. 42*(1), 137–157.

Lyddon, J., McComb, B., & Mizak, J. P. (2012). Tools for setting strategy. In R. Howard, G. McLaughlin, & W. Knight (Eds.), *The handbook of institutional research* (pp. 611–624). San Francisco, CA: Jossey-Bass.

Marginson, S. (2004). Competition and markets in higher education: A 'glonacal' analysis. *Policy Futures in Education. 2*(2), 175–244.

Marginson, S. (2006). Dynamics of national and global competition in higher education. *Higher Education. 52,* 1–39.

Marginson, S. (2010). The limits of market reform in higher education. *Higher Education Forum. 7,* 1–19.

Marginson, S. (2011). Strategizing and ordering the global. In R. King, S. Marginson, & R. Naidoo (Eds.), *Handbook on globalization and higher education* (pp. 394–414). Chelenham, UK: Edward Elgar.

McLaughlin, G., & McLaughlin, J. (2007). *The information mosaic: Strategic decision making for universities and colleges.* Washington, DC: AGB Press.

Mills, M., van de Bunt, G., & Bruijn, J. (2006). Comparative research: Persistent problems and promising solutions. *International sociology. 21*(5), 619–631.

OECD. (2012). *Education at a glance 2012: OECD Indicators.* Paris, France: OECD Publishing.

Øyen, E. (Ed.). (1990). *Comparative methodology: Theory and practice in international social research.* London, UK: Sage.

Palfreyman, D. (2008). Higher education, liberal education, critical-thinking, academic discourse, and the Oxford tutorial as sacred cow or pedagogical gem. In D. Palfreyman (Ed.), *The Oxford tutorial: 'Thanks you taught me how to think'* (2nd ed.) Oxford, UK: OxCHEPS.

Salmi, J. (2009). *The challenge of establishing world-class universities.* Washington, DC: World Bank.

Shaman, S., & Shapiro, D. (1996). Data-sharing models. *New Directions for Institutional Research. 89,* 29–40.

Shin, J. C., Toutkoushian, R., & Teichler, U. (Eds.). (2011). *University rankings: Theoretical basis, methodology, and impacts on global higher education.* Vol. 3, Dordrecht, the Netherlands: Springer.

Slaughter, S., & Cantwell, B. (2012). Transatlantic moves to the market: Academic capitalism in the United States and European Union. *Higher Education. 63*(5), 583–603.

Slaughter, S., & Leslie, L. (1997). *Academic capitalism: Politics, policies and the entrepreneurial university.* Baltimore, MD: Johns Hopkins University Press.

Slaughter, S., & Rhoades, G. (2004). *Academic capitalism and the new economy: Markets, state and higher education.* Baltimore, MD: Johns Hopkins University Press.

Stroud, J. (2010, February 26). *Understanding the purpose and use of benchmarking.* Retrieved March 2010 from www.isixsigma.com/methodology/benchmarking/understanding-purpose-and-use-benchmarking/.

Teeter, D., & Brinkman, P. (2003). Comparison groups. In W. Knight (Ed.), *The primer for institutional research* (pp. 103–113). Tallahassee, FL: Association of Institutional Research.

Teune, H. (1990). Comparing countries: Lessons learned. In E. Øyen (Ed.), *Comparative methodology: Theory and practice in international social research* (pp. 38–62). London, UK: Sage.

Tierney, W. (1988). Organizational culture in higher education: Defining the essentials. *The Journal of Higher Education. 59*(1), 2–21.

Watson, G. (1993). *Strategic benchmarking: How to rate your company's performance against the world's best.* New York, NY: Wiley.

Yanosky, R. (2009). *Institutional data management in higher education.* ECAR, Boulder, CO: EDUCAUSE Center for Applied Research.

SECTION II

National and Regional Context of Institutional Research

4

INSTITUTIONAL RESEARCH AND PLANNING IN HIGHER EDUCATION IN THE UNITED STATES AND CANADA

Gerald W. McLaughlin, Richard D. Howard, and Sandra Bramblett

> Institutional Research is an attitude. The successful practice of institutional research depends upon the individual who has a broad knowledge of diverse disciplines, an intense understanding of his institution, and, above all, an attitude which commits him to the value of his institution's purpose in society.
>
> *(Suslow, 1972, p. 1)*

Introduction

The following chapter is a brief overview of IR and planning in the US and Canada. It looks through the lens of Sidney Suslow, one of the first presidents of the Association of Institutional Research. It uses his definition of IR that includes learning assessment, institutional effectiveness, and planning. There are four sections, with the first two on our context of higher education and the last two dealing with the current and future roles of IR.

A Brief Summary of Higher Education in the United States and Canada

> While higher education is filled with skillful and committed men and women, it is not their role, as it is the institutional researcher's, to devote daily effort in the examination of the functions and processes of the institutions by means of systematic factual appraisal.
>
> *(Suslow, 1972, p. 2)*

The past 50 years since Clark and Trow's discussion of college cultures (Hendel & Harrold, 2007) has seen postsecondary education expand in the US and Canada in response to growing educational and research demands and to sustain national competitiveness. While postsecondary systems in both countries evolved independently, current academic and governance structures have many similarities. Public higher education has grown through local (state and provincial) governance and funding with indirect federal financial support. One difference is that in Canada there are a limited number of private universities, while many of the better known universities in the United States are private.[1]

Currently, United States postsecondary institutions serve approximately 21.5 million students. These students attend some 4,700 colleges and universities in the 50 states, employing some 1.5 million faculty members (NCES, 2012). In Canada, postsecondary institutions serve approximately two million students. These students attend some 280 colleges and universities, employing some 45,000 faculty members (StatCan, n.d.).

Governance

Public higher education in both countries is governed and financed at the state or provincial/territorial levels. In US public institutions lay boards are appointed by state governors. At US private institutions and at all institutions in Canada, lay boards are self-selecting. In general, a board's members reflect the geographic and demographic population primarily served by the institution and usually have ultimate authority over the institutions. An institution's operations, academic and administrative, are usually designed and managed by campus-level leadership, often through various forms of shared governance. Admissions and academic standards are set, strategic academic and financial plans are developed, and both long term and day-to-day management of all functions of the institution are the responsibility of institutional leaders. As such, individual institutions enjoy high levels of autonomy (CICICa, n.d.; Lingenfelter, n.d.).

In both countries, federal support passes through provincial or state agencies, or through direct student loan/grant programs. In Canada, the Learning Branch of Human Resources and Skills Development Canada oversees national student loan and grant programs. The Council of Ministers of Education (one from each province and territory) provide a national forum for discussions about Canadian postsecondary issues (CMEC, n.d.). In the United States, the Department of Education monitors higher education in terms of national concerns, manages federal student loans and grants, and collects institutional data (USDE, n.d.). In both countries responsibility and accountability for meeting national laws and educational goals ultimately rest with the institutions.

Federal Reporting

In both countries, institutional data are reported to a centralized federal government agency. In Canada, Statistics Canada collects institutional-level data through the Postsecondary Student Information System (PSIS). Statistics Canada also collects data annually about students and other related surveys (StatCan, n.d.).

In the United States, higher education data are collected by the Department of Education's National Center for Educational Statistics (NCES). Through the Integrated Postsecondary Educational Data System (IPEDS, n.d.), NCES collects institution-level data about colleges, universities, and technical and vocational postsecondary institutions.

Quality Assurance

In the United States, institutional accreditation is the primary means by which higher education institutions assure the public and funding agencies of their quality. There are a number of private nonprofit accrediting agencies that seek recognition from either or both the US Department of Education (USDE) (www2.ed.gov/about/bdscomm/list/naciqi.html) and/or the Council for Higher Education Accreditation (CHEA). "CHEA recognition confers an academic legitimacy on accrediting organizations, helping to solidify the place of these organizations and their institutions and programs in the national higher education community. USDE recognition is required for accreditors whose institutions or programs seek eligibility for federal student aid funds" (Eaton, 2009, p. 8). Many accrediting agencies are recognized by both agencies.

In Canada, "quality assurance" refers to the achievement of educational-program standards set by institutions, professional organizations, government, and/or governmental standard-setting bodies. "Accreditation" usually refers to the evaluation of specific university and college programs by professional bodies. All public and private "recognized" and "authorized" postsecondary institutions have been given the authority to grant academic credentials by their provincial or territorial governments. "Registered" or "licensed" institutions are monitored by the provincial or territorial government for institutional and program quality and consumer protection. "Non-registered" and "non-licensed" institutions are private commercial enterprises and are not monitored. Professional accreditation is conducted through the establishment and review of postsecondary curriculum standards set at provincial and national levels by Canadian professional-regulatory bodies (e.g., nursing, architecture, and engineering) (CICICb, n.d.).

The past 50 years have seen the growth of IR throughout higher education, supported by professional organizations in each country: AIR (www.airweb.org) in the US and CIRPA (https://cirpa-acpri.ca/) in Canada. For the history and development of IR, see Reichard (2012) and Lasher (2011).

The Current Context of Higher Education in Canada and the US

> If institutional research is incapable of perceiving those problems seen by others in the institution and focuses on myopic issues instead, its performance

will be ineffective; and if it employs data which present distorted reflections of real phenomena, its performance becomes less than purposeful.

(Suslow, 1972, p. 9)

The context in which higher education in Canada and the United States functions is both complex and dynamic. In the following we have used an environmental scanning tool, PESTEL, to very briefly describe some of the more important aspects of the context higher education must address (Lyddon, McComb, & Mizak, 2012). This tool looks at the political, economic, social, technical, environmental, and legal context of higher education.

Political Environment

The political context in which higher education exists has exerted increased pressure in both countries through national initiatives to see higher education as a competitive tool, to be concerned with access across a broad range of potential participants, and to have affordable institutions (National Commission on Accountability in Higher Education, 2005). The recent Higher Education Opportunity Act emphasized "improved consumer knowledge" and institutional accountability (Keller, 2012). Similar events occurred in Canada where provinces have pursued agendas such as the Rae Report (2005) in Ontario and the national development of Canada's Higher Education Accountability Data (HEAD) to "demonstrate accountability on the part of Canada's higher education institutions" (http://canadahead.com).

Provinces in Canada and states in the US strongly promote affordability, accountability, accessibility, increased academic rigor, and increased economic competitiveness in higher education—all to be achieved with increasing efficiency and effectiveness (SHEEO, n.d.).

Perhaps an indication of the increase in the political awareness of higher education stakeholders, a large number of non-governmental organizations (NGOs) now advocate positions regarding higher education with varying levels of transparency (McLaughlin, Pavelka, & McLaughlin, 2005). Other NGOs consist of, or are heavily funded by, foundations who gave some $10 billion to higher education in 2013 (CAE, 2014). One goal of these foundations is to increase philanthropy's impact on education policy at the local, state, and national levels (MSU, 2013).

A US political initiative particularly relevant to IR and planning has been the Common Educational Data Standards (CEDS) (Garcia, 2013). Voluntary common definitions are being developed for the entire spectrum of education for key data elements that describe student characteristics and outcomes. The goal is to create more consistent and comparable data with which to discuss the education process and for building longitudinal data files. The CEDS (n.d.) are being developed by working groups of institutions, governmental agencies, advocacy groups, and professional organizations.

Economics of Education

The core business model of education is enrollment revenue, either as state allocations or student tuition. This has always been an organizing principle, but recent declines in state appropriations and investment returns have further increased the need for funding from tuition and fees. Looking at the changes from 2005–06 to 2010–11, Aud (2013) found that "At private nonprofit institutions and private for-profit institutions, student tuition and fees constitute the largest percentage of total revenues (29 and 89 percent, respectively). At public institutions, the largest revenue sources were student tuition and fees (19 percent) and state appropriations (19 percent)." IR practitioners may already be involved, or may wish to get involved in analyses examining enrollment revenues at their institution.

One of the more persistent discussions with financial implications has involved the concept of institutions' need to contain costs and increase their efficiency while improving learning outcomes (AIR, 2014). After the economic meltdown of 2007–09, student debt has been staggering. "Outstanding student loan balances reported on credit reports increased to $1.08 trillion . . . as of December 31, 2013 representing a $114 billion increase for 2013" (FRB, 2014). These issues also call for the analytic work of IR analysts.

Social Agenda

The social agenda involves the pipeline for incoming students. In the US an echo in the baby boom caused high school graduates to reach a maximum in 2010–12 and "the era of annually increasing graduating classes through about 2011 is ending" (WICHE, 2012, p. xii). This shift will occur differently in different locations and different ethnicities with about 45 percent of the US public high school graduates being non-white by 2019–20, compared to 38 percent of those graduating in 2009 (WICHE, 2012, p. xii). The typical student is also becoming older (NCES, 2012). There are also major differences by urban density with one-third of the students enrolled in city schools in 2010–11 being enrolled in high poverty schools (Aud, 2013).

Canada also anticipates a downturn in the 18-year-old cohort, but an increase in college and university completions. From 2011–21, the enrollment in all post-secondary education in Canada is projected to increase by about 10 percent despite a drop in the 18–29 year cohort. The level of immigration is expected to grow with individuals with lower skills and the need for workers with higher level skills is expected to increase (COPS, n.d.).

Technical Aspects

EDUCAUSE sees the two top technology issues as "Leveraging the wireless and device explosion" and "Improving student outcomes using technology"

(Grajek, 2013, p. 32). It also has "Teaching and Learning" as one of its three focus areas. The National Center for Academic Transformation (http://thencat.org/) is promoting a major initiative to use technology to re-engineer and redesign classes for better learning at a reduced cost. In the next one to two years we can expect to see the growing ubiquity of social media and the integration of online, hybrid, and collaborative learning. In the next three to five years we can expect to see the rise of data-driven learning and assessment and a shift from students as consumers to students as creators.

While technology has changed how we do business, it is going to make even more of an impact in the business we do. With MOOCs, online academies like Kahn (n.d.) that award badges and "flipping the classroom," technology produces a new set of challenges on how to measure and analyze outcomes. Higher education processes will likely need to move from measuring faculty lecture hours and course credit hours to standardized metrics for competencies and student learning metrics. With expertise in data and data management, IR should be a key component in the shifting metrics of the future.

At the administrative level, IR will be expected to produce analytics and visualizations that can be modularized and ported to multiple devices. Studies will need to be based on shorter timeframes and likely with either cloud-like big data or smaller segmented groups of participants. Longitudinal data bases will become available with an accompanying need to engage in sense-making with conceptual models not yet developed.

Environmental Aspects

IR can have a major role in economic, social, and environmental sustainability. First, performance indicators and metrics are being developed and IR can have a role in developing and measuring institutional activities and events related to sustainability. This will support the work being done by the Association for the Advancement of Sustainability in Higher Education and the Global Reporting Initiative. Also multiple organizations are creating ratings for the environmental sustainability of college campuses. In addition to the sustainability of the college organization and campus, there is also the hope that student learning outcomes include developing students who are more sensitive to sustainability and more actively engaged in sustainability initiatives. IR can take an active role in measuring institutional activities and student learning outcomes (McLaughlin & Amoroso, 2012).

Legal Implications

Since states or provinces make many laws affecting higher education, there are tremendous variations in the specific laws (HECA, n.d.). Unfortunately space does not permit discussion of this topic, so suffice it to say that IR can get involved in the statistical assessment of institutional compliance (see Boon, 2012).

The Current Profile of Institutional Research in the United States and Canada: What Is Our Business?

> IR is a "constant quest for new methodologies and their purposeful applications; enthusiasm for proposals made by others for new methods and new utilizations, but a vigilant skepticism for partisan, mediocre, or reputedly consummate solutions; [and a] willingness to assume a spectrum of responsibilities and requests to provide assistance to academic and administrative functions of the institution."
>
> *(Suslow, 1972, p. 17)*

IR exists on most US and Canadian college campuses. Whether it is handled by a part-time person or a team of full-time professionals or distributed across several offices, IR is important to an institution's understanding of itself, both internally and externally. As Volkwein, Liu, and Woodell (2012) discuss, the golden triangle of IR shows the typical duties of a) institutional reporting and policy analysis; b) planning, enrollment, and financial management; and c) outcomes assessment, program review, and accreditation. Some colleges combine all of these areas and call it institutional effectiveness.

Staffing of the institutional research function varies widely. A survey conducted in 2008–09 by Volkwein, Liu, and Woodell (2012) found the typical office had an average of three professionals with 28 percent being staffed by one person and only 14 percent with more than five FTE professionals. In *Landmarks of Tomorrow* (1959), Peter Drucker first used the term "knowledge worker." In 1994, he described this person as one who has advanced formal education and can apply theoretical and analytical techniques. IR practitioners are examples of knowledge workers as evidenced in Volkwein's survey. Either a doctorate or master's degree had been earned by 70 percent of IR staff. Office heads held advanced degrees in 90 percent of those offices surveyed (Volkwein et al., 2012).

Much of what an IR office does is dependent upon its place on the college's organizational chart. With most IR offices reporting through the academic function, their duties support academic decision making related to faculty and students (enrollment trends, faculty workload, etc.). An IR organization within finance and administration would more likely study the "business" of a college in the form of human, capital, and financial resources (defining alternate revenue sources, process efficiency, etc.). The IR function that reports to the president may be primarily concerned with supporting strategic planning and reporting for external constituencies including boards, legislators, alumni, funding agencies, and business and industry.

Institutional Research Within the Institution: Accountability, Assessment, Decision Support, and Planning

While there are some common functions within IR offices, the extent to which these commonalities define IR varies at the local level. IR offices are expected to perform some level of accountability reporting, assessment, decision support, and planning. With greater calls for postsecondary institutions to justify their existence, accountability continues to shift to the forefront with associated stakeholders (government, funding agencies, students, parents, and the public in general). A variety of tools have been put into place to ensure stakeholders can find the information they need regarding an institution's profile. For example, national and state/provincial reporting efforts provide various public data about an institution's operations.

The Integrated Postsecondary Education Data System (IPEDS) in the US and Statistics Canada (StatCan) act as central data repositories for basic information such as enrollment, completions, staffing, and finance. Efforts such as the Voluntary System of Accountability, the Voluntary Framework of Accountability, the University and College Accountability Network, and the relatively new Student Achievement Measure provide ways that US institutions can make even more information about their operations available in a format that is easily accessible and understood by the public (Keller, 2012).

In terms of assessment, institutions deploy a variety of methods to ensure that they are fulfilling their mission. Evaluating outcomes through survey research, focus groups, program review, and external peer review enable institutions to close the loop in their strategic planning and implementation efforts. Assessment provides the means to identify best practices that can be continued and performance gaps that can be corrected in the next phase of planning.

It is difficult to find a definition for "decision support" that does not involve the words "systems" or "technology." Saupe (1990) defined IR as "research conducted within an institution of higher education to provide information which supports institutional planning, policy formation and decision making (p. 1)." As decision support goes, institutional researchers can be uniquely positioned on a college campus to provide analysis in support of executive leadership teams. This does not imply that the IR function should go it alone. Rather, IR can provide decision support by bringing together subject matter experts to propose solutions to campus-wide issues. Distributed networks of institutional decision support can be created to effectively share the responsibility of using analytics to inform decision making, planning, and policy formation.

Decision support implies more immediate and ongoing action while the support of the strategic planning function indicates longer term, future-focused activities. Environmental scanning, benchmarking, and establishment of measures and metrics are areas in which institutional researchers can provide sustained leadership during the formation and implementation of their institution's strategic plan. Decision support and planning must be coordinated and they must be done effectively to ensure institutional success at all levels.

Trends, Unanswered Questions, and Conclusions

> To be sought after, institutional research must demonstrate concern for the problems that are of significance to those responsible for the affairs of the institution, and it must be capable of timely response. Institutional research evaluations and analyses will bring more order and rationality to administrative and academic processes if they accurately assess commonly perceived problems.
>
> *(Suslow, 1972, p. 8)*

The Future

The World Bank (n.d.) discusses the future as being based on a knowledge economy where an educated and skilled population creates, shares, and uses knowledge and there is effective communication, dissemination, and processing of information. It is their belief that such an economy is based on an educated and skilled group of citizens. It is also apparent that achieving that level of education and training will require postsecondary education of some type. Less obvious is what that education will look like and what IR's role will be in the new knowledge economy.

What Are the Commonly Perceived Problems for IR?

The future issues and opportunities for IR are dependent on the issues and opportunities for higher education. The Society of College and University Planners (SCUP) recently identified the number one challenge in the future of higher education as *disruptive change* (SCUP, 2013). These are aspects of colleges that will change because new technology or processes are going to displace current values and ways of doing things. "Alternative (and free) educational delivery platforms, new ventures and players, dramatically decreased governmental support, greater accountability, and increasing regulations have challenged the traditional higher education model. The multiple drivers of disruption have prompted the reimagining and reshaping of higher education" (SCUP, 2013).

The forces of change include continued loss of financial support while being asked to educate more students to a higher level of success. This comes with more political pressure and changes in senior leadership. Often there seems to be no clear institutional path forward (SCUP, 2013).

If IR follows the advice of Suslow, it has to provide analytical decision support in the context of this disruptive change. The disruptive change in the institutional knowledge model will require a large number of major decisions be made in a shortened time frame and in areas of financial, physical, and personnel resources as well as student success. Decision makers will need to become part of the analytic process and IR will need to be able to anticipate decisions that will be required. This will reduce the time between identifying a problem and developing a solution. The Association of Governing Boards has outlined what it considers to be key decision areas for boards of directors at colleges and universities (Pelletier, 2013):

- *Institutional administration*: Having a sustainable revenue model, operating with productivity and efficiency, managing student financial aid, and educating students in a global world.
- *Learning*: Optimizing educational delivery, enhancing student learning, and improving student success in retention and graduation.
- *Collegial Governance*: Balancing market and mission, maintaining an energized academic workforce, and monitoring institutional risk management.

The Challenge

What challenges our ability to remain professionally relevant and to be more than a reporting function? The answers will vary by institution but the following are some thoughts.[2]

a. *Resources*: We need to maintain leverage over our key inputs. Our key inputs are data, analytical methodologies, and organizational access to academic and administrative personnel, particularly those in leadership positions.
b. *Customers*: We need to identify and meet our customers' needs. The support needs to be adequate quality, affordable, and prompt. We need a short turn-around time on requests and a consistent set of products that are available on-the-shelf.
c. *Competition and New Suppliers*: We need core competencies and value added beyond brand loyalty. Units with technology and access to university data can produce dashboards. IR's competitive advantage is that we are a pragmatic community with a very broad range of integrated knowledge. We need, as Suslow said, an "attitude of critical and systematic appraisal."
d. *Alternative Goods and Services*: Decision making and the formation of opinion can occur without data or information. We need to reduce uncertainty by using the appropriate methodology. If we provide the essential elements of information, the alternative of less data and less information should always be less desirable.

Unanswered Questions

To bridge between the present and the future and to be viable as a profession requires reflection and responsiveness and then the ability to prepare for the future.

The following are some of the questions IR needs to answer to sustain itself in the knowledge economy.

1. Will we have appropriate data of sufficient quality? The professional facilitation of data quality and information use has been our core competency. It takes time and effort to build adequate quality data. We need to be knowledgeable participants in the data management and governance at our institutions (McLaughlin, Howard, Cunningham, Blythe, & Payne, 2004).
2. Will we have the tools and technology for the knowledge economy? Historically we have been very good with using methodology and technology. Both methodology and technology are experiencing rapid change. Our profession needs to be an active learning community that includes not only basic skills but also includes expert mastery (NRC, 2000, pp. 31–50).
3. Can we leverage regulatory reporting for decision support? With requirements for greater accountability, we must provide analyses to internal and external constituents to demonstrate our institution's stewardship of student learning outcomes, research impact, economic development, and financial resources. We should turn regulatory reporting into a strategic asset for decision support (Howard, 2001).
4. Will we have the key knowledge about learning? We need to understand the intellectual aspects of learning, the concepts of effectively engaging learners, and the assessment of learning outcomes. Webinars and handbooks on basic topics are the start of the journey, not the final destination (Ewell, 1997; Kuh, Kinzie, Schuh, & Whitt, 2010).
5. Can we support and partner with strategic data-informed managers? Our colleges need to be economically sustainable with solid business models. They will need to be competitive with low cost, create a strategic niche, and/or have robust brand loyalty. Strategic institutional management will be an essential knowledge base (Lyddon et al., 2012).
6. Will we be "at the table" for strategic discussions and decision making? As data and information systems become more automated, IR professionals will need to serve as a strategic resource, supporting planning and decision making with contextual interpretations of internal and external data-based arguments and proposals (Calderon & Mathies, 2013).
7. Will we be adaptive and have the needed expertise to function within the disruptive change? We need to have experts and educate for the required expertise to be innovative. Experts can create new rules and build a "learning to learn" reality. Experts have "adaptive expertise" and are metacognitive (Terenzini, 2013).
8. Can our associations support our profession? Our associations need to be learning communities and communities of practice for our skills, providing opportunities for us to practice with presentations, collegial projects, and professional activities. They need to be networks of knowledgeable and

supportive colleagues. They need to explain what we do to external stake-holders (Suslow, 1972).

Conclusion

> If we are pretentious in our pride for our achievements to date, then let us simply accept it; if we are satisfied to rest with this achievement then we are foolish, and, if we cannot accelerate and enlarge on our achievements then, I, for one, will be damned disappointed.
>
> *(Suslow, 1971, p. 3)*

The preceding has painted a rapid picture of IR in the US and Canada. It has also provided many resources and references where additional discussions are available. The future is going to be challenging for higher education and for IR. Accountability will increase in the amount of data and complexity as the demand for postsecondary education will continue to grow while it changes character. Assessment of learning outcomes will continue to be at the center of the political conversation. Accessibility and affordability will also continue to be highly political. Institutions will need to manage tensions as the traditional markets for students and benefactors may diminish and mission agendas may conflict with new opportunities. We will definitely need to "accelerate and enlarge on our achievements." If we do, our opportunities are exciting and promise to be rewarding.

Notes

1. For more history of Canadian post-secondary education see: http://cicic.ca/421/an-overview.canada#2. For more US history see Kinzie et al. (2004).
2. Adapted from Porter's Five Competitive Forces (Lyddon, McComb, & Mizak, 2012).

References

AIR. (2014). *Delta cost project*. American Institutes for Research. Retrieved from www.deltacostproject.org/.

Aud, S. (2013). *The condition of education, 2013*. National Center for Education Statistics. Retrieved from https://nces.ed.gov/.

Boon, R. D. (2012). Regulated ethics: Institutional research compliance with IRB'S and FERPA. In R. D. Howard, G. W. McLaughlin, & W. E. Knight (Eds.), *The handbook of institutional research* (pp. 325–339). San Francisco, CA: Jossey-Bass.

CAE. (2014). Press release. *Voluntary support of education in 2013*. Council on Aid to Education. Retrieved from http://cae.org/fundraising-in-education/category/annual-press-release/.

Calderon, A., & Mathies, C. (2013). Institutional research in the future: Challenges within higher education and the need for excellence in professional practice. In Angel Calderon & Karen L. Webber (Eds.), *Global issues in institutional research* (pp. 77–90). *New Directions for Institutional Research, 157*. San Francisco, CA: Wiley.

CEDS. (n.d.). *Common education data standards.* Department of Education. Retrieved from https://ceds.ed.gov/.

CICIC. (n.d. a). *Postsecondary education systems in Canada: An overview.* Canadian Information Centre for International Credentials. Retrieved from http://cicic.ca/421/an-overview.canada.

CICIC. (n.d. b). *Quality assurance practices in Canada: An overview.* Canadian Information Centre for International Credentials. Retrieved from http://cicic.ca/658/quality-assurance.canada.

CMEC. (n.d.). Home page. *Council of Ministers of Education of Canada.* Retrieved from www.cmec.ca/en/.

COPS. (n.d.). *Canadian occupational projection system 2011 projections.* Employment and Social Development Canada. Retrieved from www.esdc.gc.ca/eng/home.shtml.

Drucker, P. F. (1959). *The landmarks of tomorrow.* New York, NY: Harper & Row.

Drucker, P. F. (1994). The age of social transformation. *The Atlantic Monthly, 274,* 53–80.

Eaton, J. S. (2009). *An overview of U.S. accreditation.* The Council for Higher Education Accreditation. Retrieved from www.chea.org/pdf/2009.06_Overview_of_US_Accreditation.pdf.

Ewell, P. T. (1997). *Principles of learning.* 1997 AAHE Summer Academy at Snowbird. Retrieved from www.intime.uni.edu/model/learning/learn_summary.html.

FRB. (February, 2014). *Quarterly report on household debt and credit.* Federal Reserve Bank of New York. Retrieved from www.newyorkfed.org/householdcredit/2013-Q4/HHDC_2013Q4.pdf.

Garcia, T. I. (2013). *In search of a value proposition: Postsecondary thoughts on the common education data standards.* State Higher Education Executive Officers. Retrieved from www.sheeo.org/resources/publications/search-value-proposition-postsecondary-thoughts-common-education-data.

Grajek, S. (June 3, 2013). *Top-ten IT issues—2013: Welcome to the connected age: EDUCAUSE Review,* 31–57. Retrieved from www.educause.edu/ero/article/top-ten-it-issues-2013-welcome-connected-age.

HECA. (n.d.). Home page. *Higher education compliance alliance.* Retrieved from http://highered compliance.org/.

Hendel, D. D., & Harrold, R. (2007). Changes in Clark-Trow subcultures from 1976 to 2006: Implications for addressing undergraduates' leisure interests. *The College Student Affairs Journal, 27*(1), 8–23.

Howard, R. D. (Ed.). (2001). *Institutional research: Decision support in higher education.* Tallahassee, FL: Association for Institutional Research.

IPEDS. (n.d.). *Integrated Postsecondary Education Data System.* National Center for Education Statistics. Retrieved from http://nces.ed.gov/ipeds/.

Kahn. (n.d.). *Khan Academy.* Retrieved from www.khanacademy.org.

Keller, C. M. (2012). Collective responses to a new era of accountability in higher education. In R. D. Howard, G. W. McLaughlin, & W. E. Knight (Eds.), *The handbook of institutional research* (pp. 371–365). San Francisco CA: Jossey-Bass.

Kinzie, J., Palmer, M., Hayek, J., Hossler, D., Jacob, S. A., & Cummings, H. (2004). Fifty years of college choice: Social, political and institutional influences on the decision making process. *New Agenda Series, 5*(3). Indianapolis, IN: Lumina Foundation for Education.

Kuh, G. D., Kinzie, J., Schuh, J. H., & Whitt, E. J. (2010). *Student success in college: Creating conditions that matter.* San Francisco, CA: Jossey-Bass.

Lasher, W. F. (2011). The history of institutional research and its role in American higher education over the past 50 years. In M. Coughlin & R. D. Howard (Eds.), *The Association for Institutional Research: The first 50 years.* Tallahassee, FL: The Association for Institutional Research.

Lingenfelter, P. E. (n.d.). *Governing bodies of higher education institutions: Roles and responsibilities.* Retrieved from www.oecd.org/edu/imhe/37378272.pdf.

Lyddon, J., McComb, B., & Mizak, P. (2012). Tools for setting strategy. In R. D. Howard, G. W. McLaughlin, & W. E. Knight (Eds.), *The handbook of institutional research* (pp. 611–624). San Francisco, CA: Jossey-Bass.

McLaughlin, J. S., & Amoroso, L. (2012). Managing sustainability. In R. D. Howard, G. W. McLaughlin, & W. E. Knight (Eds.), *The handbook of institutional research* (pp. 268–294). San Francisco, CA: Jossey-Bass.

McLaughlin, G. W., & Howard, R. D. Cunningham, L. B., Blythe, E. W., & Payne, E. (2004). People, processes, and managing data (2nd ed.). *Resources in Institutional Research.* 15. Tallahassee, FL: Association for Institutional Research.

McLaughlin, J. S., Pavelka, D., & McLaughlin, G. (2005). Assessing the integrity of web sites providing data and information on corporate behavior. *Journal of Education for Business,* *80*(6), 333–337.

MSU. (2013). Current trends in national foundation funding for education, corporate and foundation research. Michigan State University. Retrieved from www.education.msu.edu/.

National Commission on Accountability in Higher Education. (2005). Accountability for better results: A national imperative for higher education. State Higher Education Executive Officers. Retrieved from www.sheeo.org/pubs/pubs_search.asp.

National Research Council. (2000). How experts differ from novices. In *How people learn, NRC* (pp. 31–50). Washington DC: National Academy Press.

National Center for Educational Statistics. (2012). Digest of higher education statistics: 2012. NCES. Retrieved from http://nces.ed.gov/programs/digest/d12/.

Pelletier, S. (2013). Top 10 strategic issues for boards: 2013–2014. Association of Governing Boards of Universities and Colleges. Retrieved from http://agb.org/store/top-10-strategic-issues-boards-2013-2014.

Rae, B. (2005). Ontario, a leader in learning: Report and recommendations, February 2005. Scribd. Retrieved from www.scribd.com/doc/109938410/Ontario-A-Leader-in-Learning-Report-Recommendations-Honourable-Bob-Rae-February-2005.

Reichard, D. J. (2012). History of institutional research. In R. D. Howard, G. W. McLaughlin, & W. E. Knight (Eds.), *The handbook of institutional research* (pp. 22–56). San Francisco, CA: Jossey-Bass.

Saupe, J. L. (1990). The functions of institutional research (2nd ed.). Tallahassee, FL: *Association of Institutional Research.*

SCUP. (2013). Report on trends in higher education planning—2013, SCUP academy council. Society of College and University Planners. Retrieved from www.scup.org/page/resources/books/rotihep2013.

SHEEO. (n.d.). State higher education executive officers. Retrieved from www.sheeo.org/.

StatCan. (n.d.). *Surveys and statistical programs by subject. Education, Training and Learning.* Statistics Canada. Retrieved from www.statcan.gc.ca/concepts/index-eng.htm. Demographic statistics retrieved from www5.statcan.gc.ca/cansim/a05?lang=eng&id=4770019; http://publications.gc.ca/Collection/Statcan/81-582-X/institution.pdf and www.statcan.gc.ca/tables-tableaux/sum-som/l01/cst01/educ68a-eng.htm.

Suslow, S. (1971). Present reality of institutional research [Presidential address]. In C. T. Steward (Ed.), *Institutional research and institutional policy formulation: Proceedings of the 11 annual forum of the Association for Institutional Research* (pp. 1–3). Tallahassee FL: Association for Institutional Research.

Suslow, S. (1972). *A declaration on institutional research.* Tallahassee FL: Esso Education Foundation and Association for Institutional Research.

Terenzini, P. T. (2013). On the nature of institutional research revisited: Plus ça change . . . ? *Research in Higher Education, 54*(2), 137–148.

United States Department of Education. (n.d.). Overview: Mission. USDE. Retrieved from www2.ed.gov/about/overview/mission/mission.html?src=ln.

Volkwein, F. J., Liu, Y., & Woodell, J. (2012). The structure and functions of institutional research offices. In R. D. Howard, G. W. McLaughlin, and W. E. Knight (Eds.), *The handbook of institutional research* (pp. 22–39). San Francisco, CA: Jossey-Bass.

WICHE. (2012). *Knocking at the college door, projections of high school graduates.* Western Interstate Commission for Higher Education. Retrieved from www.wiche.edu.

World Bank. (n.d.). *The four pillars of the knowledge economy.* The World Bank. Retrieved from http://go.worldbank.org/5WOSIRFA70.

5

INSTITUTIONAL RESEARCH IN EUROPE

A View from the European Association for Institutional Research

Jeroen Huisman, Peter Hoekstra, and Mantz Yorke

Introduction

Those familiar with the European higher education landscape and its history know that higher education is very much a national affair (e.g., Neave, 2001), in that national governments determine, to a considerable extent, the policies for higher education and hence largely "steer" or give direction to institutional strategies of higher education institutions. National governments have also been increasingly keen to assess institutional performance on a range of dimensions. Neave, in consequence, has referred in this connection to the rise of the 'evaluative state' (Neave, 1988, 1998).

The institutions in each European system are confronted with different challenges and expectations, different stakeholders, and—importantly—different levels of institutional autonomy. Estermann, Nokkala, and Steinel (2011) show that there are considerable differences in institutional autonomy between European countries and also with respect to different facets of autonomy (financial, academic, organizational, staffing). Without going into the details of their scorecard method, they show that countries differ largely. For example, the UK scores 100% on organizational autonomy, whereas Luxembourg scores 31%, yet Luxembourg is ranked highest (91%) for financial autonomy and Cyprus lowest (23%). Further, the internal functioning of European higher education institutions differs widely, for instance with respect to governance structures. And, finally, the European higher education institutions differ significantly in terms of their heritage, with some institutions being almost a millennium old and others only recently established.

For sure, at a high level of abstraction, all these institutions have to some extent tackled issues such as access, participation, retention, research performance, and their third mission, outreach. The point is, however, that these issues are very much influenced by the particular national context. To give an example, access will be conceptualized very differently in a higher education system that has low participation rates and a very unequal participation by social-economic background of its students, embedded in a context where there is limited institutional autonomy to develop institutional strategies than if it is embedded in a higher education system in which participation rates are high and higher education institutions strongly compete for students in a market-driven environment.

If we take these different conditions and contextual factors together, it seems very reasonable to argue that institutional research plays out in very different ways in this highly diverse European landscape. We take Terenzini's (2013) intelligences as a conceptual framework to illustrate these differences in more detail.

Reflecting on institutional research in the US over a span of two decades, Terenzini (1993, 2013) argues that institutional research is 'organizational intelligence,' and stresses that three competencies are necessary:

- *Technical/analytical intelligence*, the 'toolbox,' which includes the crafts of data mining and analysis;
- *Issues intelligence*, which relates to understanding how higher education institutions function internally. Here he argues that institutional researchers need substantive knowledge (from the research literature) on the core issues that institutional research should focus on. As important, institutional researchers must be able to learn to play the institutional research game in collegial, bureaucratic, and political settings within their higher education institutions; and
- *Contextual intelligence*, which denotes a sound grasp of context and culture. This includes understanding the overarching issues of higher education as well as the specific contextual issues of a specific campus or group of institutions.

Combining these competencies with the generic role of institutional research (in shorthand: data collection for decision support) and the diversity of higher education in Europe, it is easy to see that the particular role of institutional research in European higher education institutions will differ largely. If institutional research is about decision support, it is of crucial importance to consider how much scope there actually is for making institutional strategic decisions and hence how much organizational intelligence is needed—and in which form. From the above it seems clear that painting a picture of institutional research in Europe is quite challenging and difficult to achieve within the limits of a book chapter. Our response to the challenge is based on an examination of the activities of a long-standing European organization—the European Association for Institutional Research (EAIR). The analysis focuses on how institutional research has been interpreted in practice, and by whom. For sure, this analysis only shows a tip of the iceberg, but we prefer this focus above a sketchy and patchy description of what happens at particular institutions, in particular European higher education systems. In all, it will give the reader a general insight in what institutional research in Europe entails, including its contemporary and future challenges.

We structure this chapter as follows. We first briefly describe the emergence and development of EAIR from its start in 1979. We then analyze the contributions to the annual forums, concentrating on the period 2011–13, that can be labeled as examples of institutional research. We close down the chapter with conclusions and reflections.

Background of EAIR and Its Development Over Time

There are two clearly different factors that account for the emergence and development of EAIR. First, within the International Activities Subcommittee of the US-based Association for Institutional Research (AIR), ideas were explored to broaden the association's geographical scope, a small AIR European Forum in Paris in 1979 being the result (Begg & Belanger, 2003). Subsequent forums were held in other European cities and through their successes a lively community of administrators, researchers, and policy-makers kept interest in institutional research alive in Europe. Second, that interest got a boost in the 1980s, given changing governmental views on institutional autonomy in European higher education. From the mid-1980s, national governments granted higher education institutions more autonomy in exchange for forms of accountability (Neave & Van Vught, 1991). This required the institutions to make (more) use of their internal capacity and intelligence to generate information and data in order to satisfy the government's wish to oversee the institutions. But in many systems this institutional monitoring (Neave, 2003) went hand in hand with another internal use of this intelligence, that is, to use it in the context of the institution's strategic management. Taking the intrinsic and extrinsic motivation for institutional research together, there were clear drivers for European IR activities in the broadest sense. It is therefore not a surprise that the annual forums led to the institutionalization of EAIR in 1989 as an independent membership organization (see Begg & Belanger, 2003 for vivid details).

Early Years of EAIR

Institutional research did not exist as a profession in the early years of EAIR. Indeed, the term 'institutional research' was, until recently, relatively little used in Europe. So whereas in other parts of the world associations for institutional research were seen as vehicles for professional development, EAIR became "a Society for higher education, linking research, policy and practice" (see EAIR website). In that way, EAIR attracted a broad group of participants that had some sort of engagement with IR (even though they may not at that time have acknowledged the term), which fitted with the European tradition of exchanging ideas across differing components of higher education systems and institutions. Part of the difficulties in developing an administrative profession called IR was the existing 'firewall' between academics working in the field of academic research and academics working in the administration. Many European policy-makers had the feeling that research should be exclusively done in research departments and institutes, not in the administration. This firewall constituted a barrier against the interaction between the two worlds of academic work and administration.

EAIR became more known as an acronym than as its expanded form, with—as noted above—the phrase 'institutional research' being relatively little used. The silver jubilee book reflecting on 25 years of EAIR (Begg, 2003) was called *The Dialogue between Higher Education Research and Practice*—and by 'higher education research' the authors meant the academic discipline (or better: field of study). However, EAIR was not isolated from developments elsewhere in the world, for institutional researchers from North America, Australia, and South Africa presented their work at EAIR Forums. IR became a kind of oscillation point, the point at which the conversation between research, policy, and practice fluctuated.

The Growth of IR and EAIR

In due course, IR came formally into being in some European countries. As said above, these were especially the countries where HEIs were more autonomous (United Kingdom, the Netherlands, Germany, Scandinavia). In the Netherlands the DAIR, the Dutch Association for IR, came into being, and more recently the Higher Education Institutional Research network (HEIR) was established in the UK and Ireland.

Looking back at the developments in the past decade, two issues stand out. First, from an initiative by enthusiastic AIR members and European individuals, EAIR developed into a non-profit association with a professional secretariat/executive management and a governance structure with an executive committee, president, and scope for members to discuss issues at the annual general meeting, and it launched the journal *Tertiary Education and Management* in 1995. Over the past five years, around 300 participants have attended the annual forum. Second, although adequately depicted as a kind of spin-off of AIR, EAIR matured in a particular European context. Whereas AIR continued to focus on institutional research as information collection, analysis, and utilization related to institutional strategic management (e.g., Peterson, 2003; Terenzini, 2013), EAIR, almost from the beginning, has been home to institutional researchers and to traditional discipline- and field-based higher education researchers (e.g., Teichler, 2000, for a classification of the different types of higher education researchers). This is reflected in the participation at the annual forum, with roughly 40% of the attendants being academics, 40% being institutional researchers and administrators, and about 20% policy-makers and representatives of professional organizations in higher education (as a side line, it is worth noting that many participants and members come from outside Europe). It is also reflected in the association's current strategy and mission and the strapline "Linking research, policy and practice." As such, EAIR´s activities are a reflection of higher education developments in Europe (and other parts of the world) in which both governments and higher education institutions are key players. Hence EAIR has an inclusive interest in higher education from different perspectives and stakeholders: management and other professionals within higher education institutions, academic researchers, and those involved in policy preparation and development.

Institutional Research at EAIR Forums, 2008–13

In this section we depict institutional research in Europe from the perspective of contributions to the EAIR Forums that can be labeled as institutional research due to the fact that these contributions were sent in for and accepted in an EAIR Forum-track that was called IR. In doing so, we acknowledge that in large parts of Europe, IR is not recognized as a profession in the domain of the administration (as it is in other parts of the world): while EAIR recognizes activities as IR, some participants would not label them as IR. We therefore have chosen a non-imperialistic and pragmatic approach to our analysis that respects the self-image of the forum participants.

EAIR has always shaped its annual forums in cooperation with host institutions (which could add specific topics, but had to stay within the boundaries of the policy and tradition of the association). The themes of *student experience, staff,* and *governance or management* have remained consistent across forums, with these terms appearing in track titles.

Who are the participants at EAIR Forums? Table 5.1 gives an overview of the backgrounds of the forum participants over the period 2008–13. Please note that the backgrounds are self-reported and hence there may be some ambiguity hidden in the tables: a quality manager in one institution may qualify him/herself as 'quality,' but in another institution as 'management,' whereas the actual job function may

TABLE 5.1 Background of EAIR Participants, 2008–2013

General Category	Percent	Specific Work Titles or Roles
Academic	21%	Lecturers, Professors, Principals, Emeriti, PhD-students
Management★	26%	Rectors, Deans, University Board Members, Managers
Administration	37%	Controllers, Office Manager, Administrators, Institutional Researchers
Quality	8%	Quality Assurance
Others	8%	Economics, Business, Computing, Editors, Communication

★ A number of those categorized here as managers also had policy-making functions.

be similar. Please also note the thin line that may exist between 'management' and 'administration.'

On a more restricted classification, if we define an institutional researcher as a person who is professionally working in an administrative office (analyzing institutional data on an institutional or system-level), the percentage of institutional researchers is much lower. When we accept this definition and count only offices and departments such as the Academic Practice Unit, Department of Institutional Statistics and Analysis, Office of Institutional Research and Evaluation, or the Institutional Planning and Analysis Office and job titles such as Research Officer, Analyst, Research Associate, IR Specialist, etc., the percentage of forum participants that one could define as institutional researchers is about half of the category 'Administration,' that is to say, about 15–20% of all the participants.

Institutional research tracks at EAIR Forums. The EAIR Forum did not have an explicitly labeled IR track until 2005. This constituted a belated acknowledgement of the fact that many of the forum's contributions, hitherto not specifically labeled as institutional research, would in fact be entirely consistent with the professionalized context of institutional research in the United States. At the Riga Forum of 2005 a track entitled "Institutional Research and Higher Education" was included as "the track that addressed the impact of Institutional Research—the activity that gave EAIR its name." In the invitation to submit proposals for the forum, EAIR proposal documents stated that "IR may be unknown as a concept in many European countries, but it is well known as a function. Within higher education, IR's role is to provide decision makers with essential information about their institutions and the environment in which they operate. In that way IR supports decision makers to make informed decisions and to realize their ambitions more effectively."

The track was highly successful in attracting papers—so many, indeed, that it was decided to create a double IR track. Thirty-one presenters and authors presented 18 papers and participated in a well-attended round table discussion about the effectiveness of IR. Presenters came from a wide range of countries, including the US, UK, Latvia, Netherlands, Canada, Argentina, Finland, South Africa, Australia, and Saudi Arabia.

The balance of the presenters was roughly even between those from Europe and those from outside Europe (most from North America). In other aspects, the track was balanced as well. About half of the authors were academics: professors, researchers, or lecturers; the other half were administrators: policy officers, information-analysts, and institutional researchers.

The themes that were addressed were split into two groups of fairly equal size: 10 presentations dealt with the methods and theory of IR itself. They offered contributions devoted to the development of the IR instruments, such as performance indicators and institutional dashboards, or pointed out new challenges and opportunities for IR in developments such as accreditation and internationalization. The other half of the presentations were case studies of practice, evidencing effectiveness in institutional research. The studies covered topics such as research into student satisfaction, diversity and retention, and non-traditional undergraduates. Sometimes the studies had been performed at the level of the institution; sometimes at the level of a national system.

The importance of the Riga Forum for institutional research in Europe was that it was the first time institutional research was made explicit as an activity meriting a track on its own—though much IR work had previously been located under different headings. Despite the considerable success of the institutional research track at Riga, it was not till 2010 that EAIR decided to introduce three fixed tracks that would have a stable position for a number of years. The three themes were: *Student experience, Governance, and Institutional Research.* Thus the three forums in 2011, 2012, and 2013 all had an IR track. IR has thereby been given greater visibility in the association.

The institutional research tracks at these three forums centered on different aspects of institutional research (see Table 5.2). In these three years, 35 IR papers

TABLE 5.2 Coverage for IR Topics at EAIR Forums, 2001–2013

Venue	*Year*	*Abbreviated description of track coverage*
Warsaw	2011	**Institutional Research: Working for the academic community**
		The track emphasizes strategies for gathering, analyzing, and distributing information as well as the challenges and opportunities for IR. The track offers institutional researchers, policy makers, and other members of the academic community the opportunity to exchange ideas on critical information needs in HE and on strategies and resources for improving the profession of institutional research.
Stavanger	2012	**Institutional Research: Measuring effectiveness in higher education**
		The track treated 'measuring effectiveness' sufficiently broadly to encompass measurement methodologies as well as the outcomes of measurements in respect of institutional functioning such as teaching and learning, technology transfer, and contributions to society. Particular encouragement was given to proposals that supported decision making or contributed to a better understanding of successful practices and processes to improve higher education.
Rotterdam	2013	**Institutional Research: How to measure impact**
		Proposals were sought that helped higher education institutions to better understand their overall performance or performance in specific areas such as education and research. The track covered methodologies for measurement, performance indicators and metrics, the collection and the validity of data, and the role of institutional research beyond measurement.

were presented by 64 authors/presenters. In terms of the national affiliation, these authors primarily came from the UK (17%), US (16%), Germany (14%), the Netherlands (13%), Canada (9%), Norway (9%), and 22% came from other countries. When submitting their paper proposals, the corresponding author could indicate to what extent the paper was academic, a policy-oriented/case study of practice, or a combination of these. The papers were reasonably divided among these categories, with 37%, 37%, and 26%, respectively. Where a contribution was labeled 'academic,' the research-based offerings were usually based on empirical data of various kinds and their analysis, as were the case studies. The 'discursive' and policy-oriented contributions were more conceptual in character.

In the three forums, the keywords most cited were: higher education research design and institutional performance measures (2011); institutional performance measures, governance, and assessment/evaluation (2012); and institutional performance measures and quality (2013). There is a clear dominance of attention to performance measures, not surprising given the increasing attention of many governments (and subsequently higher education institutions) to performance indicators. The keywords suggest that there is more emphasis on 'technical/analytical intelligence' and 'issues intelligence' than there is on 'contextual intelligence.' Against that, however, it should be noted that the keynote presentations at the forum typically address 'big picture' concerns—i.e., the third of Terenzini's 'intelligences.' Case studies have typically been provided by academics working in administrative roles, who presented their own practices that they considered to be good examples of projects such as effective student surveys or management information methodologies.

The use by academic researchers of institutional data builds a bridge with the administration, and with data analysts that do the collecting, the cleansing, and analyzing. The varied participation at EAIR Forums implicitly encourages such bridge-building, and invites administrators and academics to collaborate in order to strengthen practices and to make them more theoretically informed.

Institutional Research in Europe Contrasted With That in the United States

Known well to many readers, and mentioned in several chapters of this book, Volkwein's (1999) fourfold categorization of institutional research describes the roles of the IR practitioner as information authority, policy analyst, spin doctor, and scholar and researcher. Serban (2002) later added a fifth area—knowledge management—that Volkwein (2008) included in a later categorization.[1] Various writers from the US (e.g., Saupe, 1990; Howard, 2001) have stressed the role of the institutional research office as primarily 'information authority,' serving management's needs, while fulfilling some or all of the other aspects listed by Volkwein. The existence of a specialist office for institutional research provides management with a focal point to approach for data analysis and presentation. The 'spin doctor' role is probably under-represented in public presentations and writings, simply because overt acknowledgement could undermine effective practice.

The relative lack of such a formal structure in Europe (though there are specialist units in some institutions such as the University of Amsterdam), coupled with a strong tradition of academic research, has given institutional research a different coloring. An examination of contributions to EAIR Forums for the years 2011–13 shows an emphasis on two of Volkwein's categories, 'information authority' and 'scholar and researcher,' with the latter tending to dominate. Some examples of recent presentations are as follows.

IR as Information Authority

- "Be Informed," A management information system at the University of Maastricht: A case study (Dolman & Koelewijn, 2013).
- Strategic portfolio management in higher education—A practical case from the University of Stavanger (Tjelta, 2012).
- Decision support for the academia at Uppsala University (Olsson, Eriksson, & Kettis, 2012).
- Assessing the outcomes and impact of doctoral programs: Two institutional approaches (Snover, Daries, & Gordon, 2013).
- Data warehouse sharing and the changing role of institutional research (Veraart, 2011).

IR as Scholar and Researcher: (a) Reflections on Sources and Methods

- What is 'good enough?' Some practical considerations relating to the analysis of existing datasets (Yorke, 2011).
- Using productivity measures to provide feedback to academic and research programs (Snover, Carpenter-Hubin, & Rohlinger, 2012).
- Retention and withdrawal: Using longitudinal, multiple-source data to inform institutional policy (Heerman, De Wit, & Verhesschen, 2012).

IR as Scholar and Researcher: (b) Academic, Empirical Research

- The utility of assessments as predictors of study success in master programs (Van Os & Van Beek, 2011).
- The estimation of peer effects for research productivity in higher education (Opitz & Röbken, 2011).
- Identifying, characterizing and assessing new practices in doctoral education (Baschung, 2012).
- The impact of pre-entry English test results on postgraduate success (May, Forland, & Van der Sluis, 2013).

IR as Scholar and Researcher: (c) Academic, Theoretical or Discursive

- New nails in the coffin of standardized tests as comparators of institutional quality (Banta, 2013).
- Knowledge structures and patterns of external engagement. On the causality of external quality assurance in higher education institutions (Pinheiro, Garmann Johnsen, & Nordmann, 2012).

Conclusions and Reflections

The rise of the 'evaluative state' (Neave, 1988, 1998) has encouraged European higher education institutions to look at their internal functioning and at their performances as seen by the outside world, and so institutional research has grown in visibility. However, much that nowadays is labeled as institutional research was already being undertaken under different names and in units such as academic planning offices. European institutions have really been practicing institutional research without realizing it. The situation calls to mind Monsieur Jourdain in Molière's *Le bourgeois gentilhomme* who is surprised and delighted to discover that he has been speaking prose all his life without realizing it—however, the difference is that IR practitioners are not so pretentious and self-deceiving as the aspirant social climber Jourdain.

EAIR has provided a focus for activities that can be subsumed by institutional research. Indeed, the term institutional research has been increasingly used in EAIR Forum keynotes and tracks; it is becoming a term that is widely understood, even if it often lacks structural representation in institutions. The diversity of forum participants indicates that all three of Terenzini's (1993, 2013) 'intelligences' can be found in European IR, though participants vary considerably in the particular intelligence(s) they bring to the fore. However, the analysis of the keywords relating to recent forum presentations suggests that 'contextual intelligence' is the least prominent of the three. Alternatively, we could argue that the 'contextual intelligence' and 'issues intelligence' are most visible in the academic papers at EAIR, possibly somewhat disconnected from the 'technical/analytical' intelligence. Taking Volkwein's (1999) slant on institutional research, European institutional research is currently represented strongly by scholars and researchers and to a lesser extent by information authorities. In the earlier days of EAIR academic management practices were more evident in forums, and the association's journal *Tertiary Education and Management* has over the years evolved more toward an academic publication from a publication that was happy to include descriptive accounts of actual practices.

A major difference from the position in the United States is that institutional research has not developed as a profession, with all that implies for professional and career development. This may be because national systems in Europe are smaller and more diverse, making commonality more difficult to achieve, and because those whose work encompasses institutional research can be found in a variety of positions, with only a minority seeing themselves as IR professionals.

One of the strengths of EAIR has been its ability to bring together academics, administrators, and policy-makers to hear about, and discuss, research and practices in a wide variety of contexts. Academic and administrator roles are increasingly overlapping as institutions seek to deal with the implications of the evaluative state. The edging toward a stronger emphasis on academics may however create some tensions in the community. Addressing these tensions is something with which EAIR will need to deal with in the years ahead. At the same time, the diversity must be cherished as a positive, for it offers much scope for learning and exchanges between the more academically oriented and practice-oriented participants. And, in the financially troubled post-crash years, attendance at EAIR's Forums has held up well—indeed, its recent forums have proved highly attractive. EAIR is apparently satisfying a need for professional exchange regarding institutional research, which indicates the significance that institutional research has for contemporary—and future—higher education.

Note

1. However, we believe it is doubtful whether Serban's addition is distinct enough to justify its inclusion since some senior institutional researchers might be involved in knowledge management as part of their role as set out originally by Volkwein.

References

Banta, T. (2013). *New nails in the coffin of standardized tests as comparators of institutional quality*. Paper presented at the 35th Annual EAIR Forum, Rotterdam, the Netherlands, August 28–31, 2013. http://eairaww.websites.xs4all.nl/forum/rotterdam/authors.asp?achternaam=914&wat=*achternaam*.

Baschung, L. (September, 2012). *Identifying, characterizing and assessing new practices in doctoral education*. Paper presented at the 34th Annual EAIR Forum, Stavanger, Norway, September 5–8, 2012. http://eair.nl/forum/stavanger/authors.asp?keyword=166&wat=keyword.

Begg, R. (Ed.). (2003). *The dialogue between higher education research and practice*. Dordrecht, the Netherlands: Kluwer Academic Publishers.

Begg, R., & Belanger, C. (2003). EAIR in the making, in R. Begg (Ed.), *The dialogue between higher education research and practice*. Dordrecht, the Netherlands: Kluwer Academic Publishers, pp. 15–30.

Dolman, M., & Koelewijn, A. (2013). *"Be Informed," A management information system at the UM: A case study*. Paper presented at the 35th Annual EAIR Forum, Rotterdam, the Netherlands, August 28–31, 2013. http://eairaww.websites.xs4all.nl/forum/rotterdam/authors.asp?track=53&wat=track.

Estermann, T., Nokkala, T., & Steinel, M. (2011). *University autonomy in Europe II. The scorecard*. Brussels, Belgium: European Association of Universities.

Heerman, C., De Wit, K., & Verhesschen, P. (September, 2012). *Retention and withdrawal: Using longitudinal, multiple-source data to inform institutional policy*. Paper presented at the 34th Annual EAIR Forum, Stavanger, Norway, September 5–8, 2012. http://eair.nl/forum/stavanger/authors.asp?achternaam=11877&wat=achternaam.

Howard, R. D. (2001). Foreword, in R. D. Howard (Ed.), *Institutional research: Decision Support in higher education*. Tallahassee, FL: Association for Institutional Research, pp. v–vii.

May, S., Forland, H., & Van der Sluis, H. (August, 2013). The impact of pre-entry English test results on postgraduate success. Paper presented at the 35th Annual EAIR Forum, Rotterdam, the Netherlands, August 28–31, 2013. http://eairaww.websites.xs4all.nl/forum/rotterdam/authors.asp?achternaam=11441&w at=achternaam.

Neave, G. (1988). On the cultivation of quality, efficiency and enterprise: An overview of recent trends in higher education in Western Europe, 1986–1988. *European Journal of Education, 23*(1/2), 7–23.

Neave, G. (1998). The evaluative state reconsidered. *European Journal of Education, 33*(3), 265–284.

Neave, G. (2001). The European dimension in higher education: An excursion into the modern use of historical analogues, in J. Huisman, P. Maassen, & G. Neave (Eds.), *Higher education and the nation state: The international dimension of higher education*. Amsterdam, Netherlands: Pergamon, pp. 13–73.

Neave, G. (2003). Institutional research: From case study to strategic instrument, in R. Begg (Ed.), *The dialogue between higher education research and practice*. Dordrecht, the Netherlands: Kluwer Academic Publishers, pp. 3–14.

Neave, G., & Van Vught, F. A. (Eds.). (1991). *Prometheus bound: The changing relationship between government and higher education in Western Europe*. Oxford, UK: Pergamon.

Olsson, M., Eriksson, L., & Kettis, Å. (September, 2012). *Decision support for the academia at Uppsala University*. Paper presented at the 34th Annual EAIR Forum, Stavanger, Norway, September 5–8, 2012. http://eair.nl/forum/stavanger/authors.asp?achternaam=11855&wat=achternaam.

Opitz, C., & Röbken, H. (August, 2011). *The estimation of peer effects for research productivity in higher education*. Paper presented at the 33rd Annual EAIR Forum, Warsaw, Poland, August 28–31, 2011. http://eairaww.websites.xs4all.nl/forum/warsaw/authors.asp?keyword=113&wat=keyword.

Peterson, M. (2003). Institutional research and management in the U.S. and Europe: Some EAIR-AIR comparisons, in R. Begg (Ed.), *The dialogue between higher education research and practice*. Dordrecht, the Netherlands: Kluwer Academic Publishers, pp. 31–44.

Pinheiro, R., Garmann Johnsen, H. C., & Nordmann, R. (September, 2012). *Knowledge structures and patterns of external engagement*. Paper presented at the 34th Annual EAIR Forum, Stavanger, Norway, September 5–8, 2012. http://eair.nl/forum/stavanger/authors.asp?track=48&wat=track.

Saupe, J. L. (1990). *The functions of institutional research*. Tallahassee, FL: Association for Institutional Research.

Serban, A. M. (2002). Knowledge management: The fifth face of institutional research, in A. M. Serban & J. Luan (Eds.), *Knowledge management: Building a competitive advantage in higher education, New Directions for Institutional Research, No. 113*. San Francisco, CA: Jossey-Bass, pp. 105–111.

Snover, L., Carpenter-Hubin, J., & Rohlinger, M. (September, 2012). *Using productivity measures to provide feedback to academic and research programs*. Paper presented at the 34th Annual EAIR Forum, Stavanger, Norway, September 5–8, 2012. http://eair.nl/forum/stavanger/authors.asp?achternaam=1118&wat=achternaam.

Snover, L., Daries, J., & Gordon, J. (August, 2013). *Assessing the outcomes and impact of doctoral programs: Two institutional approaches*. Paper presented at the 35th Annual EAIR Forum, Rotterdam, the Netherlands, August 28–31, 2013. http://eairaww.websites.xs4all.nl/forum/rotterdam/authors.asp?keyword=203&wat=keyword.

Teichler, U. (2000). Higher education research and its institutional basis, in S. Schwarz & U. Teichler (Eds.), *The institutional basis of higher education research: Experiences and perspectives.* Dordrecht, the Netherlands: Kluwer, pp. 13–24.

Terenzini, P. T. (1993). On the nature of institutional research and the knowledge and skills it requires. *Research in Higher Education, 34*(1), 1–10.

Terenzini, P. T. (2013). "On the nature of institutional research" revisited: Plus ça change . . . ? *Research in Higher Education, 54,* 137–148.

Tjelta, M. (September, 2012). *Strategic portfolio management in higher education—A practical case from the University of Stavanger.* Paper presented at the 34th Annual EAIR Forum, Stavanger, Norway, September 5–8, 2013. http://eair.nl/forum/stavanger/authors. asp?keyword=174&wat=keyword.

Van Os, W., & Van Beek, M. (August, 2011). *The utility of assessments as predictors of study success in Master Programmes.* Paper presented at the 33rd Annual EAIR Forum, Warsaw, Poland, August 28–31, 2011. http://eairaww.websites.xs4all.nl/forum/warsaw/authors. asp?keyword=131&wat=keyword.

Veraart, F. (August, 2011). *Data warehouse sharing and the changing role of institutional research.* Paper presented at the 33rd Annual EAIR Forum, Warsaw, Poland, August 28–31, 2011. http://eairaww.websites.xs4all.nl/forum/warsaw/authors.asp?keyword= 139&wat=keyword.

Volkwein, J. F. (1999). The four faces of institutional research, in J. F. Volkwein (Ed.), *What is institutional research all about? A critical and comprehensive assessment of the profession. New Directions for Institutional Research, 104.* San Francisco, CA: Jossey Bass, pp. 9–19.

Volkwein, J. F. (2008). The foundations and evolution of institutional research, in D. G. Terkla (Ed.), *Institutional research: More than just data. New Directions for Higher Education, No. 141.* San Francisco, CA: Jossey-Bass, pp. 5–20.

Yorke, M. (August, 2011). *What is 'good enough?' Some practical considerations relating to the analysis of existing datasets.* Paper presented at the 33rd Annual EAIR Forum, Warsaw, Poland, August 28–31, 2011. http://eairaww.websites.xs4all.nl/forum/warsaw/authors. asp?keyword=121&wat=keyword.

6

DECISION SUPPORT ISSUES IN CENTRAL AND EASTERN EUROPE

Manja Klemenčič, Ninoslav Šćukanec, and Janja Komljenović

Introduction

Since the 1990s, higher education institutions[1] across Europe have obtained more autonomy from government steering. Universities were granted the right to decide by themselves on their internal organization and conduct of their operations (Klemenčič, 2012). At the same time governments have strengthened the external and internal evaluation and accountability mechanisms, prompting the universities to show responsible use of public funds through various performance evaluations and other control mechanisms (Stensaker & Harvey, 2011). The 'evaluative state' has delegated evaluative competences onto independent agencies, such as quality assurance and accreditation agencies and research funding agencies (de Boer, Enders, & Schimank, 2007). Much of these changes have occurred within the policy context of the European Union's 'modernization agenda for higher education,' which has been communicated through a series of influential policy documents and accompanying financial instruments, and which emphasizes the strategic role of higher education in promoting the competitiveness of European economies (Klemenčič, 2012; Robertson, 2008), but also in contributing to greater social cohesion. Modernization agenda for higher education has obvious neoliberal ideational foundations and promotes adoption of a new public management approach to university governance and management, including emphasis on university performance according to desired indicators and external and internal evaluations (de Boer & File, 2009). The governments' expectations as to what universities should deliver have also become more explicit when higher education became unequivocally linked to economic progress and social well-being.

These developments have increased the governments'—and their auxiliary agencies'—demand for data on university operations. Also within the universities themselves there is need for more and better 'institutional intelligence' as the institutional leaders try to figure out how to fulfill the increasing demands from various stakeholders and try to envisage the position for their university in a national and global higher education 'market place.' This is indeed prime time for institutional research in Europe, even if the term as such has not been adopted in the European higher education vocabulary. Nevertheless, at European universities we can clearly identify strengthening *practices of collecting, synthesizing, and analyzing institutional data to fulfill mandatory reporting requirements, assessment, and to support university decision making and planning*, which is indeed what institutional research is referred to in Anglo-Saxon countries. Universities in Central and Eastern Europe have not been exempt from these developments; on the contrary. They too have been granted more autonomy and are subject to more accountability checks.

This chapter investigates how practices of collecting, synthesizing, and analyzing institutional data have developed at public universities in six countries in Central and Eastern Europe: Austria, Croatia, Poland, Romania, Serbia, and Slovenia. These countries have several points in common. For all six countries, the European Union is an important common point of reference.[2] They all participate in European Union education and training and research programs. They all also participate in the European Higher Education Area (also known as the Bologna Process), an intergovernmental cooperation in the area of higher education, which initiated major reforms of degree structures, quality assurance systems, and mobility mechanisms. Like in the rest of Europe, public funding of higher education is still predominant in this region, and, hence, the role of the state continues to be significant in steering the higher education systems.

However, there are also some profound differences among the six countries. Apart from Austria, these countries have emerged from socialist systems and with different socialist arrangements (e.g., from non-allied Yugoslavia as opposed to Warsaw Pact countries). Croatia, Serbia, and Slovenia were part of the former Yugoslavia with periods of armed conflict and significant processes of nation- and state-building after the secession. As a net contributor to the European Union budget, Austria is economically notably more developed. Given its resources, cultural affinity, and geographic proximity, Austria often serves as an initiator and a partner in regional development projects. The other five are at lower stages of economic development, and have an ambition to fast-forward the higher education modernization in line with the European Union proposal mentioned above to catch up with the more developed European neighbors. These different trajectories of higher education development offer important contextual frameworks in which university reforms and the development of institutional research practices are embedded. The Bologna Process and the European Union's 'modernization agenda for higher education' have served as an important source of guidance and technical and also financial support for the reform processes in the examined countries, in particular in the areas of institutional governance, quality assurance, and funding models, all of which have had crucial implications on the development of institutional research. Indeed, the knowledge-based economy that positions universities as important and central drivers of economic development (Jessop, 2008) is strongly present in the region.

In this chapter, we explore the developments in institutional research in Central and Eastern Europe through two main aspects. First, we analyze external pressures on universities manifested through changes in the mandatory reporting requirements for universities and the implications these have on the institutional research practices. Here we expose in particular the changes in the funding models and strengthening of the external quality assurance and accreditation processes. Second, we discuss to what extent these external pressures altered internal university steering mechanisms by introducing more performance-oriented management processes. We explore how institutional research is conducted and organized within these changing university structures. Data for this section has been obtained through a fact-finding survey we developed and distributed to academic leaders and university managers at selected universities, representatives from the Ministries, and from the Quality Assurance Agencies in the six countries. We also draw on our own collaborative research on higher education reforms in the Western Balkans (Zgaga et al., 2013; File, Farnell, Doolan, Lesjak, & Scukanec, 2013).

We have to bear in mind that institutional research at universities in the region is still far from being consolidated. The changes in structures and practices of institutional research follow to a great extent the reforms of quality assurance systems and public funding arrangements. As in other areas, in this area also, the state prompts and crucially shapes institutional change in university practice through regulatory and funding arrangements. To be sure, governments have always required financial reports and other general data on operations from universities and universities have always recorded general data on students, staff, study programs, finances, etc. What has changed significantly is the type and extent of institutional micro data that is requested from regulatory and funding bodies. In addition, the neoliberal *zeitgeist* in European higher education—including the new public management approach penetrating university management—accentuates strategic and performance-oriented management practices in universities, which relies heavily on institutional research to aid institutional leaders in strategic planning and decision making. These requirements and expectations are not only raising the prominence and significance of institutional research in the region, but also profoundly changing how institutional research is conducted and organized.

The Policy Context of Strengthened Quality Assurance and Performance-Based Funding

External regulatory requirements for purposes of quality assurance and accreditation and funding arrangements have been changing dramatically since 2000. In the framework of the Bologna Process, the Ministers adopted the Standards and Guidelines for Quality Assurance in the European Higher Education Area.

These paved a way for massive reforms across European countries introducing or reforming external and internal quality assurance evaluations and accountability mechanisms, which became a norm across Europe (Stensaker & Harvey, 2011; Klemenčič & Brennan, 2013). Higher education institutions began to strengthen internal quality assurance systems, which are often managed by an internal center or unit responsible specifically for quality assurance and accreditation (Harvey & Stensaker, 2008). These units have in many institutions effectively taken on the role of institutional research; although, as it will be discussed later, institutional research takes place also in other departments of the central university administration.

Reforms of quality assurance have important implications for institutional research. The Standards and Guidelines (Bologna Process, 2009, pp. 18–19) mention explicitly that "[i]nstitutions should ensure that they collect, analyze and use relevant information for the effective management of their programs of study and other activities" and that "[i]nstitutions should regularly publish up to date, impartial and objective information, both quantitative and qualitative, about the programs and awards they are offering." Furthermore, the recommendations provide the following guidelines as to achieve this 'standard':

> Institutional self-knowledge is the starting point for effective quality assurance. It is important that institutions have the means of collecting and analyzing information about their own activities. Without this they will not know what is working well and what needs attention, or the results of innovatory practices. The quality-related information systems required by individual institutions will depend to some extent on local circumstances, but it is at least expected to cover: student progression and success rates; employability of graduates; students' satisfaction with their programs; effectiveness of teachers; profile of the student population; learning resources available and their costs; the institution's own key performance indicators.
>
> *(Bologna Process, 2009, p. 19)*

The implementation of European Standards and Guidelines both at the system and at the institutional level has been extremely diligent (Loukolla & Zhang, 2010). In all of the examined countries we observe strengthening of the external quality assurance bodies and processes on the system level, as well as further development of internal quality assurance structures and procedures, both resulting in more developed practices of data collection, analyses, and reporting on university operations.

Institutional Research Practices in Light of Changes to Funding Strategies

The changes in public funding mechanisms have also affected institutional research practices. The systems for allocating state funds to higher education institutions have been changing from the exclusively input-based models to funding schemes that include performance indicators. There are fundamental differences in the type of data and reports requested from universities by the governments in the incremental funding scheme, where allocations are based on previous years' allocations; formula funding, where allocations are calculated using standard criteria for all institutions; negotiated funding, where allocations are based on negotiations over a budget proposed by the institutions; and contract funding, where allocations are based on meeting the targets agreed on in a performance contract (Jongbloed, de Boer, Enders, & File, 2010, p. 47). Since public funding continues to be the predominant source of financing of universities, the shifts in funding models construct a whole new array of reporting requirements and fundamentally change the nature of mandatory reporting, data collection, and university financial management.

Austria was among the first to introduce funding agreements in 2004. These funding agreements are basically contracts between the federal government and the universities under which progress in the fulfillment of performance targets is monitored through annual 'Intellectual Capital Reports' (File et al., 2013). Poland, too, was among the first countries in Europe where output-based criteria played an important role in funding (Jongbloed et al., 2010). In Romania, the new Law on Education in 2011 also introduced differentiated funding based on performance. Next to core funding, which is incremental, there are also supplementary, complementary, and institutional development components, which are allocated to universities, based on the quality criteria and standards. Slovenia is combining a formula-based system, which includes output-based elements with contracts that specify targets and goals for universities (Klemenčič, 2012; File et al., 2013). In Croatia, no output criteria were used in funding arrangements until the academic year 2012–2013, but the latest reform of the institutional funding system is introducing contract-based funding, using both input-based and output/performance-based criteria (Šćukanec, 2013; File et al., 2013). In Serbia, the 2005 Law in Higher Education introduced the negotiated funding model; however, in practice "the new model has not been implemented; instead, higher education institutions have been funded through the system of direct financing [based on previous years' allocations]" (Vujačić, Đorđević, Kovačević, & Šunderić, 2013, p. 16). Funds, which are earmarked for specific use by the government, are sent directly to the academic units based on the funding category they belong to according to number of students, staff, academic programs, etc. (ibid.). But even in Serbia, as well as in other former Yugoslav countries, the reform of funding toward a more output-oriented model is in sight (Klemenčič, 2012).

The reporting requirements for universities are thus changing due to the changes in quality assurance and funding arrangements set by the governments. Consequently, these are pushing for institutional changes in structures and processes of institutional research. However, in most of the countries, with exception of Austria and Romania, the changes in regulatory mechanisms, and thus reporting requirements, have not yet been such to push for a dramatic turn to performance-based management practices at universities.

The External Pressures on the Institutional Research Practices at Universities

Similar to other European countries, institutional research conducted at universities in the examined countries serves first and foremost the purpose to fulfill the mandatory reporting requirements to the governments related mainly to funding and external quality assurance and accreditation. These mandatory requirements are stipulated in the national higher education legislation and in the regulations on quality assurance and accreditation. Apart from the Ministry responsible for higher education, also the public agencies for finances collect financial data from universities. National Quality Assurance and Accreditation Agencies collect data from universities for purposes of external quality assurance procedures, accreditation and reaccreditation, and increasingly also for the purposes of having an overview of higher education institutions and study programs within the entire higher education system. Auxiliary national funding bodies, such as research funding agencies or agencies funding internationalization activities, also request institutional reports. National research funding bodies collect data on research and development projects, knowledge transfers, and often also bibliometric data on research productivity of research units, groups, and individual researchers. Agencies responsible for coordination of European Union education and training programs that fund student and staff mobility, foreign language programs, etc. collect data on internationalization aspects of university operations. Universities, or even individual faculties, report directly to government statistical offices with general statistics as well as report data, which are forwarded from statistical offices to Eurostat and UNESCO-OECD databases.

National Data Collection Models

The changes in mandatory reporting requirements are exposing the weaknesses in the existing national systems of data collection and analyses. Most countries have different national data warehouses (national registers) into which required university data is fed. These registers tend to cover data on students, staff, finances (and infrastructure), research, accredited institutions and study programs, and international cooperation. They are managed by different units within the Ministry and by other public agencies. Data collection is in most cases supported by government information systems, which differ considerably across countries. The prevalent model in the examined countries is that of a centralized, yet, in most cases, non-integrated, national information system, where data on different activities are not gathered in one warehouse. In such systems universities' primary data collection streams feed into different data warehouses often "without an adequate correlation at the level of methods and tools" and resulting in "unsynchronized collection schedules, different reporting tools and methods, major differences regarding data categories, nomenclatures and terminology used and distinct validation procedures" (Romania, 2014, p. 1). Such non-integrated national information systems also do not drive standardization of institutional data collection at universities. The lack of reliable and transparent information systems is particularly acute in the southeast European countries where reliable data on all aspects of higher education systems is still a challenge (Zgaga et al., 2013). The ambition almost everywhere is to integrate the data warehouses into one centralized and integrated national information system, one central warehouse that would cover data from all or most of the key areas of university operations and would be—expectedly—managed by the Ministry. Among the examined countries, the closest to such system is Austria. In Romania, an integrated system is only just being implemented and work remains to be done to connect university databases with the national system.

In Austria, "Intellectual Capital Report" is a comprehensive reporting system for universities, which includes a set of indicators developed by the Federal Ministry in collaboration with the Rectors Conference. The report became mandatory in Austrian universities starting in 2006. The Romanian Government Executive Agency reports to have initiated a project that aims to "increase the capacity of public administration for evidence-based policy making in the field of higher education" by developing an "online platform with relevant data gathered from the Romanian universities" (Romania, 2014, p. 1). Elsewhere, centralized systems of data collection cover only one aspect of university operation and are not comprehensive. For example, Slovenia in 2009 introduced and in 2012 implemented the "Information system for evidence and analyses on higher education in Slovenia" (eVŠ), which is managed by the Ministry responsible for higher education. So far, eVŠ only collects data on study programs and students enrolled in Slovenian public higher education institutions. The idea is to link eVŠ directly to the National Quality Assurance and Accreditation Agency. In Croatia, the Ministry reports that they are in process of developing a central information system, which "will be linked with the higher education institutions' systems and will collect data on students and academics." Until present "[s]ome data are collected at the institutional level and only some are available at the national level and by use of different IT tools."

Other external reporting requirements come from the various ranking agencies. The European Union has sponsored development of the U-Multirank, a multidimensional international ranking system of higher education institutions that compares empirical data on institutions with similar institutional profiles on the basis of teaching and learning, research, knowledge transfer, international orientation, and regional engagement.[3] The first ranking with at least 500 higher education institutions from Europe was released in 2014. Other ranking agencies to which the universities report include QS, ARWU, THE, and Green Metric Ranking. Most of our respondents stated that preparing reports to U-Multirank and other ranking agencies requires additional data, which is in most part not readily available within their existing information systems. The only exceptions are universities from Austria, which reported that most required data to report to the international ranking bodies is readily available from the "Intellectual Capital Report," but some have to be gathered in addition.

The Practice of Institutional Research at Universities to Support Strategic and Performance-Oriented Management

A strategic and performance-oriented management approach creates enabling conditions for strengthening institutional research and crucially shapes its development. Strategy formulation at the university involves "making sense of the relationship between higher education institution and the external environment and of the higher education institution's particular state of affairs" (Frølich & Stensaker, 2012, p. 63). While all universities typically formulate some sort of institutional strategy, not every strategy automatically means strategic orientation. A more strategic and performance-oriented management of universities is prompted through aforementioned pressures from the governments through performance-based funding models and quality assurance regimes, as well as international factors, i.e., increased global competition for students, staff, and research funding. However, government policies across the countries still vary significantly in the extent that they had adopted neoliberal ideology and a new public management approach, i.e., to which extent they steer the behavior of universities by imposing performance indicators through funding and quality assurance. Furthermore, as suggested by Mathies and Välimaa (2013, p. 91), the national databases tend to "serve national needs and are rather insensitive to an institution's data needs." Similarly, the European University Association's study of quality assurance procedures at member universities reports that even in countries where national quality assurance policies are in place and information systems developed, the link between data collection for meeting reporting requirements and university strategic management still remains weak (Loukalla & Zhang, 2010).

While any university leader would certainly claim to appreciate solid 'institutional intelligence' to aid evidence-based decision making and planning, the usual problem stated is in the university 'institutional research capacity' to collect data and deliver such intelligence. As will be discussed in the following section, institutional researchers tend to be few and university information systems for data collection tend to be underdeveloped. Hence, institutional researchers are challenged to both live up to the demands of formal reporting and the expectations of their own higher education institutions.[4] With limited capacity, the former inevitably takes the precedence. In our survey several universities reported that the university collects data mainly to report to the Ministry and for reaccreditation purposes. Qualitative analyses occur only occasionally if a specific 'institutional project' had been solicited from the leadership (e.g., graduate employability) and/or when external project funding has been obtained. However, from discussions with institutional researchers in the region we are also led to question to what extent are universities really willing to institutionalize research for creation of university intelligence since the investments in institutional capacity are in most universities still rather small. The question is whether in universities led predominantly by academics, with weak or inexistent managerial leadership, support of decision making through university data intelligence is truly recognized as central or just declaratively stated as important. A further question is whether there is knowledge among institutional researchers how to develop useful university intelligence. One of our respondents commented that the software supporting their information system is too powerful for their use: many analytical functions are never used.

Another question is whether the academic leadership of universities is willing and able to engage with university intelligence for strategic planning and decision making. Developing meaningful tasks for institutional researchers to carry out is, namely, a part of the performance and strategic management systems, which we found to be still in the early stages of development in most of the examined countries. Only in responses from one university we found an explicit strategic and performance management objective underlying the establishment of a "Performance and Quality Management" unit with main focus on institutional research for data reporting and strategic analysis, including data on changes in the environment ("external changes"), benchmarking, and comparisons to other universities.

Nevertheless, we noted that universities are developing their internal standards and guidelines for quality assurance and are introducing some new data categories for measuring performance. For example, student course evaluation (in most places collected only at the faculty level rather than central university level), graduate employability, student satisfaction surveys, and surveys on academic staff satisfaction are becoming a regular practice. There are still differences among the institutions as to how comprehensive is data aggregated at the university level, and as such available to the university leadership to track performance, and which data is only aggregated on the levels of faculties and institutes. There are also differences in how and to what extent are these data used, i.e., are they carefully analyzed and certain actions taken based on it or not. It can happen that a lot of data is gathered at the central level, but it is never properly analyzed and used in decision making and planning. Most of data on student and staff profiles tends to be aggregated at the university level. However, when it comes to data on individual students' status each year, study success, student assessment of individual courses, and student satisfaction with student services, in most universities this data is only collected at the faculty level. Similarly, data on academic staff (ranked professors, lecturers, researchers) and their research productivity (publications, impact factor, patents and technology transfers, research projects, etc.) tends to be aggregated on faculty level.

The development of institutional research within central university administration is particularly challenging in the countries from former Yugoslavia due to a particular model of university governance. In these countries, the legacy of socialist self-management structures was translated into 'fragmented' universities in which faculties, art academies, and colleges had (and most of them still have) legal identity, thus making the university merely an umbrella institution without significant decision-making powers (Zgaga et al., 2013, p. 39). In a fragmented university, the position of deans is extremely strong: they are in direct contact with the Ministry regarding financing (with the exception of Slovenia). Different governmental agencies tend to obtain data directly from the academic units rather than from central administration. Governments are trying to reform this practice, but change is slow. In most cases only a 'functional integration' has been achieved, which effectively means a working cooperation between the faculties, yet still relatively weak central administration and underdeveloped central administrative services, including institutional research (Zgaga et al., 2013). In such an arrangement the capacity to make decisions on interventions is low.

All in all, the practice of institutional research to support institutional decision making and planning tends to be overshadowed by the tasks to fulfill the mandatory reporting requirements. The main reason for this lies in limited institutional capacity to undertake institutional research function. University leaders simply do not invest resources to build capacity in this area. The main reason for this seems to lie, however, in lack of incentives or pressure from the governments to university leaders to performance-oriented management of their institutions. Only in higher education systems where the state has set clear performance-based regulations for funding and quality assurance (such as in Austria and aiming in Romania) do we see systematic development of institutional research to support performance-based management across the universities in that system. Indeed, government steering is seemingly needed to drive the changes in leadership and organizational culture toward data-driven decision making and performance-based management in the Central and Eastern European context.

Where and How Is Institutional Research Conducted Within University Structures?

At the examined universities, institutional research, in the sense of data collection, is typically conducted in several 'collecting' units within the central administration: human resources, international office, student affairs, research management, library, and finance. With the consolidation and further development of internal quality assurance systems, in most universities a unit has been created in the central administration with specific responsibility for quality assurance, institutional data analyses, and reporting. This unit effectively coordinates data collection from the primary 'collecting' units, and is also responsible for analyses and reporting. In the words of one of our respondents: "On demand reports are provided by the collecting units, but the standard reporting, strategic reporting, analyses and the development of the reporting system is within the responsibility of the performance and quality management [unit]."

There are notable differences among universities in the extent of development of their university information systems for data collection on university performance. In universities with the most advanced systems the quality assurance unit provides senior management across the university with regular reports on the performance indicators and, as stated by one respondent, "secures a 'single version of the truth' by using the same standards, etc." In most universities, however, information systems are centralized, but non-integrated, which means that there are multiple warehouses managed by different departments or people at the university level. Typically these warehouses include a university system on students and study programs, human resources management system, and finance and capital management system (most universities have mentioned SAP software for this purpose). Furthermore, there exist different practices as to which data gathered at the faculty level is sent to the university level and analyzed there. Such practices are typical for fragmented universities where some data is centralized in the university information system and other is collected through separate information systems of faculties. Here, the possible intervention from the university level to the faculty in terms of requests for data is highly limited due to rather autonomous faculties. It is common that the Ministry collects reports for funding processes directly from the faculties and often also the National Quality Assurance Agency collects data directly from faculties. At present, one of the key efforts in the area of institutional research at universities in the examined countries involves efforts to strengthen their central information systems. Most universities have expressed an ambition or a concrete plan to move toward developing integrated information systems.

The quality assurance unit typically employs one or several professionals to this task: the actual numbers vary and the rule of thumb is that the more developed performance-management system it has, the better staffed is the quality assurance unit. The unit is often, but not always, connected to the IT unit or includes IT professionals. In most cases, the staff reports to one person from institutional leadership responsible for quality assurance at the university level (rector or vice-rector). In addition, there tends to be an advisory quality assurance committee composed of leadership and administration, representatives of academics, representatives of students, and possibly also external stakeholders in which professionals from quality assurance units would also participate. The quality assurance unit typically does not have any direct connection to finance units or finance reporting. The financial unit prepares its reports, which then can be merged in general university reports. The changes in the funding schemes toward performance-based and developmental funding are, however, expected to pressure universities to strengthen the connection between the units responsible for financial reporting with those responsible for quality assurance and performance indicators. In most universities, we do not yet see significant structural adjustments in this regard, except that, in operational terms, the committees responsible for finances tend to include those responsible for quality assurance.

We note from the survey that the majority of additional positions that have opened within university administrations to take on institutional research functions have taken place in the quality assurance units. We notice attempts toward centralizing data collection, analysis, and intervention, but these reforms are still in early stages, hence in rare cases we see substantial new structures for institutional research, which would entail significant human resources and technology. Most universities report that no new employments have happened (due to financial crisis) and that institutional research tasks have been delegated to the existing employees. While we cannot yet speak about a distinct professional profile of university institutional researcher, the persons hired into quality assurance units tend to be required to have some experience in data analysis, knowledge on higher education and research, and several soft skills.

Conclusion

There are major changes underway in Central and Eastern Europe as to how data on universities is collected and used. These changes are happening simultaneously at the national level and at institutional levels. Governments are trying to remedy the dysfunctionalities of their existing information systems often marked by primary data streams feeding from universities into national registers with different reporting methods and tools. In addition, existing information systems at various institutions have major differences in the basic categories of data, nomenclatures, and terminology. The trend is toward integrated information systems with a focus not only on input data, but also performance indicators. These changes are prompted by the changes in funding schemes, development of national quality assurance and accreditation systems, and through influence of European Union's modernization agenda for higher education and ranking agencies. European Union seeks to support modernization of European universities also through policy evidence, analysis, and transparency tools:

> it is essential to develop a wider range of analysis and information, covering all aspects of performance—to help students make informed study choices, to enable institutions to identify and develop their strengths, and to support policymakers in their strategic choices on the reform of higher education systems.
>
> *(European Commission, 2011, p. 11)*

The underlying principle is that of evidence-based policy making in higher education.

The changes in the government approaches are reflected in institutional practices. Universities are introducing units—typically designated as quality assurance and reporting units—with specific responsibility for collecting data from other university units, preparing strategic reports and analyses, as well as supporting the development of the internal reporting system. Universities are also seeking to develop more integrated information systems. The competencies and resources of such units very much depend on the overall strategic orientation of the respective university. In some universities, such unit is effectively the "performance and quality management unit" directly responding to the top leadership, well staffed and aided by an integrated information system. In most universities, however, institutional research is still an "add-on" function, with limited capacity in terms of people and technological resources, where most time and resources are devoted to compiling data for standard reporting and little, if any, to support strategic decision making.

Whether or not universities develop performance-based management systems of which data analytics is a vital part largely depends on government steering. If the government introduces an integrated system for data collection on universities, it will also need to support the universities to upgrade their institutional research function. The development of institutional research for data-driven management of universities depends largely on the extent of competition among higher education institutions within the national higher education systems, and of the ambitions of the universities to compete within the global higher education market.

Acknowledgement

The authors would like to thank Jeroen Huisman and the editors of this volume for their helpful comments on earlier drafts. We would also wish to acknowledge confidential responses to our fact-finding questionnaire received from 11 universities, six national Quality Assurance Agencies, and four governments from the six examined countries: Austria, Croatia, Poland, Romania, Serbia, and Slovenia. Finally, we would like to thank Nikola Baketa for his research assistance with preparation of the questionnaires.

Notes

1. In the remainder of the chapter we use the term universities equivocal to higher education institutions.
2. Serbia has obtained a status of candidate member of the European Union in 2012. Austria has been a member since 1995, Slovenia and Poland since 2004, Romania since 2007, and Croatia from 2013.
3. Available at www.umultirank.org/.
4. We thank Jeroen Huisman for his helpful comment bringing this issue to our attention.

References

Bologna Process. (2009). *Standards and guidelines for quality assurance in the European higher education area, 3rd Edition.* Helsinki, Finland: European Association for Quality Assurance in Higher Education.

de Boer, H. F., Enders, J., & Schimank, U. (2007). On the way towards new public management? The governance of university systems in England, the Netherlands, Austria, and

Germany. In D. Jansen (Ed.), *New forms of governance in research organizations—Disciplinary approaches, interfaces and integration* (pp. 137–154). Dordrecht, the Netherlands: Springer.

de Boer, H., & File, J. (2009). *Higher education governance reforms across Europe.* Brussels, Belgium: ESMU. Retrieved from: www.highereducationmanagement.eu/.

European Commission. (2011). *Communication from the commission to the European Parliament, the Council, the European Economic and Social Committee and the Committee of the Regions.* Brussels, 20.9.2011. COM(2011) 567 final. Retrieved from http://eur-lex.europa.eu/LexUriServ/LexUriServ.do?uri=COM:2011:0567:FIN:EN:PDF.

File, J., Farnell, T., Doolan, K., Lesjak, D., & Šćukanec, N. (2013). *Higher education funding and the social dimension in Croatia: Analysis and policy guidelines.* Zagreb, Croatia: Institute for the Development of Education.

Frølich, N., & Stensaker, B. (2012). University strategizing: The role of evaluation as a sensemaking tool. In B. Stensaker, J. Valimaa, & Sarrico, C. (Eds.), *Managing reform in universities: The dynamics of culture, identity and organizational change* (pp. 63–80). Basingstoke, UK: Palgrave MacMillan.

Harvey, L., & Stensaker, B. (2008). Quality culture: Understandings, boundaries and linkages. *European Journal of Education, 43*(4), 427–442.

Jessop, B. (2008). A cultural political economy of competitiveness and its implications for higher education. In B. Jessop & N. Fairclough (Eds.), *Education and the knowledge-based economy in Europe* (pp. 13–39). Rotterdam, the Netherlands: Sense Publishers.

Jongbloed, B., de Boer, H., Enders, J., & File, J. (2010). *Progress in higher education reform across Europe: Funding reform. Volume 1: Executive summary and main report.* Twente, the Netherlands: CHEPS. Retrieved from http://ec.europa.eu/education/higher-education/doc/funding/vol1_en.pdf.

Klemenčič, M. (2012). The effects of Europeanisation on institutional diversification in the Western Balkans. In P. Zgaga, U. Teichler, & J. Brennan (Eds.), *The globalisation challenge for European higher education: Convergence and diversity, centres and peripheries* (pp. 117–138). Bern, Switzerland: Peter Lang.

Klemenčič, M., & Brennan, J. (2013). Institutional research in a European context: A forward look. In Special Issue on The Past, Present and Future of Higher Education Research: Between Scholarship and Policy Making. *European Journal of Higher Education, 3*(3), 265–279.

Loukolla, T., & Zhang, T. (2010). *Examining quality culture: Part I—quality assurance processes in higher education institutions.* Brussels, Belgium: European University Association.

Mathies, C., & Välimaa, J. (2013). Is there a need for a European institutional research? *Tertiary Education and Management, 19*(1), 85–96.

Robertson, S. (2008). Embracing the global: Crisis and the creation of a new semiotic order to secure Europe's knowledge-based economy. In B. Jessop & N. Fairclough (Eds.), *Education and the knowledge-based economy in Europe* (pp. 89–108). Rotterdam, the Netherlands: Sense Publishers.

Romania. (2014). *Institutional analysis of data collection and management regarding higher education system in Romania: Conclusions and final recommendations.* Bucharest, Romania: Executive Agency for Higher Education, Research, Development and Innovation Funding (UEFISCDI). Retrieved from http://pp-is.forhe.ro/sites/default/files/conclusions_data_collection_3.pdf.

Šćukanec, N. (2013). *Overview of higher education and research systems in the Western Balkans: The case of Croatia.* HERDATA Project. Oslo, Norway: HERDATA. Retrieved from www.herdata.org/research/country-reports/68.

Stensaker, B., & Harvey, L. (2011). *Accountability in higher education. Global perspectives on trust and power.* New York, NY: Routledge.

Vujačić, I., S. Đorđević, M. Kovačević, & Šunderić, I. (2013). *Overview of higher education and research systems in the Western Balkans: The case of Serbia.* HERDATA Project. Oslo, Norway: HERDATA. Retrieved from: www.herdata.org/research/country-reports/68.

Zgaga, P., Klemenčič, M., Komljenovič, J., Miklavič, K., Repac, I., & Jakačić, V. (2013). *Higher education in the Western Balkans: Reforms, developments, trends. Key findings from field research.* Ljubljana, Slovenia: Centre for Educational Policy Studies, Faculty of Education, University of Ljubljana. Retrieved from http://ceps.pef.uni-lj.si/knjiznica/doc/hewb.pdf.

7

INSTITUTIONAL RESEARCH IN THE UK AND IRELAND

Steve Woodfield

Introduction

The practice of institutional research (IR) in the UK and the Republic of Ireland is currently a small but slowly expanding dimension of higher education (HE). IR in both countries has a relatively short history and has been rarely discussed in the local academic and professional literature beyond the work of Yorke (2004) and in a 2009 special edition of *Perspectives: Policy and Practice in Higher Education,* the journal of the Association of University Administrators (AUA) that showcases the 'state of the art' of UK IR. The inward-facing—and data orientated—dimension of UK IR is discussed by Watson and Maddison (2005) who articulate the practice of 'institutional self-study.'

In contrast to the US, IR activities in the UK and Ireland developed very much 'under-the-radar' until the late 1990s when the Britain and Ireland Association for Institutional Research (BI-AIR) was convened, an informal gathering for those work-ing in the HE sector with an interest in IR. This later evolved into the IRNetwork, supported by the Learning and Teaching Support Network (LTSN)—now part of the UK's Higher Education Academy (HEA)—in the early 2000s. Interest in IR was reignited at the end of the decade and, in 2008, the UK & Ireland Higher Education Institutional Research (HEIR) network was established to provide opportunities for institutional researchers and those working in related HE roles to share their knowl-edge, learn from others, and build networks in both nations and beyond. It achieves this through organizing conferences and thematic seminars, commissioning opinion pieces on different aspects of IR, and utilizing social networking tools.

Yorke (2004) argues that HE institutions outside the US, operating in more centrally directed HE systems, have been slow to develop 'formally constituted' IR capacity. He suggests this is because HE issues usually associated with IR were traditionally driven more by sectorial than institutional concerns, often related to accountability requirements. This means that institutional data and insights have been generated based on an 'export model' rather than been fully exploited for internal quality enhancement purposes. Yorke also suggests that even recent shifts toward a more business-like approach to HE management have failed to act as a catalyst for enhanced IR activities, and most IR in the UK and in Europe has been characterized as sector-wide 'higher education' projects on particular themes (sometimes involving institutional research) or as ad hoc IR projects at the institutional level. Increasing competition and marketization has crept up on many higher education institutions (HEIs), some of which have acted like Senge's 'frog in a bucket' (Senge, 1990) and have not realized the need for fundamental managerial and administrative change.

However, recent changes in government policy promoting a 'higher education market' have led English institutions, in particular, to recognize the need to expand their IR capacity to compete effectively for students and resources. Institutional leaders increasingly identify the potential for IR to help institutions navigate through times of turbulence and rapid change and to operate in a more resource-constrained and competitive context. Beyond the HE sector, there is research evidence that use of data and powerful business analytics to guide decision making enables companies to be more productive and experience higher return on equity than competitors that do not (Brynjolfsson & McAfee, 2012). In the UK and Ireland there has been a recent growth in interest in, and use of, 'big data' and learning analytics in HEIs (Drysdale, 2013), and Terenzini (2013) suggests that this is likely to have a strong influence on the future development of IR worldwide.

The historical development of IR in the UK has meant that the practice of IR is a 'broad church' (Chester, 2014) incorporating both academics and professional staff, working in often very different disciplinary areas or professional services departments. Very few IR practitioners have the title 'institutional researcher.' By contrast, in Ireland, most universities now have a small, dedicated IR function that provides a strong link between IR, quality assurance, and strategic planning. IR capacity is much weaker in the institutes of technology, although clusters of institutions are investigating opportunities for developing shared IR capacity.

IR activities in both the UK and Ireland range from small-scale action research projects on academic practice to policy-based research on strategic themes with resonance at the institutional and sector level (Taylor, Hanlon, & Yorke, 2013). However, although the UK and Irish IR communities come together under the auspices of HEIR, their recent trajectories related to IR have been very different.

The content of HEIR conferences from 2008–14 suggests that UK IR is built around a strong core of researchers working on student-focused research themes (e.g., retention, student satisfaction, access, and admissions) supplemented by work on other key strategic areas such as planning and resource allocation, the student experience, quality enhancement, organizational change, rankings, and institutional benchmarking. IR in Ireland is closer to the US approach to IR with a strong focus on generating and using institutional data to support decision making, and sector-wide benchmarking activities.

Defining IR in the UK and Irish Context

IR has always been a difficult activity to define, even in the US where it is more firmly established (Lyons, 1976). There is no widely shared conception or understanding of IR in the UK context and the term 'institutional research' is rarely used. Indeed terms such as 'business intelligence' and 'planning' are far more commonly used, and IR that is not focused on secondary data analysis is often conflated with action research related to teaching and learning or policy-focused research into higher education. Although institutionally centered projects focused on strategic themes are commonplace—in areas such as the 'student experience,' employability, internationalization, rankings, and flexible learning—many of these are not categorized as IR by institutions. Furthermore many practice-focused pedagogical research projects remain embedded in disciplinary contexts mitigating against wider dissemination and opportunities to scale-up research projects to support quality enhancement and improve institutional IR capacity.

Jackson (2003) highlighted the strong link with both policy and practice in his definition of UK IR as: "Research that is undertaken within an institution or higher education system to provide information to support an evidence-informed approach to policy and practice" (p. 1). The Irish Universities Quality Board (IUQB), influenced by US IR practice, defined IR "broadly as the application of social and enterprise research methods to improve institutional effectiveness by transforming institutional and other data into valid, reliable and useable information" (IUQB, 2008, p. 13).

The HEIR network was established to bring together professionals working in a variety of academic and professional roles within HE institutions who either identify themselves as engaging in IR, the collection, use, and application of institutional data, or who have an interest in higher education research taking place within HE institutions. Network members recognized their diverse research interests and perspectives and have developed an inclusive definition of IR as:

> the use of research and enquiry to provide evidence to inform policy, practice and management at all levels within higher education. This includes management information to inform policy and strategy, evaluation and pedagogic research to inform learning and teaching, and using data gathered for different purposes to better understand and manage activities within institutions, including the student experience.
>
> *(HEIR website)*

IR conceived in this way is a broad set of activities that collect, transform, analyze, and use data to generate evidence to support institutional planning, policy formation, quality enhancement, and decision making, and to help institutions meet external demands for information and data.

Such activities are well established within HEIs in both the UK and Ireland, although the specific activities undertaken by institutional researchers depend on the regulatory framework and salient policy concerns in each country. In the UK this is complicated by the fact that policy responsibility for HE is also devolved to varying degrees to the four UK governments who have created HE funding bodies to allocate funding and implement policy on HE. Furthermore the four UK countries (England, Northern Ireland, Scotland, and Wales) often have divergent policy drivers and agendas that impact the practice of IR.

The UK Context for IR

Institutional research is not undertaken systematically across the UK HE sector and there is no sector-wide approach to, or conception of, IR. Its development at the institutional level is largely dependent on the particular set of characteristics and circumstances within each institution. The UK HE sector is large and diverse and the landscape is constantly shifting. Although most HE is provided by universities, it also takes place in HE colleges and in further education (FE) institutions, where embedding the practice of IR—particularly in projects focused on teaching and learning—can provide significant institutional impact and also support scholarship and the development of an HE 'ethos' (Simmons & Lea, 2013, p. 36).

IR's relatively low profile does not mean IR activities are limited in the UK, nor does it mean that IR practice does not have a strong history. However, this is usually concentrated in pockets or expertise within individual institutions based around the activities of key individuals or teams, which tend to appear and disappear as key people move between institutions, change role, or retire. UK IR is also largely reactive, responding to external drivers for accountability around the student lifecycle (e.g., performance indicators) or quality assurance, rather than being central to institutional imperatives for continuous improvement or quality enhancement (Taylor et al., 2013).

The term 'institutional research' is also rarely used in the UK and a formal IR function remains unusual for UK HEIs, at least at the central level. Few institutions have a function labeled as 'institutional research,' and only a small number of IR practitioners have the phrase 'institutional research' in their job title. Indeed, if most institutional leaders and managers were asked about their IR function, this query would most likely be met with bewilderment. This peripheral status has implications for its potential to be utilized within institutions, as well as its wider development as a profession and a practice.

However, the operating context for UK HEIs is rapidly changing. The continuing impact of the recent economic crisis means that UK HEIs are now operating in a climate of increased competitiveness with an associated focus on providing value for money and 'doing more with less' as public funding for HE is cut. As in many countries, HEIs in the UK are facing a number of challenges, including increasing demands for higher-level skills, changing demographics, internationalization and globalization, a drive to widen and increase access to under-represented groups, increased competition for students and research contracts, and growing marketization and privatization. Successfully addressing these challenges is likely to require the development of enhanced management information and IR capabilities.

The policy context in England could perhaps be described as unique. There has been a rapid shift toward a student-centered HE system resulting in an increased focus on teaching quality, student satisfaction, graduate employability, and the growing importance of external quality measures such as student surveys and rankings. In parallel there has been a move toward the private financing of HE through tuition fees (although students are supported by government-backed income-contingent loans for tuition fees and living costs). The government has also recently announced that the current tight controls on undergraduate recruitment will be removed in 2015–16, which is likely to stimulate a more competitive mind-set in recruitment (HM Treasury, 2013). There has also been a strong policy focus on encouraging the expansion of 'alternative' or private providers in the system. Many of these changes are articulated in the 2011 BIS 'white paper' *Students at the Heart of the System* (BIS, 2011), which also places strong emphasis on providing accurate, detailed student information. This new environment and universities' own evolving strategic plans provide a rationale for developing a more evidence-based 'analytical framework' for decision making, performance measurement, and quality enhancement to ensure that decisions can be implemented effectively and resources used most efficiently.

The Irish Context for IR

Although the Republic of Ireland is a much smaller country, the Irish HE sector faces similar external challenges to the UK, but was perhaps hit even harder by the recent financial crisis. In contrast to the UK, Ireland has a binary HE system comprised of seven universities and 14 institutes of technology. Another point of difference is that Ireland's main HE agency, the Higher Education Authority (HEA), has power over both statutory planning and policy and funding allocation for HE. In England, Scotland, and Wales, these roles are split between national governments and HE funding agencies. There are no tuition charges, but in 1995–96, students began contributing to their higher education via an imposed registration fee.

The Irish experience of developing IR in recent years provides a good example of a practical case study on how to develop and embed institutional research at the national and institutional levels. The origins of this structured approach to the development of IR in Ireland lie in the establishment in 2002 of the Irish Universities Quality Board (IUQB), which, via institutional audit, provides periodic evaluation of the effectiveness of QA procedures in individual universities. IR in Ireland is considered part of a 'key triad' related to the effective management of universities that is comprised of IR, strategic planning, and quality assurance (QA) activities (Flanagan, 2011).

In 2004–05 the IUQB and the HEA commissioned a system-wide external review of the Irish university sector and individual universities that was undertaken by the European Universities Association (EUA) under its Institutional Evaluation Programme (IEP). The review findings subsequently stimulated sector-wide projects to develop national Guidelines for Good Practice in the areas of teaching and learning, research, strategic planning, and management and administration.

One of the sectorial report's key recommendations was that Irish universities "need to strengthen their capacities for institutional analysis and monitoring, in order to provide better information for strategic governance and management" and that there is "a clear need to strengthen the universities' capacity for analysis about their own situation" (European Universities Association, 2005, p. 21). The report also drew negative comparisons between Irish universities and North American universities in these areas, suggesting that they generally had incomplete information about themselves and how they benchmark their performance against competitors. In line with the North American focus on 'institutional effectiveness' it suggested that any new institutional analytic capacity should link planning, QA, staff development, and the management information systems (Flanagan, 2011).

In 2005 the seven Irish universities and the Dublin Institute of Technology (DIT) engaged in a sector-wide IUQB project on IR that involved institutional self-evaluations and analysis of internal and external review reports. The project focused on improving management practices and effectiveness and increasing awareness of the potential of IR to enhance overall organizational efficiency, and, in particular, the student experience. It involved international input from experts in the UK and the US that analyzed IR practice worldwide and identified good practice in IR relevant to the Irish context published in the 2008 *National Guidelines: Good Practice for Institutional Research in Higher Education*. A parallel set of guidelines, *Good Practice in Strategic Planning for Academic Units in Irish Universities,* was launched at the same time. In contrast to the more 'bottom up' UK approach, this comprehensive set of activities and outputs provides firm foundations for embedding IT in the Irish HE context and for future development.

Issues and Challenge for IR in the UK and Ireland

Despite the recent divergence in the development of IR at the national and institutional levels between the UK and Ireland and within both sectors, some of the key issues related to IR within institutions are broadly similar, including its activities and roles within the institution and in professional practice.

Focus and Purpose of IR

HEIs in both nations are beginning to have a greater focus on enhancing their analytic capacity and capability, or their level of 'organizational intelligence' (Terenzini, 1999). There are a range of drivers behind this shift of emphasis, which include internal requirements for enhanced efficiency and effectiveness; institutional improvement and positioning; and external requirements to control and benchmark costs, publicly demonstrate value for money and enhanced productivity, monitor access and participation, supply more sophisticated information about quality to different constituencies, and demonstrate accountability to a variety of stakeholders. Competition for resources, status, and talented students and staff also drive a need for regular scenario planning; competitor, client, and customer analyses; benchmarking processes; and trend analyses. As in other countries, the IR activities centered around 'contextual intelligence' (e.g., horizon scanning, policy analysis) are sometimes outsourced to external organizations, or are provided collectively by 'mission groups' that represent different groupings of universities. Although external perspectives can provide valuable insights, using multiple sources of contextual expertise runs the risk of creating a fragmented approach to decision support that undermines the strategic influence of IR and its ability to challenge senior management, and relegating it to a professional service rather than a strategic business function.

The UK and Irish HE sectors can already access much of the data required to improve their organizational intelligence, and the necessary expertise to undertake effective IR, but a system-wide understanding of the nature and purpose of IR remains weak, especially in the UK. A complication is that un-coordinated IR activities often appear to have contradictory purposes; for example they can be formative and help to shape internal policy and processes, and also summative through engaging in evaluation or measurement-focused activities. Longden and Yorke (2009) suggest that UK IR practitioners need to identify, define, and focus on the key questions that are crucial for the institution's success, and that can help support both single-loop and double-loop organizational learning (Argyris & Schön, 1978) if IR is to enhance practice, improve awareness, inform strategy development, assess policy, change management structures, inform further research, and serve many other purposes.

Longden and Yorke (2009) also suggest that the UK and Irish HE sectors are, like those in other countries, 'awash with data' on all aspects of HE but this is often not transformed into institutional intelligence. As mentioned in chapter 13 of this book, externally reported data is used by government (for performance indicators, legislative requirements), key stakeholders (i.e., students, employers), and commercial business purposes (for rankings, league tables) but institutional data is frequently under-exploited because the reorganization and transformation it requires to make it useful for answering key institutional questions requires significant additional resources to make it useable. A key challenge to UK IR practitioners working in secondary data analysis roles is the cost of access to more detailed HE sector data for benchmarking purposes.

IR Activities

IR practitioners in the UK and Ireland have built strong links with colleagues in the US, and it is not surprising that IR in the UK and Ireland is strongly influenced by US models, in particular the concept of using IR to enhance 'institutional effectiveness' and Volkwein's *Faces of Institutional Research* (Volkwein, 2008).

In the UK and Irish contexts, institutional effectiveness can be understood as comprising the following three elements:

1. **Inputs**—e.g., business or market intelligence in areas such as student recruitment (including fees and widening access/participation activities) and admissions policies;
2. **Outputs**—core and measurable outputs such as strategic planning, student employability and student satisfaction, change initiatives, policy development, and external and statutory reporting, and
3. **Processes**—wider areas of activity covering the 'student experience' (including progression, retention, and success), learning and teaching (including the curriculum), quality assurance, quality enhancement, and portfolio development.

Institutional effectiveness activities are embedded in UK institutions that are strongly influenced by the US system, such as the Open University, Richmond, the American International University in London, and London Metropolitan University, which are all accredited by the Middle States Commission on Higher Education. The Commission assesses accredited institutions' procedures for institutional effectiveness as part of its evaluation process.

IR can support institutional effectiveness through activities such as enrollment planning, benchmarking, developing management information systems, secondary data analysis, desk research and policy analysis, recurring and ad hoc primary research (e.g., questionnaires, focus groups, interviews), and impact evaluation projects. Such activities can be grouped under the following themes: learning and teaching; the 'student experience' (throughout the student lifecycle from recruitment to employment); quality assurance and enhancement; policy development and evaluation; strategic planning; market and business intelligence; and major institutional change initiatives (e.g., curriculum review).

Teichler (2005) suggests that, as mentioned in chapter 2 of this book, educational research (focused on higher education) has strong links to IR practice. UK HEIs have strong traditions in practice-focused academic development research (e.g., research related to teaching and learning, and the student experience). In some cases this research is cross-institutional, which carries greater external legitimacy, such as the work on assessment by the Student Assessment and Classification Working Group (SACWG). However, there are many other topics that are of relevance beyond a single institution (e.g., student retention, degree classifications) and although they are often triggered by a specific institutional need, the under-pinning theoretical frameworks or methodologies may be robust enough for them to be considered alongside more 'academic' research, and even less sophisticated or 'quick and dirty' IR studies can also serve as a basis for further, more rigorous cross-sector studies involving both IR practitioners and other academic colleagues. In such cases, the boundary between IR and educational research is often blurred and there can be tensions between institutional politics around changes to practice, and the need to provide impartial evidence to the institution and to the wider academic community. As Yorke suggests, "there may be a difficulty in bringing into institutional research a perspective that is practical but richly academic by virtue of being grounded in theory, the literature on the topic being studied, and knowledge of what is taking place in other institutions" (Yorke, 2004, p. 150).

IR as Professional Practice

Given the diversity of IR purposes and activities, it is perhaps not surprising that IR practitioners in the UK and Ireland are also a heterogeneous group, with different disciplinary and employment backgrounds, methodological and analysis skillsets, and areas of research interest (Taylor et al., 2013). For example, someone engaged in IR could categorize themselves as a data collector, a data analyst, an educational researcher, an internal consultant, or even an 'executive officer' or 'policy adviser' where they could be directly engaged in developing policy at the sector level. IR practitioners are also often involved in externally focused policy development and research activities that may, or may not, be complementary to their internal work, especially where the management and reporting of institutional data is concerned.

The largest proportion of the current HEIR network membership is engaged in academic development and academic practice roles, although there is also strong representation from planning and management information practitioners, mar-ket researchers and business intelligence professionals, and pedagogic researchers. Other members work in student support, quality, and policy development roles, and the membership also includes senior managers, registry staff, and students. Only some 3% of network members are in 'pure' IR roles.

Volkwein's (2008) five types of IR activity require different research ori-entations (technical, academic, or policy-development focused), and sometimes different combinations of these skillsets. In the UK and Ireland, many of the technical skills required by IR practitioners are also common to market, social, and academic researchers (e.g., research design, data collection and analysis, data visualization); policy professionals (working with senior people, influencing and lobbying, briefing, developing policy recommendations); and some skills are generic (e.g., report writing, presenting, teamwork). However, expertise in

IR practice requires engagement with issues and contextual intelligence that is specific to the HE sector.

Currently, there is no focused career track for institutional researchers in the UK and Ireland, meaning it can be difficult for them to progress to more senior roles within institutions, which can result in them leaving HE to develop their careers. There also tends to be only a few IR practitioners in each institution and there is thus a very limited recruitment pool should institutions seek to expand their IR capacity.

Following the IUQB good practice guidance, in Ireland there is now a small cadre of IR practitioners embedded in formalized IR functions but, in the UK, IR practitioners have either developed roles highly tailored to institutional circumstances, or work in roles that have other responsibilities and foci and may or may not consider themselves to work in IR. Most move into IR roles with experience gained from other research, policy, or data analysis roles in HEIs or sector policy agencies. While relevant research methods training courses and professionally orientated postgraduate programs focused on HE (e.g., MBAs and DBAs) are available to institutional researchers, there are no focused professional development activities or qualifications in IR; and capacity-building activities (such as workshops and seminars) at HEIR conferences and other events are usually informal and unaccredited.

Institutional Structures for IR

Six of Ireland's seven universities now have a centralized institutional research function that is aligned with strategic planning and quality functions and this function is designed to support the activities of operational planning, evidence-based decision making, performance management, and benchmarking. These tend to be based in small one- to three-person offices but have direct reporting lines into senior managers, and are supported by other functions across the institution, such as IT services, management information systems (MIS), and other data custodians. Given their place in organizational structures, they represent a move toward Volkwein's 'professional bureaucracy' model of IR office organization (Volkwein, 2008). Such offices are designed to provide high level information to inform policy formulation and strategic decision making in the university, although their influence on senior-level decision making is often constrained by a strong focus on academic leadership and perceptions of IR as a professional service function by senior managers. They undertake a range of core activities including monitoring and improving data quality, coordinating data flow, developing performance measures, staff and student research, preparing rankings data, reporting for quality reviews, and leading other ad hoc projects.

In contrast, very few UK HEIs have a central IR function, or dedicated IR roles, and when they do exist they are often very small, with limited access to complementary technical expertise within the team or limited financial resources. In the UK there are few examples of the US IR model of a central IR function that combines reporting, change management, quality assurance (for accreditation purposes), and decision support. It is not clear-cut whether following the US model would be appropriate for UK HEIs since many institutions also undertake IR activity across different units, which often works well when work is aligned, and avoids bureaucratization. However, in a climate of scarce resources, a more coordinated approach may be preferable to avoid overlap and ensure strategic focus and effective dissemination across relevant institutional stakeholders.

The majority of IR in the UK is decentralized and undertaken by a range of different units and individuals, most closely resembling Volkwein's 'elaborate profusion' model (Volkwein, 2008), although there are examples of all of Volkwein's models across the HE sector. In some institutions, IR practitioners form an 'ad hoc' or informal grouping, in others, IR activities are built around a specially convened cross-institutional group involving academic and administrative staff, while in some institutions, there is a formalized group of IR staff working in the 'center' of the institution as a specially constructed IR function. In other organizations, IR activities are linked to a wider network focused on higher education policy and practice that includes planning officers, market researchers, data specialists, educational researchers, and policy professionals. The most visible UK IR takes place in universities that achieved university status after 1992, and that generally have a more corporate approach to university management—due to their origins as public bodies with significant accountability requirements—than older universities that still retain strong elements of collegiality, and are resistant to encroaching 'managerialism.' However, IR is present in the pre-1992 sector, although usually characterized as faculty- or discipline-led research into teaching and learning or undertaken in ad hoc and more fluid 'working groups' focused on strategic themes such as the 'student experience.' IR tends to have relatively weak links with research and third-stream activity, and activities led by professional services (e.g., marketing, finance, and staffing).

IR in the UK and Ireland is an unusual activity in that it crosses the academic and administrative divide, and IR practitioners are often required to 'join the dots' between colleagues in information services departments, student administration functions, academic registries, planning departments, strategy units, or traditional academic faculties and departments. IR also transgresses traditional institutional silos and IR practitioners often operate in a complex and highly political environment where dealing with differing perspectives and expectations around research findings can be difficult, especially when they are 'counter-intuitive' (Chester, 2014). For IR to have institutional impact, practitioners need to secure access to decision-makers and the senior-leadership team, as this can help to prioritize strategic issues, manage expectations, and help to close the loop between collecting information, undertaking research, and making changes to policy and practice.

National and Institutional-Level Support for IR

The Irish experience has highlighted the important role of institutional champions, and the wider senior management or executive group, in promoting and embedding the value of IR across the institution and supporting the development of a centralized IR function. This support, when combined with an identified national-level need for improved IR capacity and an evidence-based business case, can help to unlock the resources required. However, changes in academic leadership roles, and institutional restructuring, can result in reduced budgets for IR functions that can significantly lessen their evidence-generating capacity, thus reducing their influence and impact.

In the UK, there is no sector-level commitment to the development of IR, although some institutional leadership teams are highly supportive of IR activities, especially those containing senior managers with employment backgrounds in sectors with a strong focus on strategic business intelligence and research. The changing external operating context could create the conditions where institutional senior managers are more open to the development of a coordinated IR function. UK HEIs now operate in an environment where there is increased demand for scarce resources and growing competitiveness between HE providers, making it more important than ever for institutional strategic decision making and quality enhancement activities to be soundly based on complete, accurate, and timely evidence. Where institutions are seeking to improve their external reputation with key external stakeholders in relation to comparable institutions in published league tables, there are other important drivers at play.

Where resources are available to support organizational change projects and restructuring, there will be opportunities to present a business case for the development of a systematic and integrated approach to IR (e.g., via a cost-benefits analysis, options appraisal, etc.). However, many UK HEIs—as in Ireland—are operating in a significantly resource-constrained environment and will have to find creative ways of moving from an informal arrangement to a more formalized approach to IR where different parts of the institutional community view IR as integral to achievement of their own goals. Feasible and cost-effective solutions are likely to require a mix of leadership and teamwork between individuals, professional services departments, and faculties, and openness to sourcing external income streams for both internally focused and external policy-directed IR.

Senior managers in the UK often lack understanding about the value of IR compared with disciplinary or more 'academic' research, but anecdotal evidence suggests that once IR activities are articulated in terms that they understand, they are often persuaded of the high potential impact and value of IR. However, it is the responsibility of the UK IR community to be clear about the benefits and potential 'traps' of IR around misinterpretation of data (Watson, 2009), demonstrate the ability to communicate evidence in timely and effective ways, and to focus on outcomes rather than outputs when making the case for enhanced IR capacity. As Watson and Maddison (2005) point out:

> the goals of institutional self-study include not only better strategic choices but also winning hearts and minds, inside and outside the institution; in other words, the art of persuasion.
>
> *(p. 140)*

Conclusion

Centralized institutional research remains under-developed in the UK and Ireland. IR functions, where they do exist, remain small and relatively under-resourced compared with practice in the US and Australia, limiting their potential impact on HE practice. This is a result of their historical evolution and location within institutional structures, and the status of institutional focused research and data analysis in both countries compared with more traditional 'academic' educational research on HE, which has a higher status and brings significant reputational benefits. As Macfarlane (2012) pointed out, institutional researchers are often isolated between the two main components of HE research—teaching and learning and policy and management. His *higher education research archipelago* suggests that IR is located on the isle of 'institutional research land' in the 'sea of disjuncture' close to the forgotten isle of 'development' (Macfarlane, 2012, p. 129).

Therefore, despite much good practice, the full potential of IR in the UK and Ireland is not yet fully realized, and institutions are just beginning to garner the full benefits of institutional self-study for effective organizational learning. Chirikov (2013) suggests that IR functions need to position themselves as 'information clearing houses' or 'think tanks'; however the reality in the UK and Irish contexts is much more complex, with IR practitioners undertaking either or both functions, and many more in some contexts where there can be high levels of technical and analytical expertise.

Although there is a strong community of IR practitioners in the UK and Ireland, in the UK, with some exceptions, they are loosely connected both within and across institutions and IR remains some way from being a recognized professional field (Taylor et al., 2013). The UK and Ireland HEIR network seeks to act as a bridge between IR practitioners in different institutions and countries, to bring IR closer to relevant policy-focused and higher education research, to support capacity-building, to identify and disseminate good practice, and to foster collaboration for mutual benefit in a climate of increased competition.

Ideally, the impact of recent government policy changes focused on strategically positioning and developing national HE systems in the face of growing global competition will create the optimum conditions for the growth of IR in the UK. The recent focus on developing IR practice in Ireland has demonstrated that the profile of IR practice can be significantly raised with government and sector-wide support for IR, and via engagement with good practice from other countries. Furthermore, HE institutions are becoming increasingly independent from government influence and control and should themselves recognize that the value of institutional research is to help them shape and support their future strategic direction in a rapidly changing global higher education landscape.

References

Argyris, C., & Schön, D. (1978). *Organizational learning: A theory of action perspective.* Reading, MA: Addison Wesley.

BIS. (2011). *Higher education: Students at the heart of the system.* Report presented to Parliament by the Secretary of State for Business, Innovation and Skills by Command of Her Majesty. London, UK: BIS.

Brynjolfsson, E., & McAfee, A. (2012). Big data: The management revolution. *Harvard Business Review, 90*(10), 60–68.

Chester, J. (2014). *Five pillars of institutional research.* HEIR Network. Opinion Piece Series, Number 3, March 2014.

Chirikov, I. (2013). Research universities as knowledge networks: The role of institutional research. *Studies in Higher Education, 38*(3), 456–469.

Department for Business Innovation and Skills (BIS). (2011). *Higher education: Students at the heart of the system.* London, UK: BIS.

Drysdale, R. (2013). University data can be a force for good. *Guardian Higher Education Network blog.* Retrieved from: www.theguardian.com/higher-education-network/blog/2013/nov/27/university-data-student-engagement-retention.

European Universities Association. (2005). *Review of quality assurance in Irish Universities: Sectoral report.* Dublin, Ireland: Higher Education Authority and Irish Universities Quality Board.

Flanagan, A. (2011). Chapter D 3–1: Gathering and using information for governance and leadership purposes. In S. Bergan, E. Egron-Polak, J. Kohler, L. Purser, & A. Spyropoulou (Eds.), *Leadership and governance in higher education: Handbook for decision-makers and administrators* (pp. 61–86), issue 03–2011. Berlin, Germany: Raabe Academic Publishers.

HM Treasury. (2013). *Autumn statement 2013.* London: HMSO.

Irish Universities Quality Board. (2008). *Good practice for institutional research in Irish higher education.* Dublin, Ireland: Irish Universities Quality Board.

Jackson, N. (2003). *Developing a network for institutional researchers: Working paper.* A working paper for the Learning and Teaching Support Network Generic Centre. York, England: Higher Education Academy.

Longden, B., & Yorke, M. (2009). Institutional research: What problems are we trying to solve? *Perspectives, 13*(3), 66–70.

Lyons, J. M. (1976). *Memorandum to a newcomer to the field of institutional research.* Tallahassee, FL: The Association for Institutional Research.

Macfarlane, B. (2012). The higher education research archipelago. *Higher Education Research & Development, 31*(1), 129–131.

Senge, P. M. (1990). *The fifth discipline: The art & practice of the learning organization.* London, UK: Century Business.

Simmons, J., & Lea, J. (2013). *Capturing an HE ethos in college higher education practice.* Gloucester, England: Quality Assurance Agency for Higher Education.

Taylor, J., Hanlon, M., & Yorke, M. (2013). The evolution and practice of institutional research, In A. Calderon & K. Webber (Eds.), *Global issues in institutional research* (pp. 59–75). *New Directions for Institutional Research, No. 157*. San Francisco, CA: Jossey-Bass.

Teichler, U. (2005). Research on higher education in Europe. *European Journal of Education, 40*(4), 447–469.

Terenzini, P. T. (1999). On the nature of institutional research and the knowledge and skills it requires. In J. F. Volkwein (Ed.), *What is institutional research all about? A critical and comprehensive assessment of the profession* (pp. 21–29). *New Directions for Institutional Research, No. 104*. San Francisco, CA: Jossey-Bass.

Terenzini, P. T. (2013). "On the nature of institutional research" revisited: Plus ça change . . . ? *Research in Higher Education, 54*(2), 137–148.

Volkwein, J. F. (2008). *The foundations and evolution of institutional research* (pp. 5–20). *New Directions for Higher Education, No. 141*. San Francisco, CA: Jossey-Bass.

Watson, D. (2009). The dark side of institutional research. *Perspectives: Policy and Practice in Higher Education, 13*(3), 71–75.

Watson, D., & Maddison, E. (2005). *Managing institutional self-study.* Maidenhead, UK: McGraw-Hill/Open University Press.

Yorke, M. (2004). Institutional research and its relevance to the performance of higher education institutions. *Journal of Higher Education Policy and Management, 26*(2), 141–152.

8

STRATEGIC PLANNING AND INSTITUTIONAL RESEARCH

The Case of Australia

Marian Mahat and Hamish Coates

Introduction

The relationship between institutional research and strategic planning is complex and perplexing. Large organizations can collect vast amounts of data and still run seemingly on intuition. Smaller institutions often do not have research capacity or the need for reifying the material that supports leadership. Mid-sized institutions may conduct planning-focused research yet lack the culture or leadership to convert this into planning. Such situations arise partly because not all that matters can be measured easily, and because not all that is measured or analyzed counts. Institutional culture, regulatory contexts, access to effective researchers, and leaders' discipline background also seem to influence the relationship between research and planning. It seems rational to contend that leadership is likely to be more effective when relevant research is taken into account, yet there are plenty of examples of evidence-free effective leadership, or of leadership challenges that lie beyond the research horizon.

Taking Australian higher education as a case study, this chapter explores the relationship between these two facets of higher education. The chapter looks at the development of strategic planning and institutional research, explores points of intersection between these activities, and offers suggestions for future growth. While the discussion draws on international research, this analysis focuses on Australia. The country of Australia has a substantial higher education system that is highly internationalized through deep links, particularly into North America, Europe, and Asia. The system and its institutions have several innovative features that render it interesting in its own right and also of more generalizable import. Accordingly, while the concluding remarks flow largely from the prior analysis, they can also be read with broader relevance to other systems and institutions.

The warrant for this chapter flows from broader rationales driving the book. Affirming the value of research for leadership is important for ensuring the relevance and sustainability of these fields of work. Professionalizing the science and practice of leadership is important for building broader higher education capacity. With higher education on the rise in many parts of the world, there is value in finding out more about the professions required by growing systems. The analysis also seeks to chart the current state of play, and to offer research-informed suggestions for improving future policy and practice.

A Historical Sketch of a Growing Relationship

Analyzing links between institutional research and strategic planning should be premised on understanding planning itself. Strategic planning has assumed a greater role in higher education systems and institutions over the last few decades. To frame the subsequent analysis, we consider forces shaping this change, the nature of such planning, and the increasing influence and importance of institutional research.

Higher education in Australia has grown substantially in scale over the last few decades. In 1981, the system had 19 universities and 75 colleges of advanced education (Commonwealth of Australia, 1993) with a total student enrollment of 336,702 (Commonwealth of Australia, 2000). In 2012, Australia had 40 universities and over 130 private higher education providers (TEQSA, 2013) with around 1,257,722 students and 50,423 academics being reported to the government (Commonwealth of Australia, 2013). Institutions, too, have grown in scope and scale, spanning a large range of fields and industries, functioning internationally, conducting research and teaching, carrying large and complex infrastructure, having highly diversified revenue streams, and making substantial community service contributions. Higher education has become a big business, requiring astute planning and management.

As might be expected given such change, institutions function in an increasingly complex environment. Tertiary education has moved closer to the core of public life, yielding greater political and economic attention. International operations provoke expansive, unexpected, and often perplexing uncertainties. The half-life of policies even concerning core facets of funding and regulation perpetually shrinks, requiring nimble leadership reaction and positioning. Reduced government funding requires leadership of large organizations in an increasingly commercial way. Technological reconfigurations of education and academic work are reshaping basic 'ways of doing business.'

Along with industry-specific scale and environmental complexities, higher education is also influenced by changed management dynamics. New approaches to management (see for example: Brown & Lauder, 1996; Deem, 1998) have led to growth of the (non-academic) professional workforce—roughly equal to the academic workforce—and to the delegation of institutional leadership to well-paid executive teams. Like other industries, the need to grow and diversify revenue while at the same time coordinating a host of accountabilities requires robust and timely information on past, current, and future performance. General change to the nature of 'knowledge work,' and to the contemporary organization, requires more reflective and data-driven leadership and management.

In response to these and other trends and developments, strategic planning is on the rise. Strategic planning can take a variety of forms, and for current purposes, we affirm the conception advanced by Crisp (1991, p. 3), which casts strategic planning as "the set of activities designed to identify the appropriate future direction of a college and includes specifying the steps to move in that direction." It is widely accepted that such planning generally has four stages (Bush & Bell, 2000; Taylor & Miroiu, 2002; Taylor, de Lourdes Machado, & Peterson, 2008). The first stage, **planning**, involves assessing the current status of the institution, generating forward-looking ideas, and deciding on direction. Stage two, **participating and documenting,** involves preparing the plan, achieving acceptance from stakeholders, and disseminating ideas. **Implementing**, stage three, includes merging the ideas and putting the plan into action. Finally, **monitoring,** involves assessing the success of the plan through goals and benchmarks. At each stage, evidence-based research and analysis can assist planners test and identify appropriate options.

Of course, as suggested at the outset, it is possible to do strategic planning without recourse to any kind of institutional, policy, or scholarly research. Leaders typically bring extensive contextual and institutional insight to planning deliberations and, indeed, ultimately rely on individual discretion and decision. But evidence-free planning becomes more difficult, perhaps even impossible, in large and complex settings. Hence derives the increased need for institutional research. Institutional research is generically defined as research and analysis conducted within a higher education institution to support decision making by administrators and other staff. Several formal definitions have been offered over the years (see for example: Borden & Kezar, 2012; Saupe, 1990; Suslow, 1972). The first chapter in this volume provides a comprehensive and historical review of institutional research and its derivatives. Rather than recap this analysis in general terms, we turn instead to focus on the growth of planning-relevant institutional research as it has unfolded in Australia.

Institutional Research in Australia

Traced over the last three decades, institutional research in Australian higher education can be seen as developing through several phases. As expected, institutional research has grown with reference to institutional and broader changes. We chart the broad contours of this growth and conclude with broader perspectives on links between institutional research and strategic planning.

Zimmer (1994) informs that for most of the 1980s, institutional research in Australian higher education was fairly limited in scope. Few universities had staff with specific planning or research roles, or who were performing duties beyond collating basic administrative and demographic information. Reliance on paper-based systems in a large country meant that collation and reporting were time consuming and the capacity for analysis was limited. Institutions were also comparatively small, and in academic respects servicing their local and regional environments.

The rise of new management approaches, coupled with the influence of the major structural 'Dawkins Reforms' (Commonwealth of Australia, 1988) and advances in computing technology, saw the growth of planning-related research activities in the 1990s. As charted by Coates, Tilbrook, Guthrie, and Bryant (2006) in relation to Australia's national graduate census, planning offices were established to support the provision of data to government and other agencies, and for internal support to institutional leaders and managers. Indeed, the early 1990s also saw the creation and institutionalization of several new national data collections focused on staff, finance, students, and graduates (Linke, 1991; Martin, 1994). Several indicators and statistical collections were implanted to service a suite of institutional and national requirements. A national student equity framework (Department of Employment Education and Training [DEET], 1990) was produced, for instance, to help monitor the involvement of disadvantaged groups in the system. Graduate destination and teaching satisfaction surveys were embedded within various information and monitoring frameworks. Profiles were produced for each institution to inform triennial funding agreements. Increasingly during this period, attention turned to examining how to use statistical information to monitor quality and performance.

After the turn of the century, a range of developments led to further growth of institutional research in Australia. Over a decade of experience handling national data collections brought increased confidence in using high-level indicators in more sophisticated policy and management applications. For the most part, institutional research still defaulted to the aggregation and provision of data for external reporting to government. Institutions varied enormously in the extent to which they collected and analyzed other data. Recommendations that data be used for performance funding, for instance, in the Learning and Teaching Performance Fund (Commonwealth of Australia, 2003) and as part of external quality reviews (Australian Universities Quality Agency [AUQA], 2011) placed greater pressure on institutional research staff to use data and metrics in more sophisticated ways. During the same period, the rapidly increasing onshore export of education to 'international' students (Commonwealth of Australia, 2010) led to the creation of further commercially focused data collections both within and across institutions. Several institutions moved institutional research offices into broader business and management units.

Large-scale change in the late 2000s had substantial impact on the nature of institutional research in Australian higher education. In the late 2000s, another series of major reforms, coined the 'Bradley Reforms' (Bradley, Noonan, Nugent, &

Scales, 2008), changed fundamentals of how institutions relate with each other and various government and other agencies. Most notably, rather than government and institutions setting plans for student numbers, the government implemented a voucher system that involved funding every bachelor degree student who could gain admission to a higher education institution. Facing new opportunities and fresh commercial considerations required additional support from institutional researchers for positioning and planning. During this time, the ubiquitous adoption of learning management systems (Coates, James, & Baldwin, 2005) along with the formation of research performance metrics, notably the Excellence in Research for Australia (ERA) (Commonwealth of Australia, 2014), and education performance metrics such as the Australasian Survey of Student Engagement (AUSSE) (Coates, 2009) saw increasing interest in using various forms of evidence to lead and manage higher education.

As this brief review suggests, the type of institutional research being undertaken in Australia has changed substantially over the last three decades. A more extensive analysis would likely reveal how some changes are prompted by developments in institutional research—such as new technologies and new analytical methods—but that most have been driven by changes in policymaking or management. Institutional research in Australia has grown slowly, with development tempered by the relatively small scale of the system and tight regulation of cross-institutional competition. Like many systems, but unlike the United States, outside the international arena there has been little incentive until recently for institutions to construct detailed analytics on students or research. Given an increasingly borderless higher education industry and heated domestic competition, the last few years have seen rapid advance in the field of institutional research and its link to policy and strategy. Rather than exist for the reactive provision of information to external agencies, institutions have stimulated, gathered, and probed a much larger and more nuanced range of strategic information. This, in turn, carries implications for the nature and effectiveness of planning.

Institutional Insights Into Research-Driven Planning

With the above analyses in mind, this section reviews real-world examples showing how institutional research has informed various stages of the strategic planning process: planning, documenting and participating, implementing, and monitoring. These best practice examples have been taken from institutional audit reports conducted by the Australian University Quality Agency. AUQA was established in 2000 (and closed around a decade later) to audit institutions with respect to their own objectives rather than on any externally prescribed set of standards. The reports offer a glimpse of each institution's activities and contexts. Incidentally, these best practices have been taken from the turn of the century when developments in institutional research began to proliferate in Australia.

Research-Driven Planning at the University of the Sunshine Coast: Literature on vision building has had a long history in the business sector but emerged somewhat recently in the 1980s within educational leadership (Foreman, 1998). It is not an easy process—a strong vision should incorporate an image of the future of the university and of education trends in general, embody the views of leadership on excellence in schooling, describe a process for change, and support broader university assumptions about the role of the university in education and society (Beare, Caldwell, & Millikan, 1993). Success in vision building involves multiple levels of information gathering and consensus building, including interviews of individuals representing diverse groups (Kotler & Murphy, 1981).

A fairly new university, the University of the Sunshine Coast (USC) was established in 1996 and formally received its university status in 1999. During the early years, USC drew on the experience of other Australian universities to create its institutional structures and functions. This also involved taking into consideration the strengths and weaknesses internal to the university and opportunities and threats posed by the external environment. The SWOT analysis allowed USC to find its competitive advantage while aligning its mission to serve the needs and the economic vitality of the Sunshine Coast region.

In a second wave of development from 2004, the planning process initiated by the then council, resulted in a new strategic plan. Its development involved an environmental analysis and consultative process with key stakeholder groups inside and external to the university. As a result of its environmental scan and consultative process, USC was able to develop a vision with evident commitment among staff and stakeholders to support its achievement (AUQA, 2007). By the time Professor Paul Thomas, the inaugural vice-chancellor, retired in 2010, USC had proven its viability.

From its first inception in 1996, USC was able to build a future image for the university based on information gathering at different levels. This evidence-based vision building enabled the university to build on its strengths and uncover opportunities to be exploited. USC was able to make use of 'contextual intelligence' (Terenzini, 1999) to understand the culture of higher education generally and also specifically within the region in which its campus was located. The integrated research and analysis of its internal and external environments, coupled with the ability to interpret information and provide insights to data through knowledge of higher education and its internal organization and business processes, facilitated and supported institutional strategic planning and decision making. In gathering information from a range of sources, USC was able to discern trends in the face of complexity and uncertainty as well as adaptability while still trying to shape events.

Research-Informed Documentation at Charles Sturt University: Strategic planning, obviously, seeks to develop plans that are likely to shape practice. Too many plans end up 'on a shelf' (Goldman & Salem, 2013), without influencing the activities and structure of the university. The whole university community has roles to play in carrying out the strategy once it is developed. Clear documentation and communication are essential in order for this to take place.

Incorporated in 1989, Charles Sturt University (CSU) is a multi-campus university located in New South Wales, Victoria, and Australian Capital Territory. During Professor Goulter's term as vice-chancellor, the university developed a vision of 'One University.' Its mission as articulated in its strategic plan was to be "a bold and innovative leader in providing an accessible, adaptable and challenging learning environment to develop graduates and research that meet the needs of its regional, national and international communities" (AUQA, 2004, p. 9).

Although operating across physically distributed locations and campuses, CSU was able to instill the concept and values of the vision strongly among its staff. The strategic plan document was able to effectively communicate the CSU's goals and the actions needed to achieve those goals. The ability to write an effective document begins with effective reporting (Sanders & Filkins, 2012) of institutional research and analysis. It takes into account the intended audience and specific purpose, and conveys in a practical, non-technical, and compelling way.

Through various fora, CSU also enabled effective cross-institutional discussion and information sharing. These fora helped staff foster an understanding of operating as 'One University' and was evident with staff across and for different levels, within 'far flung' campuses, and campuses with distinctive academic specializations. In particular, the special interest group fora were particularly effective in fostering relationships and discussion across the university (AUQA, 2004).

Increasingly, institutional researchers involved in supporting strategic planning of universities, and in concert with other departments such as information technology and communication offices, play key roles in documentation of strategic and other derivative plans and developing a two-way dialogue or 'engagement' with the university community. The ability for CSU to provide clear documentation and communication illustrates the integral role institutional research plays in strategic planning.

University of Melbourne Research-Driven Implementation: Bartol and Martin (1998) define strategy implementation as any management activities necessary to put strategy in motion, monitor progress, and ultimately achieve organizational goals. While it is well and good to develop a well-articulated vision, universities do not always succeed in executing their strategic plans.

Following the Growing Esteem Strategic Plan (University of Melbourne, 2005), the University of Melbourne adopted the 'Melbourne Model,' a whole-of-university curriculum restructure and redevelopment. At the time of planning, the University of Melbourne's 96 undergraduate courses were to be replaced with six 'New Generation' undergraduate degrees and professional programs. In implementing the Melbourne Model, the university was required to make changes to many aspects of its operations. New budget models, involving pooling and redistribution of teaching revenue for the six undergraduate degrees, were developed to support the cross-faculty teaching that occurred. The ways student services and advice were provided had to change. Substantial marketing and communications strategies were also applied, as the public (particularly potential students and parents) and the community grappled with the concept and the changes taking place. The University of Melbourne also undertook a major policy review.

The first cohort of students from the new generation degrees graduated at the end of 2010. That same year, AUQA commended the University of Melbourne for its commitment to obtaining and acting on continuous and immediate feedback about the implementation of its Melbourne Model (AUQA, 2010). This commitment in feedback gathering meant that the University of Melbourne was able to assess what was working and not working and implement improvements immediately.

Through open and effective communication of progress, the University of Melbourne was able to "understand the major categories of problems confronting middle and upper-level administrators in various parts of the institution" (Terenzini, 1999, p. 24). The institution was also able to understand and appreciate the essentially political character of the implementation of the Melbourne Model. This form of generalized issues intelligence is reflected in one's knowledge of the importance and role of political persuasion, of compromise, of prior consultation with important opinion makers and organizational and governance units, and personal and professional courtesy—the knowledge of how to work successfully with other people in order to accomplish goals (Terenzini, 1999).

The strategies undertaken at the University of Melbourne—marketing, communication, and collaborative interaction with various communities of interest—played a big part in ensuring the university implemented its vision well. Research-oriented investigations, undertaken outside the traditional realm of institutional research office, played an increasing and significant role in providing information and analysis to facilitate the implementation of these strategies. These provide the evidence base for the successful implementation of the Melbourne Model.

Research-Supported Monitoring at Monash University: Monitoring refers to assessing the success of the plan through benchmarks and goals. Increasingly, universities are measuring and quantifying their performance to understand their progress toward its goal and mission. Key Performance Indicators (KPIs) are incorporated into strategic planning as institutional leaders recognize the important role objective and reliable data play in terms of resource allocation, faculty evaluation, research management, etc. Yet, gathering too much data can also be expensive, overwhelming, confusing, and bury the most interesting information for organizational strategy under a pile of less useful indicators (Goldman & Salem, 2013).

Many universities, including Monash University, have developed and implemented key performance indicators as a means of monitoring performance systematically against strategic directions. Recognizing the concept of 'too much data,' in 2005, Monash developed a KPI framework with a number of core principles—the indicators had to be brief (between 10 and 20), university-wide, benchmarked, and aligned to the objectives set out in the strategic plan. The resulting framework had 20 indicators covering reputation, research, education, equity, international (students and research funding), and financial strength, each with clear stretch targets. 'Traffic-light' reporting against the targets were introduced using green, amber, and red to signify areas meeting aspirations, needing improvement, and needing critical attention. Within this new framework, Monash University also formulated an additional 52 indicators that were provided at institutional, faculty, and campus levels.

In its 2006 audit, AUQA found that the framework and resulting KPI reports were well embedded within the university (AUQA, 2006). Through the institutional research office, the university was able to make effective use of data and information to monitor and guide direction of the university; to embed further in faculty and divisional operational plans; to keep Monash University Council and the rest of the university community up-to-date with progress; and to provide a clear stimulus for staff to improve their performance. In using its 'technical/analytical intelligence' (Terenzini, 1999), Monash University was able to make use of high levels of analytical and methodological skills and competencies to analyze factual knowledge and information. In presenting the KPI report, the institutional researchers also made use of the key elements of effective reporting (Sanders & Filkins, 2012) through providing information in an efficient and visually engaging way.

Additionally, Monash was able to create a clear alignment of the various levels of strategic planning system (institutional, campus, faculty, and divisional) to monitor accomplishments toward goals in an effectual way. The institutional research office played a key role in implementing the Monash Planning Pyramid (Monash University, 2013)—a planning architecture that helped conceptualize various aspects of planning in terms of 'reach' and time; from short-term operational through medium-term strategic to long-term vision; and making sure the use of KPIs cascaded through every level.

Future Opportunities and Challenges

Together, the above deliberations carry myriad implications for institutional research and strategic planning and, hence, for higher education as a whole. In the penultimate section of this chapter, we offer broad perspectives arising from the preceding analysis, observations on building capacity, and insights on growing planning-relevant forms of institutional research.

Broadly, this chapter highlights that over the last few decades, institutional research and higher education leadership have grown closer. There is still much leadership that has little to do with planning, and much planning done for practice and policy rather than institutional leadership. But in general, leaders today rely more on research-informed planning, which in turn calls for more planning-focused research. Growing evidence-based management implies increasingly sophisticated approaches to higher education, and increased expectations. To be sure, there is ample scope for further growth and in this section we review a small selection of improvement prospects.

In an era of 'big data' higher education institutions are awash in information. A core challenge for institutional researchers is to shift expertise and focus from data collection toward analysis and interpretation. This is challenging, for until recently the collection of data—for instance, via surveys, administrative records, and paper-based assessments—was a major facet of institutional research. The onus now is on higher-order work that applies complex 'learner analytics' or 'people analytics' to distill salient insights from masses of information. This requires new forms of expertise and methodological insight to deliver the new potential.

As relevant experts, institutional researchers need to ensure that, particularly in an era where information is vast and easy to find, the 'right' things are being measured in valid, reliable, and efficient ways. Reporting information to management is meaningless if the information is not focused on the areas that count. The need to build new impact-oriented metrics on learning outcomes and research impact continues to heighten, though progress is being made (see for example: Coates & Mahat, 2014; Higher Education Funding Council for England [HEFCE], 2012). With the greatest capacity to bridge practice with policy and strategy, it is vital that institutional researchers play a shaping role in advancing work in these core fields. As higher education moves beyond input- and process-oriented metrics, ensuring provision of salient and robust outcome-oriented metrics is critical.

Of course, along with the production of new metrics, higher education is also experiencing an unprecedented boom in new forms of transparency and reporting. International and other forms of strategically relevant rankings continue to proliferate, as do more regulatory focused forms of reporting and various internally initiated benchmarking exercises. Together, these call for greater institutional research capabilities around ensuring the integrity of data and reporting processes, and understanding the strategic and operational environments being navigated by institutions.

Most if not all of these improvement prospects go to a broad need to improve and build a larger and more effective tertiary workforce. This broad point was affirmed within Australia in 2006 in the initiation of the LH Martin Institute (LH Martin Institute, 2014a). More capacity in institutional research is required, as endorsed through development over recent years of a specialized training program in Institutional Research in Tertiary Education (LH Martin Institute, 2014b). But building research capacity alone would be pointless without broader progress in other areas of management and leadership. It is not entirely untrue to suggest that Australia's high-growth higher education system has been led over the last three decades largely by people working 'out of field'—very few of the country's current institutional leaders, or policymakers, have been trained in the field of tertiary education, and many have received only light-touch management training. In an increasingly competitive international higher education context, this is not necessarily an approach that will replicate well into the future. Such training takes structured, less formal, and ad hoc forms (Scott, Coates, & Anderson, 2008). Initiation of professional conferences and meetings (for instance, the Higher Education Planning in Asia Forum—see http://hepa.ust.hk) along with more coherent forms of professional recognition is important.

Concluding Insights

In a keynote address in 1990, the Chair of the National Board of Employment, Education and Training identified strategic planning as creating an opportunity for institutional research to contribute to improve understanding and functioning of Australian higher education (Ramsey, 1990). The above analysis and case studies point to just that. The growth of institutional research in Australia provides context on how the field has advanced over the last three decades. The case studies offer evidence on how institutional research has supported strategic planning in Australian universities. The emergence of professional development courses and forums in planning and research and the need for new metrics, forms of transparency, and reporting, as articulated in the last section, indicate that institutional research will continue to grow in strength in Australia as well as other parts of the globe.

This chapter considered the role and influence of institutional research on strategic planning, taking Australian universities as a case study. In tandem with the other chapters in this section, we have mapped out practices specific to Australia and outlined the extent to which research and planning have contributed to understanding and supporting decision making in Australian higher education. Drawing threads across these kinds of national insights contributes to broader pictures of the nature and settings of institutional research and, indeed, of strategic planning.

Significant forces are reshaping higher education, leading to new business and education models, and new forms of governance, provision, and knowledge, which links directly to institutional, policy, and scholarly research (Coates & Mahat, 2014). As the higher education landscape continues to change the role research-evidence decision-making plays should continue to be documented. The recent growth of higher education in Australia enables institutional research practices and processes to be further detailed and, more importantly, acknowledged. As the role research plays in positioning universities within a highly competitive and globalized environment continues to grow in strength, it becomes more critical than ever that a volume and the chapters within, such as this, continues to bring prominence to research in higher education.

References

Australian Universities Quality Agency (AUQA). (2004). *Report of an audit of Charles Sturt University*. Melbourne, AU: Australian Universities Quality Agency.

AUQA. (2006). *Report of an audit of Monash University*. Melbourne, AU: Australian Universities Quality Agency.

AUQA. (2007). *Report of an audit of the University of the Sunshine Coast*. Melbourne, AU: Australian Universities Quality Agency.

AUQA. (2010). *Report of an audit of the University of Melbourne*. Melbourne, AU: Australian Universities Quality Agency.

AUQA. (2011). *Audit manual version 8.0*. Melbourne, AU: Australian Universities Quality Agency.

Bartol, K., & Martin, D. (1998). *Management*. New York, NY: McGraw-Hill.

Beare, H., Caldwell, B., & Millikan, R. (1993). Leadership. In M. Preedy (Ed.), *Managing the effective school* (pp. 141–162). London, UK: Chapman.

Borden, V.M.H., & Kezar, A. (2012). Institutional research and collaborative organizational learning. In R. D. Howard, G. W. McLaughlin, & W. E. Knight (Eds.), *The handbook of institutional research* (pp. 86–106). San Francisco, CA: Jossey-Bass.

Bradley, D., Noonan, P., Nugent, H., & Scales, B. (2008). *Review of Australian higher education*. Canberra, AU: Department of Education, Employment and Workplace Relations.

Brown, P., & Lauder, H. (1996). Education, globalization and economic development. *Journal of Education Policy, 11*, 1–24.

Bush, T., & Bell, L. (Eds.). (2000). *The principles and practice of educational management*. London, UK: Paul Chapman Publishing.

Coates, H. (2009). Development of the Australasian Survey of Student Engagement (AUSSE). *Higher Education, 60*(10).

Coates, H., James, R., & Baldwin, G. (2005). A critical examination of the effects of learning management systems on university teaching and learning. *Tertiary Education and Management, 11*, 19–36.

Coates, H., & Mahat, M. (2014). Threshold quality parameters in hybrid higher education. *Higher Education*, 1–14. doi: 10.1007/s10734–014–9729–x.

Coates, H., Tilbrook, C., Guthrie, B., & Bryant, G. (2006). *Enhancing the GCA National Surveys: An examination of critical factors leading to enhancements in the instrument, methodology and process*. Canberra, AU: Department of Education, Science and Training.

Commonwealth of Australia. (1988). *Higher education: A policy statement*. Canberra, AU: Australian Government Publishing Service.

Commonwealth of Australia. (1993). *National report on Australia's higher education sector*. Canberra, AU: Australian Government Publishing Service.

Commonwealth of Australia. (2000). *Higher education students time series tables, 2000*. Retrieved 24 February 2013, from www.education.gov.au/selected-higher-education-statistics-time-series-data-and-publications.

Commonwealth of Australia. (2003). *Our universities: Backing Australia's future*. Canberra, AU: Australian Government Publishing Service.

Commonwealth of Australia. (2010). *Stronger, simpler, smarter ESOS: Supporting international students*. Canberra, AU: Department of Education, Employment and Workplace Relations.

Commonwealth of Australia. (2013). *Higher education statistics data cube (*uCube). Retrieved 26 February 2014, from www.highereducationstatistics.deewr.gov.au/.

Commonwealth of Australia. (2014). *ERA 2009 Trial development.* Retrieved 26 February 2014, from www.arc.gov.au/era/era_2009/archive/development.htm.

Crisp, P. (1991). *Strategic planning and management.* Blagdon, UK: The Staff College.

Deem, R. (1998). 'New managerialism' and higher education: The management of performances and cultures in universities in the United Kingdom. *International Studies in Sociology of Education, 8*(1), 47–70.

Department of Employment Education and Training (DEET). (1990). *A fair chance for all: Higher education that's within everyone's reach.* Canberra, AU: Australian Government Publishing Service.

Foreman, K. (1998). Vision and mission. In D. Middlewood & J. Lumby (Eds.), *Strategic management in schools and colleges.* London, UK: Paul Chapman Publishing Ltd.

Goldman, C. A., & Salem, H. (2013). *Strategic planning methods for building world-class university.* Paper presented at the 5th International Conference on World-Class Universities, Shanghai, China.

Higher Education Funding Council for England (HEFCE). (2012). *Research excellence framework.* Retrieved 28 February 2014, from www.ref.ac.uk/.

Kotler, P., & Murphy, P. (1981). Strategic planning in higher education. *The Journal of Higher Education, 52*(5), 470–489.

LH Martin Institute. (2014a). *About the Institute.* Retrieved 26 February 2014, from www.lhmartininstitute.edu.au/about-the-institute/overview.

LH Martin Institute. (2014b). *Institutional Research in Tertiary Education.* Retrieved 26 February 2014, from www.lhmartininstitute.edu.au/professional-development-programs/single-subjects/135-institutional-research-in-tertiary-education.

Linke, R. D. (1991). *Report of the research group on performance indicators in higher education.* Canberra: Department of Employment, Education and Training.

Martin, L. M. (1994). *Equity and general performance indicators in higher education.* Canberra: Australian Government Publishing Service.

Monash University. (2013). *Monash University planning pyramid.* Retrieved 21 February 2014, from www.monash.edu.au/about/monash-directions/assets/pdfs/planning-pyramid-2013.pdf.

Ramsey, G. (1990). *Directions for institutional research in higher education.* Paper presented at the Australasian Association for Institutional Research Forum, Rockhampton, AU.

Sanders, L., & Filkins, J. (2012). Effective reporting. In R. D. Howard, G. W. McLaughlin, & W. E. Knight (Eds.), *The handbook of institutional research* (pp. 594–610). San Francisco, CA: Jossey-Bass.

Saupe, J. L. (1990). *The functions of institutional research* (2nd ed.). Tallahassee, FL: Association for Institutional Research.

Scott, G., Coates, H., & Anderson, M. (2008). *Learning leaders in times of change: Academic leadership capabilities for Australian higher education.* Sydney: Australian Learning and Teaching Council.

Suslow, S. (1972). *A declaration on institutional research.* Tallahassee, FL: Esso Education Foundation and Association for Institutional Research.

Taylor, A., & Miroiu, A. (2002). *Policy-making, strategic planning and management of higher education.* Papers on higher education. Bucharest, Romania: UNESCO-CEPES.

Taylor, J., de Lourdes Machado, M., & Peterson, M. (2008). Leadership and strategic management: Keys to institutional priorities and planning. *European Journal of Education, 43*(3), 369–386.

TEQSA. (2013). *National Register of higher education providers.* Retrieved 22 April 2013, from www.teqsa.gov.au/national-register.

Terenzini, P. T. (1999). On the nature of institutional research and the knowledge and skills it requires. In J. F. Volkwein (Ed.), *What is institutional research all about? A critical and comprehensive assessment of the profession, No. 104* (pp. 21–29). San Francisco, CA: Jossey Bass.

University of Melbourne. (2005). *Growing esteem.* Melbourne, AU: University of Melbourne.

Zimmer, B. (1994). Institutional research in Australia: Recent developments at a time of system-wide restructuring. *Journal of Institutional Research, 3*(2), 1–12.

9

INSTITUTIONAL RESEARCH IN SOUTH AFRICA IN THE SERVICE OF STRATEGIC AND ACADEMIC DECISION SUPPORT

Jan Botha

Introduction

Since its transition to a democracy in 1994, South African society has gone through a comprehensive transformation process. The planning and policy development processes in higher education during this period, and the concomitant demands on institutions to respond to and to implement these policies, have made a deep impact on the role of institutional researchers in South Africa. This tendency is continuing. Increasing reporting requirements by government as well as increasing demands for research outputs to be used for evidence-based decision-support in institutions can be expected. South Africa is not isolated from the global trends and challenges to higher education. South Africa is the eleventh largest host country in the world for incoming international students in higher education (UNESCO Institute of Statistics, 2012). As in other parts of the world, South Africa is experiencing general global higher education trends such as accountability and competition, new stakeholder expectations, and rapidly changing technologies. In addition to the challenges related to these trends, however, and given the critical development needs of South Africa and the region, there are also high expectations that higher education will make a significant contribution to the economic development of the country and contribute to the well-being and quality of life of all its citizens (Badat, 2013).

In 2012, about 91% of the 950,000 higher education students in South Africa (population 51.8 million) were enrolled in the twenty-three public higher education institutions. The approximately eighty small private higher education institutions catered for the remaining 9% (Council on Higher Education, 2014).

The first section of this chapter consists of a historical overview of the policies regulating higher education, with the focus on the policy changes during the early years of democracy (post-1994) when major strategic decisions were taken that made a deep impact on the higher education sector. Against this background, a more detailed discussion of the work of the Southern African Association for Institutional Research (SAAIR) during the first two decades of the democratic dispensation (1994–2014) is presented. In the final section, I venture a number of pointers to what institutional research (IR) professionals and planners in South Africa can expect in the years to come.

Higher Education in South Africa Before the Advent of Democracy in 1994

Although institutionalized higher education in South Africa goes back to the 1850s, the first two independent universities were established only in 1919. By the mid-1940s there were four independent universities in South Africa. Following World War II and shortly after the beginning of the apartheid era (1948), four more colleges received full university status.

The apartheid ideal that there should be separate institutions for different population and racial groups determined the developments between 1948 and 1994. Two more universities for whites and a number of universities for the black population groups were established. By the end of the apartheid era there were thirty-six higher education institutions in South Africa (Cooper & Subotzky, 2001).

A number of significant developments in higher education during the 1970s and 1980s contributed to the initial development and role of institutional research for decision support during the apartheid era. These developments continue to form the basis of institutional research activities during the democratic dispensation. In 1974 the report of the Van Wyk De Vries Commission of Inquiry into Universities was published. It set out the views of the government on higher education and laid the foundations for the trinary structure of higher education in South Africa, namely universities, technikons, and vocational colleges (Bunting, 1994). The technical work on the higher education data on which this report was based was undertaken by H.S. Steyn, a PhD graduate of the University of Edinburgh and a Professor of Statistics at the University of South Africa, and his team of co-workers. Under his guidance a number of highly qualified statisticians, physicists, mathematicians, and educationalists became involved in research on the university system and individual institutions. Although the Commission granted some measure of independence to universities, the report stated that the university was "brought into existence by the state, its functions are defined and prescribed by the state and its existence can in the end be terminated by the state" (quoted by Bunting, 1994, p. 12). This close link between the state and higher education must be kept in mind to understand the subsequent development of the higher education system and, within that, the role of institutional research. The government accepted that it is responsible to provide financial and other resources necessary for the operation of the universities and technikons.

The Origins of Institutional Research in South Africa

In order to fulfill this responsibility, the state needed to have good data on universities and technikons and this led to the development of the South African Post-Secondary Education (SAPSE) system and the Classification of Education Subject Matter (CESM) system. Both systems were implemented in 1982. In each public higher education institution a SAPSE Office (or similarly named unit) was established in the Registrar's Office or in the Finance Department. In many institutions these SAPSE Offices later developed into Institutional Research and Planning offices. The government officials responsible for the development of SAPSE undertook study tours to the US and different European countries to study best practices elsewhere. Through these tours and other capacity-building activities, institutional research expertise in South Africa received a major boost.

In 1999 the SAPSE system was replaced by the Higher Education Management Information System (HEMIS). The CESM system was revised in 2010. However, the principles and structure of SAPSE still form the basis of the generation, reporting, and analysis of higher education information in South African higher education. So, for example, Bunting's (1994) exposition of the state of higher education in South Africa at the end of the apartheid era was based on SAPSE. It included analyses of the data regarding the size and shape of the system (student enrollments in the different categories of institutions), student outputs, staffing resources, and finances. The SAPSE system laid the foundation for much of the institutional research and evidence-based strategic decision making and policy-formation in higher education in South Africa during the period of transformation after the advent of democracy in 1994.

The Transformation of Higher Education During the First Two Decades of the Democratic Dispensation

During the early years of democracy there was a flurry of strategic planning and policy development activities. The following chronicles some of the major events that helped transform higher education during this time.

The period following the release of Nelson Mandela from prison in February 1990 was characterized by significant policy developments in almost all spheres of society. In 1991, the National Educational Coordinating Committee (NECC) approved the National Education Policy Investigation (NEPI). It was a project aimed at providing policy options for different aspects of education, including higher education. NEPI's goal was to build indigenous capacity through research into and analysis of policy options (Badat, 1995).

One of the early initiatives of the Mandela presidency was the appointment of the National Commission on Higher Education (NCHE) with the brief to, *inter alia*, formulate a vision for the future of South African higher education. The NCHE Report published in 1996 was an important milestone. The report was informed by expert technical teams who analyzed higher education data and consulted with international experts. The Commission's recommendations included the establishment of a single and nationally coordinated higher education system based upon (a) a National Qualifications Framework, (b) a system of cooperative governance, and (c) the introduction of focused, goal-oriented funding to support transformation goals such as increased enrollments to broaden access to higher education in particular for black South Africans. Other recommendations included interventions to enhance the ability in higher education to respond through the production of knowledge to the needs of society and communities. This is necessitated by the urgently needed economic growth and technological development in South Africa (see the summary by Baumert, 2014).

Further growth of IR resulted from the publication of the *Education White Paper 3: A Programme for the Transformation of Higher Education* (1997) and promulgation of the Higher Education Act of 1997 (Department of Education, 1997). The Act gave legal effect to many of the recommendations of the National Commission on Higher Education (NCHE) as well as the government's intentions as formulated in *White Paper 3*. It provided, *inter alia*, for the establishment of the Council on Higher Education (CHE) in 1998, a statutory body with advisory and quality assurance functions, the latter through the establishment of a permanent Higher Education Quality Committee (HEQC) in 2001.

Higher education institutions (HEIs) were now expected to develop and submit three-year rolling plans to the government in which they set out their enrollment planning with reference to an agreed-upon institutional mission statement. These submissions also had to include plans for quality improvement, for the promotion of equal opportunities through the hiring of more black and female faculty and staff, plans for the development and academic support of students, and plans for research development. In order to meet these new national planning requirements, many higher education institutions had to increase their planning capacity and in particular their capacity to gather and interpret data.

This led to a significant enhancement in the professionalization of institutional research and related support services. Whereas all institutions had by then, for more than a decade, technical experts responsible for reporting in terms of the SAPSE (and, later, HEMIS) systems to their avail, the reporting of only the student, faculty, staff, and space data of previous years was no longer sufficient. This data now had to be aggregated and interpreted and there were various new data requirements. Staff members responsible for reporting institutional data through SAPSE and, later, HEMIS were expected to contribute to the institutional plans. However, additional skills and additional capacity beyond the traditional SAPSE/HEMIS functions were urgently needed. In some institutions the new function of institutional planner(s) came into being. In many institutions the Research Development Directors, or Directors of Centers for Teaching and Learning, or Directors of Academic Planning Units, or Executive Assistants to the Vice-Chancellor, or other high-level administrators and experts were called upon to provide leadership and technical expertise in the development of the institutional plans. Institutional research received a major boost. The first institutional plans were submitted in 1998, followed by two further rounds in 2000 and 2001. At the national level, there was also an urgent need for institutional research expertise to support the government in the interpretation of the institutional plans and in the preparation of the Department's responses to institutions. After 2006, the three-year rolling plans were replaced by a more detailed process of enrollment planning.

These intensive planning activities were needed to underpin and support the comprehensive transformation agenda in higher education. Much richer data on the higher education system and on individual institutions became available.

The National Plan on Higher Education (2001) and Institutional Mergers

Despite the enhanced planning activities of the late 1990s, it was evident that more direct government interventions were needed to transform the higher education system in South Africa. The massification predicted by the NCHE in 1996 did not materialize. Whereas there were 605,000 students enrolled in 1996, the number had shrunk to only 564,000 in 1999. While black students were beginning to enroll in significant numbers in the historically white institutions, the problems that plagued the historically black institutions increased, and the system as a whole remain skewed and inefficient.

In 2001, the Department of Education published the *National Plan for Higher Education* (Department of Education, 2001). This plan provided the framework and the mechanisms for the implementation of the goals of the white paper. Radical changes in South African higher education were announced. A process of institutional mergers driven by the national government was implemented during 2002–2005 and the number of higher education institutions in the country was reduced from thirty-six to twenty-three, namely eleven universities, six comprehensive universities, and six universities of technology. The mergers caused major upheaval in institutions. HEMIS officers and institutional planners worked under great pressure to provide the data needed by the merger processes. Information systems of different institutions had to be merged. Reporting of institutional data of new institutions (now merged into new configurations) was required. Due diligence studies and various other forms of analyses had to be undertaken. The stakes were very high.

The Role of Institutional Research Professionals in Quality Assurance

Simultaneously with the developments discussed above, the Higher Education Quality Committee of the Council for Higher Education (CHE) supported the provisions of the Higher Education Act by establishing a national system for quality assurance. In 2004, the CHE published the *Framework for Programme Accreditation* (Council on Higher Education, 2004a). Since then, all new programs of public and private higher education institutions were accredited in terms of these new stringent regulations that called for more elaborate data at the program level. The higher education data experts and institutional researchers were called upon to provide the evidence to substantiate the submission of programs for accreditation.

The CHE followed up on this with the publication of the *Framework for Institutional Audits* (Council on Higher Education, 2004b). On the basis of these criteria, comprehensive institutional audits of all twenty-three public institutions, as well as eleven private higher education institutions, were conducted between 2004 and 2011. These audits confronted higher education institutions with a range of new data needs. In addition to the data generated by the institutional researchers in the higher education institutions, the CHE also enlisted expert research units, such as the Centre for Research on Evaluation, Science and Technology (CREST), to undertake detailed analyses of institutional as well as system-level data on research and publication statistics.

Due to the introduction of the Quality Assurance system, the group of the planning and institutional research professionals appointed in the late 1990s was joined in the first half of the 2000s by the appointment of a cohort of quality assurance officers. In some cases, the professionals and support staff responsible for planning, quality assurance, institutional research, institutional effectiveness, and HEMIS reporting were located in the same units in higher education institutions.

Recent Examples of National Investigations and Interventions

From this overview it is evident that the transformation agenda set in motion by the advent of democracy was very ambitious and many changes for HEIs were introduced simultaneously at different levels. Toward the end of the 2000s, the system began to mature and to stabilize. It has become standard practice that higher education data experts are called upon to provide decision-support for the government, the CHE, and for higher education institutions themselves as well as other role players in higher education in the ongoing process of higher education provision in South Africa.

A number of recent examples of the role of decision support in strategic planning are mentioned here to illustrate the ever-increasing importance of the role of institutional researchers in South African institutions.

- In 2013, the CHE published a study report on undergraduate curriculum reform with the proposals to replace the current three-year first bachelor degree with a four-year program (Council on Higher Education, 2013). This report included perhaps the most detailed data analyses and financial modeling ever undertaken in South African higher education.

- Various studies of research outputs from the databases developed by CREST were undertaken to underpin the National Innovation Initiative. Studies by the Academy of Science in South Africa (ASSAf) on the state of doctoral education in the country were commissioned (Academy of Science in South Africa, 2010; Centre for Research on Evaluation, Science and Technology, 2012).
- The White Paper on Post-Secondary Education and Training (PSET) (Department of Higher Education and Training, 2014) contemplates, *inter alia*, an ambitious project to develop an integrated PSET Management Information System integrating and aligning information of all the bodies and institutions (including the universities) in the postsecondary system.
- Instead of another round of institutional audits of quality assurance arrangements in institutions, the Council on Higher Education decided to implement a Quality Enhancement Project (QEP) during 2014–2019 (Council on Higher Education, 2014).

The National Development Plan

With 2030 as its planning horizon, the National Development Plan (NDP) has established ambitious targets for higher education (National Planning Commission, 2012). Decision support systems are expected to play a key role to plan and monitor the progress toward the achievement of these targets. The NDP targets include: (a) an increase in the participation rate in higher education of the eighteen to twenty-four age group to 30% by 2030, which will raise total headcount enrollments about 50%; (b) a 25% increase in the graduation rate by 2030; (c) to quadruple the headcount of freshmen enrollments in science, technology, engineering, and mathematics by 2030; (d) to aim for 1,000 PhD graduates per annum per million of the total population by 2030; and (e) to increase the percentage of faculty members in the higher education system as a whole with PhD qualifications from 34% in 2010 to 75% by 2030. The feasibility of these ambitious targets has been criticized by higher education experts (e.g., Mouton, 2012). Undoubtedly, institutional research officials will play a key role in monitoring progress toward these targets.

In the next part of this chapter the focus moves from official IR activities at national and institutional levels to the work undertaken by IR professionals in the context of their own volunteer professional association, the Southern African Association for Institutional Research (SAAIR), 1994–2014.

The Southern African Association for Institutional Research was established in November 1993 (Minnaar, 2003) "to benefit, assist, and advance institutional research leading to improved understanding, planning and operation of institutions of higher education" (SAAIR Constitution Article 2.1, 1994). The first annual forum was held in 1994 at the University of South Africa. The SAAIR has developed into one of the most robust volunteer associations of professionals

TABLE 9.1 2010–2013 Participants at SAAIR Capacity-Building Events

EVENT	2010	2011	2012	2013
HEMIS Institute	76	72	96	68
HEMIS Foundations Workshop	–	68	56	37
Quality Institute	57	57	68	46
Institutional Research Institute	20	–	25	40
HEMIS Foundations Regional Workshop	–	60	75	32

in higher education in South Africa. Forums held in major urban centers tend to attract more participants. Almost all South African higher education institutions (as well as a small number of institutions in neighboring countries such as Botswana and Namibia) are represented in the membership of SAAIR. A number of the data analysts working in government and statutory bodies are also members.

In addition to its annual forum, SAAIR also organizes a number of capacity building events, called institutes. The numbers of participants shown in Table 9.1 indicate that these institutes are well fairly attended and suggest a growing number of informed IR practitioners in the region.

During its first twenty years of existence a total of 490 papers were presented by 448 individuals at the annual forums of SAAIR. A number of people have presented more than one paper and many papers had co-presenters. There was a good blend of presenters by gender, race, and professional role or title. A noted goal is to attract more black individuals to institutional research as a profession. It is therefore encouraging to note that the majority of the participants in the SAAIR capacity-building foundations institutes and workshops are black. The members of SAAIR hail from a range of institutions, although the representatives from the public institutions in South Africa are by far the majority. SAAIR struggles to involve more individuals working in countries in sub-Saharan Africa outside South Africa.

SAAIR has managed to attract many of the influential national higher education leaders in South Africa as well as a number of international experts to present keynote papers at the annual forums. Many of them play a leading role at the national level and were responsible for the generation of the evidence that informed the strategic planning processes in South African higher education discussed in the first part of this chapter.

Classification of Papers Presented at SAAIR Forums (1994–2013)

The topics of the papers presented at SAAIR Annual Forums in 1994–2013 are classified in order to illustrate the scope of the work of higher education data experts, institutional researchers, quality assurance managers, and planners. As a starting point for the classification, the four areas for institutional researchers to focus on in order to "get out of the box and out of the office" suggested by

TABLE 9.2 Frequency of Concepts in the Titles of SAAIR Forum Papers (1994–2013)

Planning, information and implementation, management		40%
Strategic planning at system and institutional levels	6%	
Environmental scanning	4%	
Institutional transformation and change (including mergers)	9%	
Enrollment planning and management	3%	
Performance indicators	4%	
Management information and business intelligence for decision-support and reporting	10%	
Subsidy, funding, fees	4%	
Quality assurance and evaluation		10%
Quality assurance policy and arrangements	7%	
Institutional audits, program reviews, and program accreditation	2%	
Reviews of institutional organizational units (e.g., departments, schools, support units)	1%	
Teaching and learning and curriculum development		26%
Student preparedness	3%	
Language of instruction	1%	
Interventions to enhance the quality of student learning and improve student success	10%	
Student experience and student engagement	2%	
Student satisfaction studies	1%	
Tracking student success and follow-up studies	8%	
Knowledge production by universities (the research function)		4%
Community engagement		1%
Postgraduate studies		2%
International benchmarking and learning		3%
Practice and instruments of Institutional Research		16%
Institutional research practice	10%	
Information and communication technology tools, instruments, and models in IR	6%	

Voorhees and Hinds (2012, p. 80) were used; namely strategic planning, assessment, accreditation, and curriculum development. The 490 papers presented at SAAIR Forums were analyzed to determine to what extent they could fit into these four areas. In this process, a broader and more detailed framework was developed. The classification scheme in Table 9.2 shows the number of papers in each category, and illustrates the relative interest of IR professionals in the different issues. Some of the papers fit into more than one category.

Considering the history of higher education in South Africa in the period 1990–2014 presented in the first part of this chapter, it is clear how the topics

FIGURE 9.1 Word Cloud of Titles from SAAIR Forum Papers 1994–2013.

of the papers and other activities during the annual forums related to prominent developments in higher education during this period. When the titles of all 490 papers presented at SAAIR Forums were combined and a word count is done, it yields the data visualization of paper frequency in Figure 9.1.

Future Challenges for Institutional Researchers in South Africa

In the final section of this chapter I venture a number of pointers to what can possibly be expected from South African institutional researchers over the short and medium term. (For another list of "to do's" for institutional research professionals in South Africa, see Badat, 2013.)

Based on national emphases and goals, I believe student access and student success will remain high on the agenda in South Africa and on the African continent beyond South Africa for the foreseeable future. I believe actionable information will be expected on the in-class as well as the out-of-class learning environments, geared to track and enhance student success and support student development.

Institutional researchers can expect demands to generate more, better, richer actionable information to support and enhance teaching and learning at the *level of programs and courses.* The gap between institutional level information (mostly prepared by IR professionals in institutional offices for institutional executives and for external reporting) and course and program level information (often prepared by faculty members themselves) will have to be narrowed. The CHE's Quality Enhancement Project during 2014–2019 will confront institutional researchers with this challenge.

Efficiency and accountability demands in institutional governance will require more sophisticated tools to generate and report organizational intelligence, including sets of performance indicators aligned with institutional missions and goals. Institutional researchers can expect to be called upon not to merely generate information, but to interpret the information and to give advice to decision-makers.

Government reporting demands can be expected to intensify even more, with more detail to be reported at shorter intervals. This will have an impact on the scheduling of routine tasks of HEMIS officers and institutional researchers. Relatedly, government reporting can be expected to become more comprehensive, with an expectation of integrated information systems covering all the components of the post-secondary system (and not only universities). Institutional researchers will need a good understanding of the system as a whole beyond their own institutions.

Existing and new legislation requiring compliance efforts will have an impact on the work of institutional researchers, including, for example, legislation on access to information and legislation on the protection of personal information. Institutional researchers will be expected to be familiar with the requirements of these and other related pieces of legislation. They will be expected to play a leading role in the development and implementation of appropriate compliance measures.

Higher education is expected to become ever more global and transnational. Institutional research in South Africa will, therefore, also internationalize more.

Institutional researchers will have to understand and lead processes to respond prudently and timeously to the possibilities and opportunities (but also to the possible threats) emanating from various forms of so-called "disruptive technologies." Technological changes and possibilities impacting on the practices and instruments of institutional researchers will become ever more far-reaching.

Conclusion

Although the higher education system in South Africa is small in comparison to many other countries of the world, it has a number of pockets of excellence. The country has a vibrant community of professional higher education experts working in higher education institutions, in government, in statutory agencies, and in other environments with a stake in higher education. The international trend of enhanced evidence-support for decision making in higher education is clearly present in South Africa. Due to the ambitious and far-reaching transformation activities that characterized higher education in this country during the past two decades, high levels of professional activity have been achieved. All indications are that this trend will not only continue but will become even more important in the years to come.

References

Academy of Science in South Africa (ASSAf). (2010). *The PhD study: An evidence-based study on how to meet the demands for high-level skills in an emerging economy*. Pretoria, South Africa: Academy of Science.

Badat, S. (1995). Educational politics in the transition period. *Comparative Education, 31*, 141–159.

Badat, S. (2013). Theses on institutional planning and research at universities. *South African Journal on Higher Education, 27*(2), 295–308.

Baumert, S. (2014). University politics under the impact of social transformation and global processes—South Africa and the case of Stellenbosch University 1990–2010. (Doctoral dissertation). Available from SUNScholar.

Bunting, I. (1994). *A legacy of inequality. Higher education in South Africa*. Rondebosch, South Africa: UCT Press.

Centre for Research on Evaluation, Science and Technology (CREST) and Council on Higher Education (CHE). (2012). *Postgraduate studies in South Africa: A statistical profile*. Stellenbosch, South Africa: Stellenbosch University.

Cooper, D., & Subotzky, G. (2001). *The skewed revolution: Trends in South African Higher Education*. UWC Education Policy Unit.

Council on Higher Education. (2004a). *Framework for programme accreditation*. Pretoria, South Africa: Council on Higher Education.

Council on Higher Education. (2004b). *Framework for institutional audits*. Pretoria, South Africa: Council on Higher Education.

Council on Higher Education. (2013). *A proposal for undergraduate curriculum reform in South Africa: The case for a flexible curriculum structure*. Pretoria, South Africa: Council on Higher Education.

Council on Higher Education. (2014). *Framework for institutional quality enhancement in the second period of quality assurance (QEP)*. Pretoria, South Africa: Council on Higher Education.

Department of Education. (1997). *Education White Paper 3. A programme for the transformation of Higher Education*. Government Gazette General Notice 1196 of 1997. Pretoria, South Africa: Department of Education.

Department of Education. (2001). *National plan for higher education (NPHE)*. Pretoria, South Africa: Department of Education.

Department of Higher Education and Training. (2014). *White Paper for Post Secondary Education and Training. Building an Expanded, Effective and Integrated Post School Education System*. Government Gazette No 37229, 15 January 2014.

Minnaar, P. (2003). Early days of the Southern African Association for Institutional Research recalled. *SAAIR News, 4*(2), 3–4.

Mouton, J. (2012). South African doctoral graduate production: Statistics, challenges and supervisory management. Presentation to the Cape Higher Education Consortium (CHEC), 10 July 2012, Cape Town, South Africa.

National Commission on Higher Education (NCHE) (South Africa). (1996). *NCHE Report. A Framework for Transformation:* Pretoria, South Africa.

National Planning Commission. (2012). *National Development Plan for South Africa. Vision for 2030*. Pretoria, South Africa: National Planning Commission, The Presidency, Pretoria, South Africa.

Southern African Association for Institutional Research (SAAIR). (1994). Constitution of the SAAIR. (Amended in 2013). Pretoria, South Africa: SAAIR.

UNESCO Institute of Statistics (UIS). (2012). Inbound mobile students by country, destination and inbound mobility rate. Retrieved from www.uis.unesco.org.

Voorhees, R. A., & Hinds, T. (2012). Out of the box and out of the office. Institutional research for changing times. In R. D. Howard, G. McLaughlin, & W. E. Knight (Eds.), *Handbook for institutional research* (pp. 73–86). San Francisco, CA: Jossey Bass.

10

INSTITUTIONAL RESEARCH IN LATIN AMERICA

F. Mauricio Saavedra, María Pita-Carranza, and Pablo Opazo

Introduction

Higher education has not only continued to grow in Latin America, but it has also experienced several changes during the last few decades (Balán, 2013; Bellei, Poblete, Sepúlveda, Orellana, & Abarca, 2012). According to the UNESCO Institute for Statistics (www.uis.unesco.org), the number of enrollments in Latin American countries exceeded 23 million students in 2012. Concerning growth, Bellei et al. (2012) explain that when examining the number of students enrolled in higher education for every 100,000 inhabitants living in the different Latin American countries, the average rate of 2,316 students in year 2000 went up to 3,328 students in year 2010. This represents an increase of more than 40% for that decade. Overall, Latin American governments have sought ways to improve their education systems, especially due to the importance of the knowledge economy (Balán, 2013; Bellei et al., 2012). Such attempts have usually resulted in policy changes related to accountability with the desire to improve quality. Saavedra (2012), for example, writes about Ecuador's most recent higher education reform where several structural changes are mentioned pointing to the central government's high priority on regulation and accountability. In spite of the increase in enrollment and the attempts to improve quality, Latin American higher education continues to face challenges related to the latter due to issues concerning teaching and learning, graduation rates, graduate programs, research production, and not enough involvement in science and technology (Balán, 2013). As in higher education systems in other regions of the world, the practice and development of institutional research (IR) functions are able to provide reliable data and valid information for decision makers concerning these areas by continuously examining, responding to accountability demands, and reporting on related measures for assessing the effectiveness and efficiency of institutional processes and programs (Howard, 2001).

In this chapter, the authors examine the origin, development, and practice of IR in Latin America. They consider some of the challenges facing the field and offer suggestions for its advancement. Particular situations concerning the practice of IR in Argentina, Chile, Colombia, Mexico, and Ecuador are mentioned.

The Origin of Institutional Research in Latin America: Its Development and Current Practice

Institutional research is most commonly known as institutional analysis in Latin America. Although IR offices are not usually found across Latin American higher education, the IR functions, mainly fulfilling reporting mandates, are evident in different administrative units under several different names throughout the Latin American higher education system. The origin of IR in Latin America can be traced to assessment and accreditation practices that were established given the need for higher education quality assurance (Fernández-Lamarra, 2005; Lange, Saavedra, & Romano, 2013; Rama, 2005). Such need, initially, came about in the 1990s as a result of governments' initiatives in almost all Latin American countries, seeking to improve higher education quality due to the strong diversification of higher education, the spread of private universities, and the heterogeneity of quality between institutions (Fernández-Lamarra, 2005). Assessment and accreditation have continued to develop in Latin American countries through the implementation of different quality assurance systems based on self-evaluation, peer review, and external evaluation practices (Fernández-Lamarra, 2005; Rama, 2005). These systems were different among the Latin American countries introducing them and have continued to develop according to the needs, characteristics, and culture of the Latin American country implementing them (Lemaitre & Mena, 2012; Romero, 2009). Table 10.1 shows some of these entities as a result of the approval of different higher education laws in several Latin American countries.

Higher education accreditation in Latin America is mandatory in some countries and voluntary in others. However, for the latter, there are certain restrictions to public funding if universities and their programs are not accredited (Lemaitre & Mena, 2012). Thus, it is in the best interest of the higher education institutions to fulfill accreditation demands, which are for the most part related to data requests. As such, meeting data request mandates enforces the IR function of data reporting.

National Higher Education Information Systems in Latin America

The introduction of different assessment and accreditation entities in Latin America, eventually, led to the implementation, in some countries, of national higher education information systems used for the collection, integration, and

TABLE 10.1 Higher Education Laws Leading to Agencies for Quality Assurance in Latin America

Country	Higher Education Law	Year Law was Approved	Notes	Main Agencies for Quality Assurance	Agencies, Institutions, & Programs Being Regulated
Argentina	Higher Education Law N° 24.521	1995	Implemented an assessment and accreditation program focused on evaluation for institutional improvement, graduate and regulated undergraduate programs, the creation of new public universities, and the operation of private universities. (Pita-Carranza, 2012)	Comisión Nacional de Evaluación y Acreditación Universitaria (CONEAU) (Lemaitre & Mena, 2012)	Agencies, institutions, undergraduate and graduate programs
Brazil	Law 10.861	2004	While, in the late 70s, Brazil had already established accreditation processes for graduate programs, since 1990, Brazil began a series of initiatives aimed at institutional assessment, which culminated with the creation of System Avaliação da Educação Superior Brasileiro (SINAES). (Polidori, Marinho-Araujo, & Barreyro, 2006)	Sistema Nacional de Avaliação da Educação Superior (SINAES) Coordenação de Aperfeiçoamento de Pessoal de Nível Superior (CAPES)	Institutions, programs Graduate programs
Chile	Higher Education Law N° 20.129	2006	Established a National System for Quality Assurance that examined universities' structure, undergraduate and graduate programs, and accrediting agencies. (Ministerio de Educación Gobierno de Chile, n.d.)	Consejo Nacional de Educación (CNED) Comisión Nacional de Acreditación (CNA) Other agencies (Acredita CI, Acreditacción, Akredita QA, Qualitas, aadsa, Apice Chile, Acreditadora de Chile, aacs, adc, Aespigar) (Comisión Nacional de Acreditación—CNA Chile, n.d.)	New institutions Agencies, institutions, undergraduate and graduate programs Undergraduate and graduate programs

Country	Law	Year	Description	Agency	Scope
Colombia	Law N° 30	1992	Created a National System for Accreditation to ensure that universities fulfilled quality requirements, as well as the universities' goals for improvement (Cifuentes-Madrid & Pérez-Piñeros, 2000). The system placed priority in accrediting the academic programs first and then the university as an institution (Consejo Nacional de Acreditación, n.d.). Institutional accreditation sought mainly to assess the ability of the university to maintain its educational mission given environmental changes. For this reason, Colombian universities had to develop their own quality assurance system. (Cifuentes-Madrid & Pérez-Piñeros, 2000)	Consejo Nacional de Acreditación (CNA)	Institutions, undergraduate and graduate programs
				Comisión Nacional Intersectorial de Aseguramiento de la Calidad de la Educación Superior (CONACES)	Institutions, undergraduate and graduate programs
				Instituto Colombiano de Fomento de la Educación Superior (ICFES)	Undergraduate programs
				Ministerio de Educación	Undergraduate and graduate programs
				(Lemaitre & Mena, 2012)	
Ecuador	Ley Organica ade Educacion Superior	2010	Most recently, a higher education law established a new entity for accreditation: Consejo de Evaluación, Acreditación y Aseguramiento de la Calidad de la Educación Superior—CEAACES (Registro Oficial No 298, 2010). This new entity's mission was to accredit all universities within the higher education system (public and private) at the institutional and program levels for both undergraduate and graduate programs. (CEAACES, 2014)	Consejo de Evaluación, Acreditación y Aseguramiento de la Calidad de la Educación Superior (CEAACES)	Undergraduate and graduate programs

(Continued)

TABLE 10.1 (Continued)

Country	Higher Education Law	Year Law was Approved	Notes	Main Agencies for Quality Assurance	Agencies, Institutions, & Programs Being Regulated
México			For evaluation and accreditation, see: www.ses.sep.gob.mx/sitios-de-interes/sistema-nacional-de-evaluacion-acreditacion-y-certificacion. Information on legislation can be found at: www.ses.sep.gob.mx/acerca-de-la-ses/normatividad.	Comités Interinstitucionales de Evaluación de la Educación Superior (CIEES)	Undergraduate and graduate programs
				Consejo para la Acreditación de la Educación Superior (COPAES)	Agencies, undergraduate programs
				Asociación Nacional de Universidades e Instituciones de Educación Superior (ANUIES)	Institutional
				Federación de Instituciones Mexicanas Particulares de Educación Superior (FIMPES)	Institutional
				Disciplinary accreditation agencies	Undergraduate programs

(Lemaitre & Mena, 2012)

dissemination of higher education data. Not all countries in Latin America have such systems. For the most part, Latin American countries that have created these data management systems have, at the same time, mandated that their universities (public and private) provide data on a regular basis (Lange et al., 2013). Such is the case of Mexico, Chile, Colombia, and, most recently, Ecuador.

From the countries mentioned above, Colombia has been recognized as one of the most advanced Latin American countries in its national higher education data management system (Gazzola, 2010), while Ecuador continues developing its system and the implementation process for making data accessible to the public. Mexico includes a longitudinal database that contains student information from kindergarten to graduate education (Secretaría de Educación Pública—SEP, 2010). Chile has been developing its system and currently reports data on four general areas: the labor market, country finance, academics, and technology (DIVESUP/MINEDUC, 2012). The need to continually update the different national higher education information systems in Latin America has encouraged the IR function of centralizing and reporting data, as well as conducting analyses on various indicators.

Higher Education Information Systems and Administrative Units Within Universities

In order for higher education institutions in Latin America to respond to data requests, mainly due to accreditation purposes, they found it necessary to develop both information systems and administrative units able to manage institutional data. To that end, government funding played a critical role in the development of such units and, consequently, has influenced the way information management was carried out in universities. Several examples exist: in 1995, Argentina provided funding for their public universities with the purpose of creating and improving higher education information systems (Gurmendi & Williams, 2006). In Chile, higher education institutions had the opportunity to compete for funding related to strategic planning and quality assurance, which were connected to the development of institutional analysis practices and self-evaluation (Reich et al., 2011). Mexico implemented programs that allowed public higher education institutions to articulate planning, assessment, and financing processes in their attempt to improve quality (Buendía-Espinosa, 2012; Ibarra-Colado, 2009; Rubio, 2006). Government funding determined the direction, functions, and structure adopted for the development of information management units in the different universities. Argentina, for example, placed emphasis in data reliability, improving data management, and providing more information for external requirements, while Chile promoted the creation and expansion of units dedicated to institutional analysis.

IR's Organizational Structure

IR's organizational structure across Latin America is complex in that, although it is possible to find some commonalities across units doing some of this work in Latin American universities, there are no set definitions, norms, and specific functions assigned to this area of work. Nonetheless, given the ever-increasing accreditation and quality assurance demands, units carrying out functions related to IR have emerged in Latin American universities under areas known as university statistics, institutional evaluation, planning, planning and development, quality assurance, institutional development, assessment and accreditation, accreditation and development, and institutional effectiveness, among others. Reporting lines for these offices vary. Many are found within academic affairs while others reside within information technology. These offices usually report to a vice president or directly to the president, but in some cases they report to specific areas such as academic affairs, economic affairs, and even to areas related to information technology (IT).

Overall, administrative units in Latin America with IR-related functions are responsible for activities related to accreditation, assessment, quality assurance, strategic planning, institutional effectiveness, data reporting, and data analysis. Even though a common denominator across the Latin American higher education system entails reporting for assessment and accreditation purposes, different countries in Latin America have guided their IR-related administrative units toward separate goals creating particular situations for the different regions. As it is the case, Argentina, which focused on improving data management systems, has been successful in gathering great amounts of data, but has failed in establishing organizational structures for managing data across their higher education system. Data management in Argentine universities is decentralized in different administrative units and the respective IR-related units are only relevant to the university when it comes to reporting data for accreditation purposes (Corengia, 2010). Chile, on the other hand, succeeded in establishing offices of institutional analysis for data management across their system (Fernández, 2010), but the offices have failed to obtain legitimacy and acceptance from other units on campus, and have not integrated their data systems across the higher education system.

Colombia, which focused on quality assurance and on improving the information systems, has become aware of the importance of data for decision making. Nonetheless, the use of this data is not observed in the decision-making processes aimed at improving the quality of the instruction (OECD, 2012), which may be attributable to a lack of organization for the IR-related administrative units. Mexico placed emphasis on institutional effectiveness, guiding their universities to fulfill their mission and objectives by seeking ways to improve their programs and services. However, greater use of information systems is required for Mexico to attain a similar impact to that seen in Colombia or Chile (Lemaitre & Mena, 2012).

Challenges Facing the IR Field in Latin America

The field of institutional research in Latin American higher education is currently in a developmental stage. When several different reporting demands came about, universities realized they had to promptly assign the task to administrators able to respond. This resulted in the creation of offices with staffing coming from different administrative units across campus. In turn, universities were forced to revisit, examine, and improve their information systems so as to be able to fulfill the reporting requirements on a continuous basis.

Overall, universities and government officials in Latin American have yet to realize that this situation has created an opportunity for the professionalization of IR where ample training is needed in areas such as data management systems, higher education administration, assessment, and analysis. This opportunity has the potential to turn IR-related administrative units into an organized activity across Latin American universities, as it is in other regions within the global context. This includes professionalizing IR and creating a more structured organization with centers and associations dedicated to providing support, training, and a space for personnel working in these units to have the opportunity to share experiences, seek ways to improve, and establish networks. In the last couple of years, some action was carried out to gather higher education professionals and universities from different Latin American countries, encouraging the creation of a Latin American association for institutional research; nonetheless, it was not possible to establish such an association. The purpose of the association was to provide some of the opportunities mentioned above. However, a phenomenon currently seen in Latin American IR-related administrative units is the lack of stability from personnel leading such offices. Officials in these units, across Latin America, are constantly shifting positions or moving to other units or other institutions. This situation generates instability for the profession and makes it difficult to sustain an IR-related association. The reason for the constant turnover would seem to be due to the lack of support and understanding from government and university officials for the development of the IR profession in Latin American higher education.

Another area of concern, as with any IR office anywhere in the world, is data reliability and the ability to efficiently provide information for decision making out of robust data warehouses coming from well-defined transactional data systems. Such activity encompasses visiting and revisiting the current transactional data systems, continuously cleaning the data, restructuring data warehouses, employing Business Intelligence/Analytics, and creating efficient reporting by the implementation of dashboards and other graphically rich data displays. Currently and in most instances, Latin American universities use transactional data for decision support, which is not convenient due to the complexity of the transactional data structure. Several different efforts have gone forth at both the institutional and government levels with the intent of implementing stronger data warehouse systems, as well as Business Intelligence/Analytics and dashboards for reporting.

Nonetheless, lack of support and understanding from government and university officials have not allowed these projects to yet be successful, in most instances. However, Chile has more recently invested toward this effort and is seeking to develop this area further.

Data reliability, professionalization of IR, and having a more structured organization for this profession in Latin American higher education needs to be enforced and supported by both university presidents and government officials in order for the IR profession to move forward in its development. Such investment should come about when considering the impact of IR-related administrative units on Latin American higher education when providing information on quality assurance and accreditation and feeding their respective national higher education information systems. By practicing these activities, Latin American higher education is impacted as university and government decision makers follow the data, track reported indicators related to different higher education measures such as graduation rates, and establish policies to improve these indicators.

Implications for IR Professionals in Latin America

Lacking a data driven culture, where data analysis is taken into consideration prior to making decisions and establishing policy, lies among the main challenges facing Latin American higher education and, in turn, the IR profession in this region. Institutional and public policy emphasizing the importance of data analysis for decision support is needed to strengthen the IR function. As such, university administrators and government officials in charge of the higher education system in the respective Latin American country need a more clear understanding of the functions of IR and the positive impact these functions can have on higher education via data analysis for decision support.

Currently, and for the most part, data reporting has become part of a bureaucratic process rather than an essential component for decision support. This situation has placed many IR-related administrative units within Latin American higher education at risk of becoming providers of bureaucratic mandated reporting alone rather than providers of knowledge for decision making and, as such, agents of change. Given the preceding, IR-related administrative units in Latin America struggle with obtaining legitimacy and being recognized by other units on campus as an important part of the everyday university process. As pointed out by Lange et al. (2013), the challenge of setting up and developing IR offices in Latin American universities include support from university leaders foremost, having trained staff available, communicating the importance of IR on campus, and "getting the different academic and administrative units to collaborate" (p. 31). We are hopeful that IR will achieve a new level of support and integration into higher education in Latin America as needs for assessment requirements and data-driven decisions continue to increase.

References

Balán, J. (2013). Latin American higher education systems in a historical and comparative perspective. In J. Balán (Ed.), *Latin America's new knowledge economy: Higher education, government and international collaboration* (pp. vii–xx). Institute of International Education.

Bellei, C., Poblete, X., Sepúlveda, P., Orellana, V., & Abarca, G. (2012). *Situación Educativa de América Latina y el Caribe: Hacia una educación para todos 2015.* Oficina Regional de Educación para América Latina y el Caribe (OREALC/UNESCO Santiago).

Buendía-Espinosa, A. (2012). Cuarta parte. Informes de impacto por país. Resumen Ejecutivo: México. In M. J. Lemaitre & M. E. Zenteno (Eds.), *Aseguramiento de la Calidad e Iberoamérica. Educación Superior. Informe 2012.* Santiago de Chile: Centro Interuniversitario de Desarrollo (CINDA)–Universia.

CEAACES. (2014). *Misión.* Retrieved from www.ceaaces.gob.ec/sitio/mision/.

Cifuentes-Madrid, J. H., & Pérez-Piñeros, M. D. (2000). Sistema de acreditación colombiano, visión analítica. In *Acreditación de Programas, Reconocimiento de Títulos e Integración.* Santiago de Chile: CentroInteruniversitario de Desarrollo (CINDA).

Comisión Nacional de Acreditación—CNA Chile. (n.d.). *Comisión Nacional de Acreditación— CNA Chile.* Retrieved from www.cnachile.cl/.

Consejo Nacional de Acreditación. (n.d.). *Sistema Nacional de Acreditación en Colombia.* Retrieved from www.cna.gov.co/1741/article-186365.html.

Corengia, A. (2010). *Impacto de la política de evaluación y acreditación de la calidad en universidades de la argentina. Estudio de casos.* Unpublished Doctoral Thesis, Universidad de San Andrés, Escuela de Educación, Argentina.

DIVESUP/MINEDUC. (2012). Informe Nacional de Antecedentes. "El Aseguramiento de la Calidad de la Educación Superior en Chile," Comité de Coordinación. Sistema Nacional de Aseguramiento de la Calidad de la Educación Superior en Chile (SINAC-ES), Santiago de Chile. Retrieved from www.divesup.cl/usuarios/1234/File/2013/ocde/InformeAntecedentesAseguramientodelaCalidaddelaESVisitaOCDE.pdf.

Fernández, E. (2010). Análisis Institucional. *Boletín PPES N° 11 del Programa de Políticas de Educación Superior—Anillo de Ciencias Sociales.* Centro de Políticas Comparadas de Educación, Universidad Diego Portales.

Fernández-Lamarra, N. (2005). La educación superior en América Latina y el Caribe y la evaluación y acreditación de su calidad. Situación, problemas y perspectivas. Paper presented at the *Primer congreso nacional de estudios comparados en educación "Retos para la Democratización de la Educación. Perspectiva Comparada."* Buenos Aires, Argentina, November 18–19, 2005.

Gazzola A. L. (2010). Sistemas de Información-Educación Superior [Video]. Retrieved from www.youtube.com/watch?v=7yBOkzaqUos.

Gurmendi, M. L., & Williams, R. (2006). *Desarrollo informático colaborativo en el sistema universitario: La experiencia SIU-Guaraní.* Documento SIU. Retrieved from www.siu.edu.ar/que-es-el-siu/documentos-de-interes-consorcio-siu.

Howard, R. D. (2001). *Institutional research: Decision support in higher education.* Tallahassee, FL: Association for Institutional Research.

Ibarra-Colado, E. (2009). *Aseguramiento de la calidad: Políticas públicas y gestión universitaria. Informe Final México.* Documento LAISUM. Retrieved from www.laisumedu.org/.

Lange, L., Saavedra, F. M., & Romano, J. (2013). Institutional research in emerging countries of Southern Africa, Latin America, and the Middle East and North Africa: Global frameworks and local practices. In A. Calderon & K. Webber (Eds.), *Global issues on institutional research. New Directions for Institutional Research, Issue 157* (pp. 23–38). Wiley.

Lemaitre, M. J., & Mena, R. (2012). Aseguramiento de la calidad en América Latina: Tendencias y desafíos. Introducción. In M. J. Lemaitre & M. E. Zenteno (Eds.), *Aseguramiento de la Calidad e Iberoamérica: Educación Superior Informe 2012* (pp. 21–71). Chile: Universia.

Ministerio de Educación Gobierno de Chile. (n.d.). El Valor de la Acreditación. Retrieved from www.mifuturo.cl/index.php/calidad/acreditacion.

OECD. (2012). *La Educación Superior en Colombia 2012. Evaluaciones de Políticas Nacionales en Educación.* OECD y el Banco Internacional de Reconstrucción y Fomento/el Banco Mundial.

Pita-Carranza, M. (2012). *Aspectos y alcances de la 'investigación institucional' en distintos contextos regionales.* Unpublished Master's Thesis in Policy and Education Administration. Universidad Nacional de Tres de Febrero.

Polidori, M., Marinho-Araujo, C., & Barreyro, G. (2006). SINAES: Perspectivas e desafios na avaliação da educação superior brasileira. *Ensaio: Avaliação e Políticas Públicas em Educação, 14*(53), 425–436. Retrieved from www.scielo.br/scielo.php?script=sci_arttext&pid=S0104–40362006000400002&lng=en&tlng=. 10.1590/S0104–40362006000400002.

Rama, C. (2005). Los sistemas de control de la calidad de la educación superior en América Latina en la III reforma universitaria. La evaluación y la acreditación de la educación superior en América Latina y el Caribe. Documento UNESCO-IESALC. Retrieved from www.academia.edu/5279329/Los_sistemas_de_control_de_la_calidad_de_la_educacion_superior_en_America_Latina_en_la_III_Reforma_universitaria.

Reich, R., Machuca, F., López, D., Prieto, J. P., Music, J., Rodríguez-Ponce, E., & Yutronic, J. (2011). Bases y desafíos de la aplicación de convenios de desempeño en la educación superior de Chile. *Ingeniare. Revista chilena de ingeniería, 19*(1), 8–18.

Romero, C. (2009). Relación entre la evaluación/acreditación de programas y de instituciones. Presented in *Primer Congreso Chileno de Investigación en Educación Superior.* Universidad de Talca, Santiago de Chile.

Rubio, J. (2006). La Mejora de la Calidad de las Universidades Públicas en el Periodo 2001–2006 (1st ed.). Secretaría de Educación Pública, México.

Saavedra, F. M. (2012). Higher education reform in Ecuador and its effect on university governance. In H. G. Schuetze, W. Bruneau, & G. Grosjean (Eds.), *University governance and reform: Policy, fads and experience in international perspective* (pp. 161–175). Basingstoke, UK: Palgrave Macmillan.

Secretaría de Educación Pública—SEP. (2010). *Acerca de la SEP.* Retrieved from www.sep.gob.mx/.

11

INSTITUTIONAL RESEARCH IN ASIA

Jang Wan Ko

Introduction

Institutional research has evolved over the past 50 years, and institutional researchers have explored the roles and scope of institutional research. Institutional research (IR) has spread beyond the US and become a global trend. There are already many IR associations across the world, including CIRPA (Canada), EAIR (Europe), MENA-AIR (Middle Asia), SAAIR and HERPNET (Africa), and AAIR (Australia). Nevertheless, Calderon and Webber (2013) remind us of the need to further expand knowledge and practice in IR in the globalized higher education environment.

While institutional research is distributed throughout the world, IR in Asian countries has not been emphasized until recently. IR in Asian countries is not yet widely visible to the higher education community, nor has the community paid IR much attention. However, with a changing landscape of higher education in Asia—including its rapid expansion and growing concerns about social accountability—IR has been recognized by college administrators and higher education professionals as playing a critical role in the present as well as in the future of higher education in Asia.

Higher Education in Asia

Higher education enrollment worldwide has increased from 32.6 million in 1970 to 182.2 million students in 2011 (UNESCO Institute for Statistics, 2014). In particular, higher education in Asia has experienced explosive growth over the past 20 years (ADB, 2011; World Bank, 2012). For instance, the enrollment ratio of college students increased from 23.2% to 42.5% in Japan and from 26.8% to 67.5% in Korea between 1990 and 2011. During the same period, there had also been a dramatic increase in some other countries whose enrollment had been traditionally lower, including those in Sri Lanka, Malaysia, India, and Thailand (UIS, 2014). In 2007, the number of students in Asian higher education institutions accounted for 45% of all college students in the world (UIS, 2009). Furthermore, the expansion of college students in Asia will continue, and the total number of students in Asia will be over 160 million by 2030 (Calderon, 2012).

While enrollments and unit costs have increased, public funding has not kept pace, resulting in a further financial strain on universities in most countries (Johnstone, 2009). This is especially true for Asian countries because of the dramatic increase of the student population and higher education's dependence on direct funding by the governments.

In addition to the ongoing expansion of higher education enrollment and the considerable financial pressure that accompanies it, Asian higher education institutions (HEIs) are facing new issues in restructuring the higher education system—for example, internationalization of higher education as students and faculty cross national borders, global competitiveness, and demands for quality assurance. All these issues add pressure and present some challenges and opportunities for HEIs. However, institutional responses to the challenges and opportunities depend mainly on the capacity of institutions.

The Origin and Development of Institutional Research in Asia

Because of the regional diversity of Asian countries in the development of higher education systems, it is hard to trace the exact origin of institutional research in Asia. Probably the oldest institutional research unit was established in Thailand. According to Wuwongse (2013), the first IR unit in Thailand was founded at Chulalongkorn University in 1971. The IR unit (often entitled by a number of names and not usually 'Institutional Research' per se) had three main functions: collecting data for the planning, development, and management of the university; conducting internal research required by the university stemming from its regular responsibilities; and disseminating information in different forms. After that, other Thai universities established their own IR units, and the number of IR units increased over time. In 2000, the Association of Institutional Research and Higher Education Development was established to provide a platform for collaboration among IR units in Thai universities.

In Japanese universities, IR offices were established in the late 1990s (Funamori, 2013). In the early 1990s, when Japan had economic difficulties, the Japanese government decreased public spending, including funding to universities; the emphasis was on efficiency and transparency of public funding. Japanese universities foresaw the need for institutional research in response to this emphasis on accountability of university management. In particular, the shrinking public funding for higher education made clearer than ever the need for and the importance of institutional research offices. Thus, IR was established in both public and private universities (Funamori, 2013).

Although a few scholars introduced IR in China in the 1980s and 1990s, the first IR unit in China was established at Huazhong University of Science and Technology in 2000 (Zhang & Chen, 2012). Changes in higher education, including the massification of higher education, the requirement for social accountability, and the need for institutional-based research, contributed to the ongoing establishment of IR in Chinese HEIs. In 2003 China Association for Institutional Research (China AIR) was established, gaining government approval in 2007. Since 2003, China AIR has held annual national and international conferences and workshops and has actively engaged in IR. Activities include compiling and publishing books about IR, offering IR courses in higher education programs in selected universities, and recently creating some provincial IR associations such as Sichuan AIR, Guangdong AIR, and Shanxi AIR (Zhang & Chen, 2012).

Although Korean universities faced circumstances similar to those of universities in other Asian countries, the development of IR in Korea is more directly related to government policy on higher education evaluation and the funding mechanism. Over the past two decades, the Korean government has provided financial support to higher education based partially on institutional capacity and performance. Recently the performance-driven funding mechanism became the foremost element in the higher education financial support system. Consequently, HEIs must provide evidence of their qualifications and performance in order to receive government funding. As a result, the first institutional research office in Korea, the Center for Institutional Effectiveness at Sungkyunkwan University in Seoul, was founded in 2010 to devise measurement tools for student development, conduct institutional effectiveness and program evaluation, and to monitor institutional performance indicators (Ko, 2014).

The ASEAN (Association of Southeast Asian Nations) countries have developed IR through a regional association. As an international association, the South East Asian Association for Institutional Research (SEAAIR) has provided critical contributions to institutional research in ASEAN countries such as Thailand, the Philippines, Malaysia, and Indonesia. In 2000, a group of college administrators and professors in ASEAN countries met to discuss the possibility of forming a regional association for institutional research, and, consequently, the first annual general meeting of SEAAIR was held in 2001 in Kuching, Malaysia (SEAAIR, 2014). The major purposes of SEAAIR are to benefit, assist, and advance research leading to improved understanding, planning, and operations of institutions of postsecondary education in the region. The SEAAIR also encourages the application of appropriate methodologies and techniques from many disciplines, and comparative research into national higher education systems in South East Asia. SEAAIR, which is now a regional chapter or affiliate of the Association for Institutional Research in the US, has relationships with IR associations around the world, such as the European Association for Institutional Research (EAIR), the

Australasian Association for Institutional Research (AAIR), Dutch AIR, and the Canadian Association (CIRPA-ACPRI).

Despite the unique origin of IR in each county, the development of IR in Asian countries shares some common features, especially among those countries establishing IR recently. First, the increase in enrollments and number of higher education institutions over the past two decades is the primary reason why the IR function is needed in Asian universities. This massification required university administrators to depart from traditional management practices and use more data-driven approaches and focus on systematic management of the university. HEIs must generate accurate and meaningful data and maintain a well-developed data management system, and, accordingly, institution-based research is needed. Second, HEIs need to respond to the demand for external accountability; therefore, IR must expand its role to include, for example, quality assurance. Recently HEIs in many Asian countries were granted more institutional autonomy by their governments, but they faced greater competition in a climate of reduced funding for HEIs. Therefore, HEIs must not only exhibit more efficient and transparent institutional management systems to the public—including the government, students, and parents—but must also convince the public that they maintain high-quality programs and excellent institutional performance. This is somewhat different from IR in the US, where quality assurance was not initially the main function.

The Role of IR in Asian Institutions

To describe the roles of IR in Asian countries, it is important to describe what the roles or functions of institutional research are in a broader sense. While IR in the US has over 50 years of history and has followed its own developmental stages from gestation to maturation (Coughlin & Howard, 2011), IR in Asian countries has developed more recently and therefore reflects the emerging challenges that higher education faced over the past two decades.

The functions and roles of IR might be categorized differently, depending on the definition and perspectives of institutional research. In general, the roles and functions of institutional research in Asian universities are broader than those of IR offices in the US identified by previous studies (Volkwein, 1999, 2008; Volkwein, Liu, & Woodell, 2012). IR professionals in Asian countries mainly conduct the evaluation of institutional performance or performance indicators, quality management, and accreditation roles. They focus less on data management and reporting and institutional studies to support university decision making. Among the golden triangle of IR (Volkwein et al., 2012), the tasks that are primarily emphasized in Asian institutions are outcomes assessment, effectiveness, and accreditation functions.

Data management and analysis are considered to be basic and essential functions of IR in its support of decision making as well as routine management of the institution. In fact, 72.7% of all IR offices in Japanese private universities reported that they offer data management and data reporting functions (Funamori, 2013). Some universities in other areas, such as the Open University of China and the Hong Kong University of Science and Technology, also reported that they provide university senior administration with data and data analytical reports.

However, IR units generally do not emphasize tasks to generate, manage, and disseminate data and information to internal and external constituencies; rather, they focus more on performance evaluation and the accreditation function. Reasons for this focus include a shortage of data management systems in the university, existing decentralized data management systems throughout the departments and offices without a campus-level integrated system, and failure to recognize the importance of institutional data on decision-making processes (Funamori, 2013; Zhang & Chen, 2012). Lacking these basic and analytical databases, Chinese universities mainly utilize the case study methods and monographic study to support university decision making (AIR, 2012).

Other main functions of IR are to provide valuable data and information for decision-making and to conduct institutional studies that aid policy formation. The IR units in some Chinese universities report that they provide data and information for university decision making and the development of university strategic planning (Zhang & Chen, 2012). For example, the Hong Kong University of Science and Technology and the University of Hong Kong also report that they provide data and analytical reports to facilitate decision making, and they conduct projections and data analysis on budget affordability and risk scenarios. They also support academic and resource planning to assist with recommendations for the university senior administration. De La Salle University in the Philippines states that it, too, conducts research analysis for the university's strategic planning. For those cases, IR units usually contain 'planning' in their titles, e.g., Office of Planning and Institutional Research (the Hong Kong University of Science and Technology); Strategic Planning and Provost's Office (the University of Hong Kong); and Institutional Research, Planning and Advocacy (De La Salle University).

But in other countries, such as Japan and Korea, IR offices are not fully involved in decision-making processes. Funamori (2013) argued that Japanese IR offices generally lack the functions to support policy formation and decision making. For instance, Kominato and Nakai (2007) analyzed the functions of IR in three Japanese national universities and found that while all three universities perform data management, data analysis, internal reporting, and assessment support, none of the three universities support decision making or policy formation. In addition, Japanese IR offices do not report to the highest-ranking administrators such as the president or provost. Even when the IR offices are located under the president, it is mainly for formal university evaluation and accreditation purposes and does not lead to supporting university decision making (Funamori, 2013). In the case of private universities, support for teaching and learning is the main function of IR offices, which gives them only indirect influence on high-level decision makers.

Finally, outcomes assessment, effectiveness, and accreditation are emphasized as the main IR functions in Asia for the purpose of fulfilling institutions' quality assurance needs. Most IR units in Asia perform the role of 'quality manager.' For instance, IR offices in Japan, especially in the national universities, are established at the central administration level and focus primarily on university evaluation and accreditation procedures linked to governmental funding (Funamori, 2013; Kominato & Nakai, 2007). In addition, many universities in ASEAN countries have quality units or offices that respond to changes in public funding policy and fulfill internal and external accountability requirements. Traditionally, governments in Asia (including ASEAN countries) have controlled HEIs. However, governments in Asia have recently begun granting more autonomy to the HEIs (Johnstone, 2009; Zhang & Chen, 2012) while retaining the power to introduce performance standards and change funding policies. Accordingly, institutions need to follow government guidelines to receive funding, and they must develop and maintain performance indicators set by the government and other external constituencies. This also includes analyzing institutional rankings and conducting comparative studies.

Challenges and Further Directions for IR in Asia

Institutional research in Asia is a new profession and still in its initial stage, which explains its many shortcomings. It is important to recognize the identity of IR in the Asian context. While some universities in Japan and Hong Kong use the term institutional research, many IR units do not use those words in their titles. Rather, they use titles that reflect the IR roles required by the university and society, such as 'planning,' 'quality management,' 'research and development,' and 'development and planning.' The expansion of IR functions from regular institutional management to more research- and policy-oriented functions and to quality assurance seems reasonable, as it reflects the emerging trends of higher education. However, many IR offices in Asia do not have regular data management functions. The current role of IR offices lacking these functions is routine institutional management utilizing data and information. This disparity raises a fundamental question: what should be the roles of institutional research in Asia?

Two different approaches have been discussed to answer this question. One is to build a national- and institutional-level database system to strengthen data management functions. This approach would follow the US style of IR by supplementing the current weakness of Asian IR (lack of data management) while retaining the extended role of quality management. In China, for instance, integrated operational databases and analytical databases are very rare at universities, and many databases are not open to the public. Therefore, institutional researchers in China have discussed how to promote the development of a national integrated higher education data system—the National Undergraduate Teaching Data System—and how to encourage institutions to focus on integrated rather than isolated databases (Zhang & Chen, 2012).

The second approach is to redefine the role of IR in the Asian context. Because of the different purposes of IR and its unique organizational relationship to the decision-making process, 'Asian-style IR' could be more appropriate in Asian universities. Funamori (2013) argues that, using Japanese cases, 'Japanese-style IR' might be effective for now because of incomplete data management systems in HEIs, decentralized decision-making processes across the departments, and the lack of awareness about IR functions by top university administrators. Moreover, institutional management is not based mainly on regular institutional management practices, but rather on special initiatives and events such as university internationalization and the establishment of research centers. Hence, Funamori (2013) suggests a different approach for the future direction of IR in Japan: first conduct and strengthen strategic planning and institutional studies to get administrators' attention, and then motivate administrators to build and utilize the regular intuitional management system. This approach might work for IR in Asian countries because Asian universities share common features.

Institutional research in Asia is in its initial stage and has already faced many challenges. However, it has great potential to grow in Asia's current higher education environment. Within this environment, university administrators are starting to recognize the importance of IR functions and realize the benefits IR can bring to their universities. The higher education community also values data-driven decision making and university management, and the number of IR professionals in Asia is growing due to ever-growing decision support needs. All these changes will contribute to the development of institutional research in Asia.

References

Asian Development Bank (ADB). (2011). *Higher education across Asia: An overview of issues and strategies*. Manila, the Philippines: ADB.

Association for Institutional Research (AIR). (December 2012). Interview with Junchao Zhang and Min Chen, *e-AIR Newsletter, 32*(12). Tallahassee, FL: Association for Institutional Research.

Calderon, A. (2012). Massification continues to transform higher education, *University World News,* 237.

Calderon, A., & Webber, K. L. (2013). *Global issues in institutional research, New Directions for Institutional Research, 157.* San Francisco, CA: Jossey Bass/Wiley.

Coughlin, M. A., & Howard, R. D. (2011). *The Association for Institutional Research: The first fifty years.* Tallahassee, FL: AIR.

Funamori, M. (2013). *Institutional research in a university without regular institutional management: The case of Japanese national universities.* 2013 Second IIAI International Conference on Advanced Applied Informatics. Japan.

Johnstone, D. B. (2009). *Worldwide trends in financing higher education: A conceptual framework.* Retrieved from the Graduate School of Education, University at Buffalo the State University of New York website: http://gse.buffalo.edu.

Ko, J. (2014). Activities and accomplishment of the Center for Institutional Effectiveness at Sungkyunkwan University. Paper presented at the Education Excellence Forum, February 14, 2014. Seoul, Korea.

Kominato, T., & Nakai, T. (2007). Institutional Research at National University Corporations: The cases of Nagoya University, Ehime University, and Kyushu University, *Research on Academic Degrees and University Evaluation*, 5, 19–34.

SEAAIR. (2014). www.seaairweb.info/.

UNESCO Institute for Statistics. (2009). *Global education digest 2009: Comparing education statistics across the world*. Paris, France: UNESCO.

UNESCO Institute for Statistics. (2014). *Higher education in Asia: Expanding out, expanding up*. Paris, France: UNESCO.

Volkwein, J. F. (1999). The four faces of institutional research. In J. F. Volkwein (Ed.), *What is institutional research all about? A critical and comprehensive assessment of the profession. New Directions in Institutional Research*, no. 104. San Francisco, CA: Jossey-Bass.

Volkwein, J. F. (2008). The foundations and evolution of institutional research. In D. G. Terkla (Ed.), *Institutional research: More than just data. New Directions for Higher Education*, no. 141. San Francisco, CA: Jossey-Bass.

Volkwein, J. F., Liu, Y., & Woodell, J. (2012). The structure and functions of institutional research offices. In R. Howard, G. McLaughlin, & W. Knight (Eds.), *The handbook of institutional research* (pp. 22–39). San Francisco, CA: Jossey Bass.

World Bank. (2012). *Put higher education to work*. Washington, DC: The World Bank.

Wuwongse, V. (2013). *History and challenges of IR activities in Thailand*. 2013 Second IIAI International Conference on Advanced Applied Informatics. Japan.

Zhang, J., & Chen, M. (November 2012). The history, role and characteristics of IR in China. Paper presented at the 37th CAIR Annual Conference, November 7–9, 2012. Orange County, CA.

12

INSTITUTIONAL RESEARCH AND PLANNING IN THE MIDDLE EAST

Diane Nauffal

Introduction

While all societies value the economic and social benefits that come from knowledge, the value of education enjoys a particularly long history in the Middle East and Northern Africa (MENA) regions. The MENA region gave birth to some of the world's major religions that played a critical role in the production of knowledge in fields such as philosophy, medicine, astronomy, and mathematics. The held value for knowledge in the region has recently prompted a sharp expansion of higher education, followed by subsequent growth in the use of institutional research (IR) and planning in higher education settings. In the changing landscape of higher education in the Middle East—including the region's rapid expansion, goals for economic strength, and concerns about social accountability—led to IR and planning functions now being recognized by higher education leaders as critical in the present, as well as in the future, of higher education. In this chapter, I discuss the recent growth of higher education in the MENA regions. As in other parts of the world, institutions in these regions show an increasing value for professionals who strengthen higher education through their IR, decision support, and academic planning roles.

Higher Education's Growth in the MENA Region

The MENA region is composed of two interrelated groups of developing countries. The first group consists of the oil-producing Gulf States including Libya and Algeria, while the second group comprises the remaining Arab states of the Levant and North Africa including Lebanon, Jordan, Syria, Iraq, Egypt, and Yemen. Both groups are similar in many ways and have been described as relatively unproductive and highly vulnerable to external shocks (Alissa, 2007). While both groups are facing a number of common challenges in their higher education sectors, the first group can mobilize their considerable wealth generated from the export of a single natural resource to effect change. Among current efforts are plans to foster a more diverse economy base and implement a labor nationalization program supported by substantially improved secondary, vocational, and higher education (Davidson, 2008). The aggressive plans of these oil-producing countries will impact the economies of the predominantly non-oil producing Arab countries that are heavily reliant on foreign aid, loans, and, more importantly, on remittances from expatriate workers particularly from the Gulf States (Salehi-Isfahani & Dhillon, 2008). This is especially true in the field of education where citizens of these Arab states, in particular Egyptians and Palestinians, constitute the majority of the cadre of instructors and are gradually being replaced by competitive local instructors (Davidson, 2008).

For countries across the MENA region, perhaps the most important factor that acted as a catalyst for the development and expansion of national systems of education and, in particular, higher education, is the end of colonialism. Higher education is a key economic and social driver for the establishment of a corps of indigenous school teachers necessary for educating future generations and formalizing the type of knowledge needed by civic servants to successfully hold the significant administrative responsibilities in the corporate, government, and education sectors. This gave rise in the second half of the twentieth century to the creation of ministries of education and the establishment of higher education systems characterized by a distinct dominance of public institutions whose prime concern was the development of their country's human capital.

Currently, a number of economic, social, and political issues face the region and affect MENA's higher education sector. Some of these issues include the global economic recession, the regional political tensions, the rapid growth in the youth population, growing enrollment in higher education, limited resources, poor alignment between universities and industry, high levels of unemployment among graduates, and the outmigration of intellectual human capital. However, according to the 2008 World Bank report, *The Road Not Travelled: Education Reform in the Middle East and North Africa,* the average public spending on education for the MENA region was 5.3% of GDP for the period spanning 1995–2003, a figure that is comparable to international standards. Higher education officials are hopeful that regional spending on higher education will remain, if not rise, in the near future.

In recent years, many countries in the region have embarked on the road of reform, embracing Western notions of education and the concept of building knowledge-based societies where knowledge diffusion, production, and application drive economic growth, sustainability, and productivity (Kirk, 2010). The pace and level of intensity with which reform is taking place varies considerably across the region. A range of strategies have been adopted to address the gaps for attaining full and productive participation in the global knowledge economy. One strategy involves privatizing higher education through innovative public institutions such as Al-Akhawayn University established in Morocco in 1995, which offers liberal-arts curriculum based on the American system, and King Abdallah University of Science and Technology in Saudi Arabia in 2009. Partnership programs with foreign universities have also been established, such as the German-Jordanian University in 2005 where undergraduate and graduate programs are oriented to the German "Fachhochschule" model.

While higher education systems across the MENA region are similar in a myriad of ways, deviations from the norm exist. Unlike most countries where the higher education system was founded by public institutions, foreign missionaries established three private universities in Lebanon. The American University of Beirut was established in 1866, Saint Joseph University in 1875, and the Lebanese American University, now a coeducational institution, was established in 1924 as a women's college offering associate degree programs. Similarly, an American missionary founded the American University in Cairo in 1919. These renowned institutions stand out as longstanding milestones of academic excellence and are usually at the forefront of change. With the support of their IR office and quality assurance units, these institutions embraced academic planning as a means of linking their mission, priorities, and varied resources in a system of evaluation, decision making, and action to shape and guide the organization.

Over the past three decades, private higher education providers also became predominant in the Gulf States. States such as the United Arab Emirates, Qatar, and Bahrain have developed free educational zones to promote education that will stimulate local research capacity and position the states to take a leading role in contributing to the global knowledge economy. Each state has adopted a unique partnership model with foreign degree-granting branch campuses reflecting the different economic and social priorities arising from incongruent levels of wealth (Witte, 2010). While Dubai pursued partnerships with universities like Michigan State University (US) that operate on a self-sustaining financial model, Abu Dhabi forged partnerships with institutions such as New York University (US), a publicly funded research university. Other universities in the region include Monash University Dubai (Australia), Middlesex University Dubai (UK), Paris-Sorbonne University Abu Dhabi (France), and Weill Cornel Medical College Qatar (US).

Significant achievements have been realized in higher education in the MENA region as a result of the policy recommendations provided by international organizations. Higher education systems have become increasingly diversified to include public and private, national and foreign, and local programs and partnership programs with foreign universities, with the number of institutions of higher education doubling over the past decade. Tertiary gross enrollment increased from 10% to 24% from 1980 to 2003, with Bahrain lying on the high end of the gross enrollment scale with a ratio of 34% and Oman at the lower end with a ratio of 13%. IR and quality assurance professionals have an important role to play in helping their institutions respond to these challenges by generating essential data and information to facilitate the development of clear policy strategies and interventions when necessary.

The Growth of IR and Higher Education Planning in MENA

The rapid growth in the higher education sector triggered concerns for quality in the MENA region, and this, too, created a greater need for personnel who are skilled in assessment and evaluation. Countries in the region have adopted varied strategies to ensure the quality of their institutions and their academic offerings. Several MENA countries have established national commissions for accreditation and quality assurance such as the Commission for Academic Accreditation (CAA) in the UAE, the National Commission for Assessment and Academic Accreditation (NCAAA) in Saudi Arabia, and the National Evaluation, Quality Assurance and Accreditation Authority in Tunisia. Some universities have sought institutional and program accreditation by international accreditation bodies usually selected relevant to their referential educational model, including accrediting agencies such as the New England Association for Schools and Colleges (NEASC) and Evalag (Evaluation Agency Baden-Württemberg) for institutional accreditation, and the Accreditation Board for Engineering and Technology (ABET) and the Royal Institute of Architects of Ireland (RIAI) for program accreditation. The influence of quality assurance agencies on the development of institutional research is substantial at the institutional and, in some instances, at the national level between institutions. They have acted as a vehicle disseminating concepts such as quality assurance and institutional effectiveness among higher educational professionals and governing bodies based on their norms and standards, thus typifying the quality assurance and IR experience accordingly.

Overall, the institutional research function has been confined to the individual institutions and little has been achieved by way of developing collective data-naming conventions and data sharing across institutions or across countries. The different educational models adopted by institutions across the region and the coexistence of national and foreign institutions of higher education, in particular in the Gulf States, that are subject to a reporting system in their country of origin makes central collection of data in the region complex.

Elementary institutional research tasks have been conducted by various units within MENA institutions for many years; in some locations such as Lebanon and Cairo, basic data collection and reporting has occurred for over 20 years. Functions that involved basic statistics about the institution such as number of applications, admissions, and enrollments led many to view institutional researchers as 'number crunchers.' IR offices and quality assurance units were established within institutions to consolidate and centralize the dispersed and isolated institutional research activities. For the majority of universities in the region, the establishment of these offices accompanied the accreditation exercise where the standards clearly elucidate the role of institutional research within institutions, as is the case with the Commission for Academic Accreditation in the United Arab Emirates, or where the standards require officials to track institutional data covering the continuum of functions in higher education (Lange, Saavedra, & Romano, 2013).

As it became important for institutions in the region to understand the global, social, political, and economic currents shaping societies at large, local institutional researchers needed to develop their research expertise and basic skill sets. To this end, they initially sought valuable professional development and networking opportunities with international organizations such as the AIR in the United States. The need for similar networking opportunities and collaborations among institutions at the regional level soon became evident to institutional researchers in the area and concerted efforts led to the establishment of MENA-AIR, an affiliate organization of AIR, which held its inaugural conference in 2009. In less than a year of its establishment, MENA-AIR welcomed more than a hundred members from over 45 institutions from seven MENA countries (MENA-AIR, 2014).

The Roles of Institutional Research and Planning in MENA

With the increase in quality assurance and accreditation, mechanisms of accountability for demonstrating institutional effectiveness to internal and external stakeholders led to the need for institutional research in the MENA region. Volkwein's (2008) view of IR as the focal point for all of the university's analytics activities has been used as a guide in MENA, and some individuals see the outcomes of the IR function as strands of institutional intelligence that support institutional learning and an essential ingredient of sound university governance (Saupe, 1990).

According to a study on the classification of higher education institutions in the region, higher education data was not collected or organized in a way that facilitated reporting (Bhandari & El-Amine, 2012). With the recent establishment of IR offices and quality assurance units after the turn of the new millennium, institutional researchers sought to provide operational definitions of data to facilitate common understanding within their institutions. They provided support for the development of their data management systems and improved their decision support reports by adopting the latest technologies and software. AIR and MENA-AIR have played a crucial role in introducing IR professionals to the tools and best practices through forums, conferences, and workshops.

Institutional researchers in the MENA region provide useful insights in areas such as accreditation (institutional and program); planning (strategic and academic); enrollment management, assessment, and evaluation (academic, administrative, and support units); data management; reporting (internal and external); and, to a lesser extent, special research initiatives and policy formulation as revealed through content analysis of IR mission statements and goals. Following international trends, other areas that have gained importance recently in the region are outcomes assessment and student success gauged by indicators such as retention, persistence, attrition, and graduation rates, as revealed in topics covered in presentations in successive MENA-AIR forums. These observations are confirmed by the findings of a study conducted in 2009, which also shed light on areas where IR professionals are less involved to include academic affairs and research analyses such as faculty workload, scholarly productivity, and salary equity studies as well as administrative and financial analyses such as staffing needs and fundraising statistics. With the majority of IR offices linked to the chief executive officer as compared to the chief academic executive, one can appreciate the important role IR plays in planning and operations (El-Hassan & Cinali, 2009).

The IR function in the MENA region embraced these developments in the role of IR over a period of less than two decades. Today through trend analysis, modeling, forecasting, comparative analysis, environmental analysis, survey analysis, and benchmarking exercises, IR offices convert data into information to provide a meaningful and comprehensive picture of the institution—students, faculty, staff, alumni—to effectively support decision making. The impact of one benchmark study initiated by the Lebanese American University on human resources (faculty and staff) in 2011 was profound, providing insights into their market competitiveness, the effectiveness of their policies, and the efficiency of their operations.

Challenges and Further Directions for IR in the Middle East

Institutional research in the Middle East is a relatively new field and still in its initial stage. However, it is noteworthy to recognize the growing identity of IR in the context of the region. As noted in chapter 1 of this book, some colleges and universities use the term institutional research, but many IR units do not use those words in their titles. Rather, they use titles that reflect the IR roles required by the university and society, such as 'planning,' 'quality management,' 'research and development,' and 'development and planning.' The expansion of IR functions from regular institutional management to more research- and policy-oriented functions and to quality assurance seems reasonable, as it reflects the emerging trends of higher education. However, many IR offices in MENA do not have regular data management functions. The current role of IR offices lacking these functions is routine institutional management utilizing data and information. This disparity raises a fundamental question: what should be the roles of institutional research?

The need for IR is on the rise globally and so is the need for professionals with a diverse set of skills, an expanded knowledge base in higher education, and familiarity with technologies. This is particularly true for the MENA region where the concern for the quality of higher education provision in many countries and the demand for accountability are on the rise. Initially, institutions engaged in rigorous self-study in the pursuit of accreditation that is considered a form of documented quality. Now these same institutions and others are being enticed to enter the race of higher education rankings and league tables, which will undoubtedly require the efficient management of data and generation of information (Lange, Saavedra, & Romano, 2013). The nature of efforts in ranking may lead institutions to become more effective and efficient as they strive to enhance their reputation, financial position, and competitiveness, however it may also limit the diversity of approaches to quality resulting in institutional similarity (Taylor, Webber, & Jacobs, 2013). According to these authors, it is the role of institutiónal researchers to alert senior administrators to the positive and possible negative consequences that rankings might have on strategic direction and the culture of the institution. As ranking agencies such as *QS World University Rankings* and *US News and World Report Rankings* initiate regional ranking projects for the Arab World and the MENA region, this heightened IR role should become even more critical.

The increasing impact of higher education rankings and subsequent emphasis on international higher education affects MENA IR practitioners as well. According to Altbach (2006), internationalization supports a market-based model of higher education where higher education is viewed as a commodity for trade, a service easily transferrable across borders, and a private good to be purchased. Advances in communication and technology have also contributed to worldwide trade in educational services (Calderon & Tangas, 2006). With the emergence of diversified institutional types, in addition to the national public universities, private not-for-profit, private for-profit, foreign, and partnership programs with foreign universities in the MENA region, global education is progressing forward quite steadily. The internationalization of higher education, which is continuously gaining impetus, and the benchmarking projects covering various aspects of higher education not only require standardization of data across systems, they require an in-depth knowledge of the specific institutional and national contexts as well as international trends in higher education. It seems clear that IR professionals have a significant role to play in producing information and knowledge needed to respond to the challenges of higher education and essential for decision making, planning, and assessment.

Although the Middle Eastern oil-producing countries are more economically equipped to grow and answer the challenges of higher education, the non-oil producing Arab countries of the Levant and North Africa have additional challenges due to economic instability, paucity of resources, and ongoing internal and external conflict influenced by regional political tensions. The consequences of these challenges have resulted in brain drain and diminished intellectual leadership (El-Ghali, Chen, & Yeager, 2010). Despite the often turbulent and disruptive conditions, these countries have progressively sought to develop their educational systems in an attempt to preserve their competitive position in higher education regionally and globally based on the conviction that the future of their citizens is dependent on the full development of their human capital. Planning in such an unstable political, social, and economic environment is a challenging task fraught with a high level of uncertainty; however, it is essential to effect change. Institutions have invested in IR to address societal needs and to respond to the ever-changing economic and political conditions.

In its early stages of growth, institutional research in MENA has already faced many challenges. However, it has great potential to grow in the current higher education environment. University administrators are starting to recognize the importance of IR functions and realize the benefits IR can bring to decision making for the institution. The higher education community also values data-driven decision making and informed institutional management. In addition, there is growth in the number of IR professionals, their perceived value, and the function itself. All these changes will contribute to the successful development of institutional research and higher education planning in the MENA region.

References

Alissa, S. (2007). *The challenge of economic reform in the Arab world: Toward more productive economies.* Washington, DC: Carnegie Endowment for International Peace.

Altbach, P. (2006). *International higher education: Policy and practice.* Boston, MA: Boston College, Center for International Higher Education.

Bhandari, R., & El-Amine, A. (2012). *Higher education classification in the Middle East and North Africa: A pilot study.* New York, NY: Institute of International Education.

Calderon, A., & Tangas G. (2006). Trade liberalization, regional agreements, and implications for higher education. *Higher Education Management and Policy, 18*(1), 79–104.

Davidson, C. (2008). Higher education in the Gulf: A historical background. In C. Davidson & P. Mackenzie-Smith (Eds.), *Higher education in the Gulf States: Shaping economies, politics and culture.* London, UK: Saqi.

El-Ghali, H. A., Chen, Q., & Yeager, J. (2010). Strategic planning in higher education in the Middle East: The case of non-Gulf countries. In D. Obst & D. Kirk (Eds.), *Innovation through education: Building the knowledge economy in the Middle East.* New York, NY: Institute of International Education.

El-Hassan, K., & Cinali, G. (2009). MENA-AIR survey results. Presentation at the MENA-AIR Inaugural Forum, Zayed University, United Arab Emirates.

Kirk, D. (2010). The "Knowledge Society" in the Middle East. In D. Obst & D. Kirk (Eds.), *Innovation through education: Building the knowledge economy in the Middle East.* New York, NY: Institute of International Education.

Lange, L., Saavedra, F. M., & Romano, J. (2013). Institutional research in emerging countries of Southern Africa, Latin America, and the Middle East and North Africa: Global frameworks and local practices. In A. Calderon & K. L. Webber (Eds.), *Global issues in institutional research, New Directions for Institutional Research, 157* (pp. 23–38). San Francisco, CA: Wiley Periodicals, Inc.

MENA-AIR. (2014). Retrieved from: www.mena-air.org/AboutUs.html.

Salehi-Isfahani, D., & Dhillon, N. (2008). *Stalled youth transition in the Middle East: A framework for policy reform.* Washington, DC, and Dubai, United Arab Emirates: The Wolfensohn Center for Development and the Dubai School of Government.

Saupe, J. L. (1990). *The functions of institutional research,* 2nd ed. Tallahassee, FL: Association for Institutional Research.

Taylor, B., Webber, K., & Jacobs, G. (2013). Institutional research in light of internationalization, growth and competition. In A. Calderon & K. L. Webber (Eds.), *Global issues in institutional research, New Directions for Institutional Research, 157* (pp. 5–22). San Francisco, CA: Wiley Periodicals, Inc.

Volkwein, J. F. (2008). The foundations and evolution of institutional research. In D. G. Terkla (Ed.), *Institutional research: More than just data. New Directions for Higher Education, 141* (pp. 5–20). San Francisco, CA: Jossey-Bass.

Witte, S. (2010). Gulf State branch campuses: Global student recruitment. *International Higher Education, 58,* 5.

World Bank. (2008). *The road not travelled: Education reform in the Middle East and North Africa.* Washington, DC: World Bank.

SECTION III

Themes of Institutional Research Practice

13

BUSINESS INTELLIGENCE AS A DATA-BASED DECISION SUPPORT SYSTEM AND ITS ROLES IN SUPPORT OF INSTITUTIONAL RESEARCH AND PLANNING

Henry Y. Zheng

Introduction

In higher education, it is widely recognized that data analytics is an organization's strategic asset and key enabler of strategic planning and organizational management. As noted by Gusza and Lucker (2001), "Successful analytic projects do not begin with data and end with models; rather, they begin with strategy and end with models and decision making and business process" (p. 41). In his seminal book, *Competing on Analytics*, Harvard scholar Tom Davenport argues that organizations can no longer compete on products and services alone; they must rely on data analytics to differentiate themselves to gain unique competitive advantage. Analytics enables organizations to become more agile and effective.

The increasing importance of data analytics is not lost on higher education leaders who face a multitude of challenges, including increasing operating costs, dwindling state support, limits to tuition increases, stagnant research funding growth, and increasing competition from the for-profit sector and online education. To navigate their institutions through these challenges, higher education leaders have begun to place more emphasis on the utilization of data to support decisions. In a recent EDUCAUSE survey of college and university leaders, 86% of respondents believed that analytics will be more important in the years to come (EDUCAUSE, 2012).

Several trends converge to highlight the imperatives for developing data analytics: more electronic devices are used in personal and business activities to collect data seamlessly behind the background, and this collection is projected to generate 44 times greater data volume from now to 2020 (Manyika et al., 2011); phenomenal growth of social media in cyberspace adds more contextual data;

more technology options are available that cost less; and all these are leading to the emerging of the so-called "big data" revolution. Gartner (2012) defines big data as: "high volume, high velocity, and/or high variety information assets that require new forms of processing to enable enhanced decision making, insight discovery and process optimization."

With data accumulating at a breakneck speed, big data makes today's analytical environment more complex and challenging. Organizations that are able to leverage data resources effectively to support decision making are more likely to have a competitive edge. This chapter discusses the concept of business intelligence as a form of data-based decision support systems. I discuss different stages in the development of business intelligence. I also explore institutional researchers' role and responsibility in promoting the effective use of business intelligence to support organizational decision making and performance management.

The Concepts of Decision Support System and Business Intelligence

In developing data analytics capabilities, the terms decision support system and business intelligence are interconnected. Decision support system (DSS) is a concept introduced and developed long before business intelligence became fashionable. Several scholars credited the concepts involved in DSS as first articulated by Michael S. Scott Morton (1971) in his 1971 book *Management Decision Systems: Computer-Based Support of Decision Making* (Power, 2007; Sprague, 1980). From an organizational management perspective, a decision support system is a computer-based information system that supports business or organizational decision making activities. DSS systems provide the data, analysis, reporting, and projection capabilities to facilitate operations and planning.

Sprague (1980) believes that the true value of DSS is in the improvement of organizational performance and not the storage of data. DSS supports management reporting and ensures that it gets the right information to the right people at the right time. Knowledge workers are the ultimate clientele of DSS and, therefore, DSS specifically focuses on features that make them easy to use by non-computer people in an interactive mode. A survey of DSS literature suggests that an effective DSS should have the following basic characteristics (Power, 2000; Silver, 1991; Sauter, 1997):

- The ability to work in both semi-structured and unstructured decision situations. If the decision situation is very structured, the decisions may be automated by using computer programs. For example, collecting evaluation of instruction can be a very structured task but analyzing narrative comments in the data is semi-structured;
- It supports and enhances managerial decisions but cannot replace human judgment and experience. For example, a DSS supporting student financial

aid applications may have the basic information and processing parameters but the financial aid officer can still make discretionary decisions within the parameters;

- It introduces the use of models and analytical techniques to supplement conventional data storage and retrieval. For example, a university's budget system may tap into the enrollment management model to run different revenue scenarios; and

- It has interactive features that empower analytical processing to all levels of an organization in a user-friendly manner.

In the higher education environment, examples of DSS can be found in every functional area. For example, Bresfelean and Ghisoiu (2009) illustrate how DSSs are widely used in higher education. From enrollment management to faculty evaluation and from employee management to academic research evaluation,

TABLE 13.1 Summary of DSS Modules in Higher Education

DSS MODULE	Students Module	Teaching Module	Research Module
	• Students' enrollment • Studies reclassification • Tuition • Choosing a specialization	• Syllabi and teaching materials • Course schedule • Choosing optional courses	• Scientific research, evaluation • Performance issues and standards
DECISIONAL SITUATIONS	• Scholarships • Students' dorms • Issue certificates • Web information and announcements • Students' transfer • Expelling students • Interruption of studies • Extension of studies • 2nd or more specializations • Diploma exam in other institutions • Career guidance	• Tutoring activities • Teaching-learning activities • Students' practical work • Preparation for the bachelor exam • Evaluation of the teaching staff • Exam schedule • Partial exams during the semester and final exams • Students' grading management • Contestation of the evaluation results • Bachelor final exam	• Salary coefficients • Human resources strategy • Job opening and interviewing for research positions • PhDs activity and evaluation • Grants' continuation and management, etc.

Source: Bresfelean & Ghisoiu (2009)

DSS is engrained in many aspects of our work. DSS is so pervasive that we take it for granted that our system of management relies on human-computer interfaces that tap into servers, databases, terminals, and electronic cables. In Table 13.1, Bresfelean and Ghisoiu (2009) describe a summary of DSS in higher education that includes student, teaching, and research modules. For example, DSS student modules start with the student admissions process and move through enrollment, fee payment, financial aid, scheduling, and degree completion. DSS teaching modules include situational factors such as syllabi and teaching materials, tutoring activities, evaluation of teaching staff, and exam schedules. All of these situations used to support decisions are captured in enterprise data management systems that can be integral parts of DSS.

Compared to DSS, business intelligence (BI) is a relative new but similar concept. As an extension of DSS, Negash and Gray (2008) believe business intelligence is a data-driven DSS that combines data gathering, data storage, and knowledge management with analysis to provide input to the decision process. In a BI environment, knowledge workers use large databases, typically stored in a data warehouse or data mart, as their source of information and as the basis for sophisticated analysis. BI enables analysis that ranges from simple reporting to slice-and-dice, drill-down, answering ad hoc queries, real-time analysis, simulations, and forecasting (Negash & Gray, 2008). The key difference between the concepts of BI and DSS is that BI is a data-driven DSS while DSS is a broader concept that includes non-data driven and heuristic-based DSS systems. A DSS can be communications-driven, focusing on enhancing interactive and collaborative decision-making processes such as a SharePoint or Google Docs site. A DSS can also be knowledge-driven that provides specialized problem-solving expertise stored as facts, rules, procedures, or in similar structures (Power, 2002).

A BI system is data centric and data driven. Adapted from Chaudhuri, Dayal, and Narasayy (2011), Figure 13.1 presents a BI model that includes five components that can be summarized as: 1) source data; 2) data management; 3) data warehousing; 4) data delivery; and 5) business intelligence generation. Source data can come from different sources—typically from multiple operational databases across departments within the organization, as well as external vendors. A particular issue in BI development is the integration of different data sources into one system. Different sources contain data of varying quality and use different definitions, codes, and formats. All of these need to be reconciled before they can be truly useful.

Loading and standardizing source data is a major task and, as new data arrives daily and even hourly, it is important to have an efficient and quality data management process. The commonly known Extract-Transform-Load (ETL) process includes three key steps: *E*xtracts data from outside sources; *T*ransforms it to meet operational and analytical needs; and *L*oads it into an operational data store or data warehouse. A common tool for storing and querying warehouse data is relational database management systems (RDBMS). According to Chaudhuri, Dayal, and Narasayy (2011), large data warehouses typically deploy parallel RDBMS engines

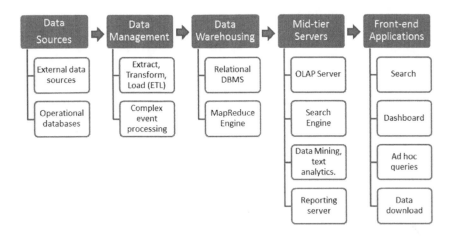

FIGURE 13.1 Business Intelligence Architecture

Adapted from Chaudhuri et al. (2011).

so that structured query language (SQL) queries can be executed over large volumes of data.

Data delivery is generally handled by set of mid-tier servers that provide specialized functionality for different BI scenarios. For example, online analytic processing (OLAP) servers provide a multidimensional view of data to applications or users and enable the common BI operations such as filtering, aggregation, drill-down, and pivoting. Reporting servers enables the generation of administrative and analytics reports to meet different needs of the organization. Enterprise search engines support the keyword search paradigm over text and structured data in the warehouse and enables data mining using keywords and data attributes to find data nuggets in the sea of data. Text analytic engines can analyze large amounts of text data and extract valuable information that would otherwise require significant manual effort.

The front-end applications in a typical BI system can include spreadsheets, web portals, canned reports, dynamic drill-down query tools, and other performance management tools such as IBM's Cognos or Oracle's Business Intelligence Enterprise Edition (OBIEE) that enable the development of performance scorecards using visual dashboards. In the age of social media and mobile technologies, new BI applications such as web analytics and mobile analytics and reporting tools are also added to the front-end tools of BI platforms.

Business Intelligence Maturity Models

Business intelligence is receiving increased attention from higher education institutions. One of the driving forces behind this development is the gradual expansion in IR's scope of work from the traditional roles of data reporting and ad hoc analysis to more advanced planning and organizational development roles. In these expanded roles, IR offices use BI tools to provide analytics that support strategic planning, long-range financial modeling, organizational effectiveness assessment, and operational improvement. Business intelligence is taking shape as a data-driven platform with the capability to describe, analyze, explain, plan, predict, and solve problems. It is a toolbox that helps "increase organizational knowledge, provide information to the decision process, enable effective actions, and support establishing and achieving business goals" (Wells, 2008, para. 8).

Not all organizations are equally well established to leverage the power of business intelligence. Industry experts use "maturity models" to describe, explain, and evaluate an organization's BI growth life cycles. A maturity model typically describes several stages or phases of BI development, which need to be completed by the organization to achieve a certain level of maturity. In developing BI, it is almost impossible for organizations to skip key development stages to be very mature. BI maturity comes through experience, investment, cultural transformation, and other enabling factors.

There are several major BI maturity models in the industry. They typically utilize a standard questionnaire supplemented by on-site interviews and other communication tools to assess an organization's BI development stage. For example, the Data Warehouse Institute (TDWI, 2014) provides an online assessment tool for organizations to evaluate their BI's maturity level. TDWI's model concentrates on the technical viewpoints, especially in the data warehouse aspect. TDWI's model has five stages: Nonexistent → Preliminary → Repeatable → Managed → Optimized. Chuah and Wong (2011) provide a concise comparison of key models available and their relative strengths and weaknesses.

The most popular model is perhaps Gartner's BI maturity model. Figure 13.2 is adapted from Gartner's model, which also has five progressive stages. Gartner proposes that maturity moves along a path from: Unaware → Tactical → Focused → Strategic → Pervasive. Each stage is viewed from several perspectives: process, people, technology, leadership, and culture of performance measurement (Gartner, 2008).

In the first stage, "Unaware," organizations are in "information anarchy." This stage is characterized by the lack of consistent data resource and management practices, incorrect and inconsistent data definition and interpretation, and knowledge workers struggling to pool data from sources. In this stage, spreadsheets are often the analytics tool of choice and there are no defined metrics for organizational performance measurement. In this stage, an organization is unaware of the importance of analytics and business intelligence.

In the "Tactical" stage, organizations start to recognize the value of analytics and start investing in BI tools. Metrics are usually used on the department level only. Common metrics do not exist or are inconsistent. Most of the data, tools,

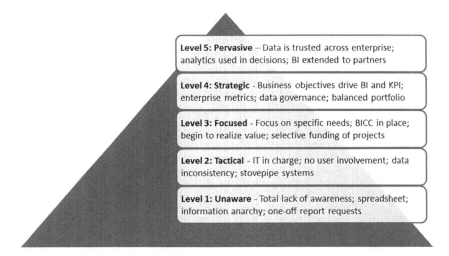

FIGURE 13.2 Gartner's Business Intelligence Maturity Model

Adapted from Gartner Research (2008).

and applications are in "silos." Companies at this level often use off-the-shelf software, with few or no modifications, to accommodate company needs. Management has yet to trust the quality and consistency of the information provided.

In the "Focused" stage, organizations begin to push for using standard reporting tools. Sponsorship of BI projects usually comes from a department or IT leaders. Management dashboards are often requested at this level. Their goal is to optimize the efficiency of individual departments or business units, but is not related to the broader organizational goals. Data is not integrated at this stage and inconsistencies in metrics and/or goals of individual business units or departments are very common.

In the "Strategic" stage, organization leaders have a clear appreciation of and understand the importance of BI strategy. Top management wants BI to become a critical organization process and push for decision analytics to be available at all levels of the organization. Management process is created to include experts from functional areas and IT. BI projects have enough resources and funding to achieve their goals. An organization's strategic goals, operational imperatives, and performance metrics are aligned for integrated development. Data management policy and data quality metrics are in place.

In the "Pervasive" stage, data quality control and flow are well-managed and trusted throughout the organization. The use of data analytics to support decision making and performance management is pervasive at every level of the organization. Results are measurable and linked to specific goals, while use of BI is extended to suppliers, business partners, and customers.

Achieving Business Intelligence Maturity in Institutional Research and Planning

The progression from "unaware" to "pervasive" use of data analytics to assist decision making and performance management is a slow and incremental process. For institutional researchers and planners in higher education organizations, the goal should be achieving the "pervasive" stage. However, very few colleges and universities have actually come close to this "pervasiveness." Most are making the journey, but they are constrained by a number of factors that hinder them from BI maturity. Such constrains include: slow pace in creating a performance and accountability culture; lack of an organization-wide data governance model, which leads to inconsistent data definitions and interpretations; and unwillingness to commit scarce resources to build the necessary infrastructure and platform for organization-wide implementation.

Regardless of your institution's current status in BI development and the constraints that you may be facing, there are a number of essential elements that you must consider when developing BI capabilities along the maturity pathway.

Common Data Definitions and Shared Data Resource Management

"How many faculty members does your college have?" This seemingly simple question often solicits several more counter-questions from an institutional research office. "Do you want to include all faculty ranks or just regular, tenured or tenure-track faculty members? Do you want headcount or FTEs (full-time equivalent)? Do you want to include clinical or courtesy appointments (if your university has an academic medical center)?" Depending on how you answer these questions, you receive different faculty numbers. In data reporting, some requesting agencies may have different data definitions and, therefore, the numbers are reported consistent with definitions. For example, *US News and World Report's* definition of faculty count is different from IPEDS's (Integrated Post-secondary Education Data System) definition. All of these numbers can be technically correct, but are distinct nonetheless.

The need for standardization and documentation of data definitions and data interpretations is often under-appreciated and poorly coordinated in many organizations. Without an effective data governance structure, many colleges and universities rely on their IT department and institutional research office to play this coordination role. In the business intelligence environment, this role needs to be substantially strengthened and coordinated. A formal data governance structure with all major data producing and user groups participating is often a good facilitating condition for effective business intelligence management. Under the data governance model, data stewards from all functional areas are expected to do their job to clarify and document how data elements are defined. Often, a data element can be defined differently because there may be different needs or requirements. Given the varied contexts for defining a data element, it is imperative that all data users have a way to understand why and how data are defined. Sharing data dictionaries and data definitions among users are therefore a vital first step in promoting effective business intelligence from an organizational perspective.

An effective business intelligence development requires organizations to follow sound principles for organizational data management. Seiner (2005) believes that the first principle is to establish the common understanding that organizational data is the property of the enterprise and is not "owned" by any individual or business unit. Data (both structured and unstructured) and the meta-data about that data are business and technical resources owned by and used by the organization. Together with data definitions and dictionaries, enterprise data shall be readily accessible to all, except where determined to be restricted. If data access restrictions need to be made, the data governance committee or functional area data stewards are accountable for clearly defining who should be granted access and at what levels the access should be granted. Organizational leaders and institutional researchers and planners should not be put in the position to go "trick-or-treating" for data or have the data access but without sufficient support to understand and fully utilize the data.

Integration of Data Resources From All Functional Areas

An effective business intelligence platform requires that data from different functional areas are connected and shared. In many higher education organizations, it is not uncommon for functional areas to maintain their own database operations or data warehousing capabilities. There are historical and operational reasons for functional areas such as admissions, registrar, enrollment management, financial aid, human resources, faculty affairs, and finance to maintain their own data resources for both online transactional and analytical processing (OLTP and OLAP). However, these data islands must be connected through bridges so that data users such as institutional researchers can travel to different islands efficiently. In business intelligence, the bridge that connects the scattered data islands together is the enterprise data warehouse.

As defined earlier, business intelligence is a data-driven decision support system that combines data gathering, data storage, and knowledge management with analysis to provide input to the decision process. In such a data-intensive process, the data warehouse plays the vital role of pulling and connecting data resources throughout the enterprise and organizing it together into one place (or virtually using connectivity). A data warehouse not only provides scale efficiency but, more importantly, a standard process for data quality control, data production, data delivery, and data utilization. The ideal state is the enablement of a "single version of truth" in which data resources for decision support are coming from a reliable source and are trusted throughout the organization—a key indicator of a mature BI system.

In the age of "big data," developing an integrated approach to data resource management is vitally important. For example, in the growing area of learning analytics, student data from admissions to degree completion should be integrated for data mining and analysis. Once the life cycle of a student's learning experience is pieced together and insights are gained, appropriate interventions and services can be individualized to meet the unique needs of the students. Data points capturing a student's learning experience from admissions to course enrollment, from campus life to experiential learning, are like the trail of breadcrumbs left by Hansel and Gretel in the fairytale. String them together; these data points paint a full picture of a student's pathway through their college life. Not making all the relevant data points available to institutional researchers and program leaders limits an organization's ability to promote student success and program development.

In an EDUCAUSE (2012) report of advances in data analytics in higher education, University of Washington shares its model on institutional data management. Figure 13.3 shows that a higher education institution's data universe includes six broad categories: academics, research, human resources, finance, advancement, and services and resources. Each category includes subsets of functional area data elements. An effective enterprise business intelligence system must be able to integrate key data elements from these sources to support institutional decision making, teaching and learning, research and discovery, operational management, and performance improvement.

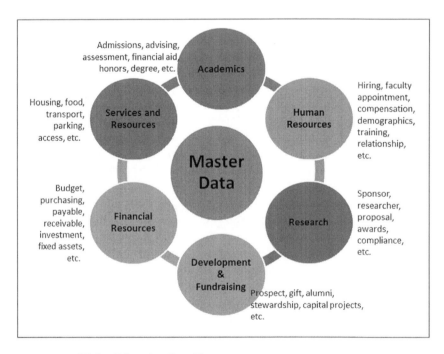

FIGURE 13.3 Higher Education Data Types

Adapted from Educause (2012).

Leveraging the Advances in Technical Capabilities

In addition to traditional data resources, business intelligence development can also benefit from new data sources and analytics tools such as social media, web analytics, mobile technology, and data visualization. Compared to business organizations, higher education organizations are slower in collecting and using data coming from social media and web traffic and treat them as part of their business intelligence data collection. Many of these new data sources can be effectively harnessed for institutional research. For example, the website Collegeconfidential.com has a "Campus Vibe" section where parents and prospective students visiting college campuses can express their opinions and impressions of each of the campuses they visited. This website is a gold mine of textual data that can help college admission and marketing officers understand how their colleges are perceived by external stakeholders and how their college is compared to other colleges. Institutions can collect such feedback from post-visit surveys, but such surveys are typically too structured to yield unfiltered data.

Another new source of information for business intelligence is web analytics. Web analytics is a generic term describing the measurement and study of the impact of a website on its users (Webopedia, 2014). Web analytics can be used to measure how many people visited a website, how many of those visitors were unique visitors, how they came to the site (i.e., if they followed a link to get to the site or came there directly), what keywords they searched with on the site's search engine, how long they stayed on a given page or on the entire site, what links they clicked on, and when they left the site.

From a business intelligence standpoint, web analytics help organizations right-target or personalize their web contents or other responses based on web visitors' unique characteristics. Amazon.com is one of the pioneers in this area and any visitor to Amazon's search engine can expect recommendations for other products based on his or her search terms. Similarly, higher education officials who like business intelligence books will likely be asked to recommended data warehouse books. In web analytics, search logics are based on pattern recognition and semantic associations. Business intelligence can leverage web analytics tools to help infer certain characteristics based on web visit behaviors and recommend changes to meet visitor needs. For example, web analytics may help student life administrators find out what students are interested in on various parts of their website and what student activities get the most visits and by what types of students. They can then optimize their web contents and activities to meet students' needs and interests.

As the volume of data increases and more advanced analytics tools are introduced in business intelligence development, another important development is the use of visualization to make data presentations more effective. Most commercially developed BI platforms today come with amazingly easy to use and impressive visualization capabilities. Used effectively, new data visualization tools and well-thought-out scorecard and dashboard designs help transform large and complex data sets to simple and effective data summaries for better decision making. In Figure 13.4, Terkla (2012) demonstrated how different performance data can be

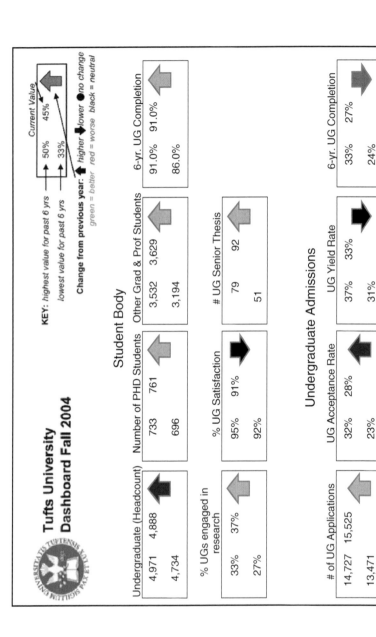

FIGURE 13.4 Tufts University Performance Dashboard

Source: Terkla (2012)

displayed visually to concisely convey performance data on a student body. A simple dashboard like this can display multiple data points effectively, often using just one page. Organizational leaders who are constantly struggling with competing priorities and issues surely can appreciate the elegance of highly summarized data visually so that they can grasp the performance statistics quickly every month or quarter.

Building a Culture of Data-Driven Decision Making and Performance Management

An effective business intelligence development process requires corresponding changes in leadership and organizational culture to base management decisions on data evidence without forcing data to justify decisions. A common quote in the institutional research community is more to the point: "if you torture the data long enough, it will confess to everything." This may seem humorous, but it reveals some actual practices in which researchers are asked to find the best data angles or hide the worse data points to support a leader's points or decisions. A business intelligence system that democratizes the data reporting and sharing process will make such data manipulations less likely. After all, data access enables data transparency, which in turn enhances accountability.

A more mature business intelligence environment requires a greater respect and acceptance for data-driven strategic and decision insights. This means that organization leaders will have a clear appreciation and understand the importance of data sharing and data-based decision making. They will appropriate sufficient resources to build effective data governance structures and business intelligence capabilities to make their organization an analytics-savvy organization. In the ideal state, the use of data analytics to support decision making and performance management should be natural and pervasive at every level of the organization. Results are automatically measured and accessible through BI portals and visualized for effective management reporting.

A huge benefit of an effective business intelligence system is the enablement of changes in institutional research and planning functions. Many IR offices are inundated with basic data gathering and reporting and hardly have the time to truly analyze data in depth to gain analytical and actionable insights. A more mature BI system will reduce the basic data management tasks for institutional researchers and help them focus on more advanced analytical projects such as predictive modeling, long-range planning, performance scorecard and dashboard, and scenario development and simulations.

Barton and Court's (2012) analysis of business organizations concluded that companies that used data analytics and invested more resources had productivity and profit gains that were 5–6% higher than those of their competitors. Guszcza and Lucker (2011) believe that data analytics can be a source of competitive advantage if an organization embraces data intelligence to support decision making and performance management. "Uncovering the realities that lie behind the data is what business analytics is all about. Precisely because they are hidden to the casual observer, they lend competitive advantages to the organizations that discover and implement them in business first" (Guszcza & Lucker, 2011, p. 32). As higher education organizations move to become more competitive in the global marketplace, it is imperative that leaders of these organizations recognize the importance of analytics, invest in sufficient resources to build business intelligence capabilities, and support the use of data analytics in decision making and performance management. Organizations that fail to do so will be operating at a disadvantage.

Concluding Remarks

Institutional research and planning as a field is relatively young and its golden age has yet to come. The emergence of analytics as an organizational competency and data resources as strategic assets puts institutional researchers all over the world in an enviable position. This field is on the verge of a data analytics and business intelligence revolution. In their highly influential article in *Harvard Business Review*, Davenport and Patil (2012) call data scientists "the sexiest job of the 21st century." Data researchers are "akin to the Wall Street 'quants' of the 1980s and 1990s" (p. 76). With such a high praise and high expectations, institutional researchers must leverage their data resources and business intelligence tools to deliver value-added, actionable insights for organizational decision making and performance improvement. As the higher education industry becomes more competitive, such decision insights are not only important, but mission critical.

References

Barton, D., & Court, D. (2012). Making advanced analytics work for you. *Harvard Business Review, 90*(10), 78–83.

Bresfelean, V. P., & Ghisoiu, N. (2009). Higher education decision making and decision support systems. *MPRA* Paper No. 26698. Retrieved February 3, 2014 from http://mpra.ub.uni-muenchen.de/26698/.

Chaudhuri, S., Dayal, U., & Narasayy, V. (2011). An overview of business intelligence technology. *Communications of the ACM, 54*(8), 88–98.

Chuah, M., & Wong, K. (2011). A review of business intelligence and its maturity models. *African Journal of Business Management,* 5(9), 3424–3428.

Davenport, T. H., & Patil, D. J. (2012). Data scientist: The sexiest job of the 21st century. *Harvard Business Review, 90*(10), 70–76.

EDUCAUSE. (2012). Analytics for enterprise efficiency and effectiveness. Retrieved February 4, 2014 from www.educause.edu/library/resources/analytics-enterprise-efficiency-and-effectiveness.

Gartner Research. (2008). Q&A: Seven questions every business intelligence leader must answer. Gartner Research White Paper, April 2008. Publication ID Number: G00156821.

Gartner Research. (2012). The Importance of 'Big Data': A definition. Retrieved February 2, 2014 from www.gartner.com/doc/2057415.

Guszcza, J., & Lucker, J. (2011). Beyond the numbers: Analytics as a strategic capability. *Deloitte Review*, Issue 8. Retrieved from www.deloitte.com/view/en_US/us/Insights/Browse-by-Content-Type/deloitte-review/index.htm.

Manyika, J., Chui, M., Brown, B. Bughin, J., Dobbs, R., Roxburgh, C., & Byers, A. H. (2011). Big data: The next frontier for innovation, competition, and productivity. McKinsey Global Institute. Retrieved at: www.mckinsey.com/insights/business_technology/big_data_the_next_frontier_for_innovation.

Morton, M. S. (1971). *Management decision systems: Computer-based support of decision making.* Boston, MA: Harvard University Press.

Negash, S., & Gray, P. (2008). Business intelligence. In F. Burstein & C. Holsapple (Eds.), *Heidelberg handbook on decision support systems*, Vol. 2 (pp. 175–192). Berlin, Germany: Springer Berlin Heidelberg.

Power, D. J. (2000). *Web-based and model-driven decision support systems: Concepts and issues.* AMCIS 2000 Proceedings. Paper 387.

Power, D. J. (2002). *Decision support systems: Concepts and resources for managers.* Westport, CT: Greenwood/Quorum.

Power, D. J. (2007). A brief history of decision support systems. Version 4.0. Retrieved February 2, 2014 from http://DSSResources.COM/history/dsshistory.html.

Sauter, V. L. (1997). *Decision support systems: An applied managerial approach.* Chichester, New York: John Wiley.

Seiner, R. S. (2005). Data steward roles & responsibilities. *The Data Administration Newsletter*, July 1, 2005. Retrieved January 31, 2014 from www.tdan.com/view-articles/5236/.

Silver, M. (1991). *Systems that support decision makers: Description and analysis.* Chichester, New York: John Wiley.

Sprague, R. H., Jr. (1980). A framework for the development of decision support systems management. *Information Systems Quarterly*, 4(4), 1–26.

Terkla, D. G. (2012, Winter). Institutional dashboards: Navigational tool for colleges and universities. *AIR Professional File*, Number 123. Tallahassee, FL: Association for Institutional Research.

The Data Warehouse Institute. (2014). BI maturity model. Retrieved on January 30, 2014 from http://tdwi.org/pages/maturity-model/maturity-model-home.aspx.

Webopedia.com. (2014). What is web analytics? Retrieved on February 8, 2014 from www.webopedia.com/TERM/W/Web_analytics.html.

Wells, D. (2008). The changing face of business intelligence. Retrieved on February 4, 2014 from www.b-eye-network.com/view/9007.

14

STRATEGIC PLANNING IN A GLOBAL UNIVERSITY

Big Challenges and Practical Responses

Julie Wells

Introduction

What does it mean to claim to be a 'global university' and what might such an entity look like? Given massively increased international student mobility over the past two decades, and the fact that more and more universities are describing their values, their mission, and their research and other academic activity as 'global,' it may seem an unnecessary question. University rankings tools point to a number of indicators—most notably international diversity of staff and students—as defining characteristics, and it is relatively easy to find other recognized measures: student and staff mobility across borders, for examples, or the number and value of international teaching partnerships and research collaborations.

But the 'global university' and the internationalization of higher education itself are not end points we have reached; rather they are evolving concepts that progressively reflect the effects of globalization, and are shaping the strategies of universities. The 'global university,' therefore, is more than a bundle of characteristics that reflect international activity. It can be used to describe an institutional form or forms that are still taking shape, linked to the internationalization of higher education more generally. This chapter reflects on that evolution, considering what it might mean to be a 'global' university now and in the future, and in particular the challenges it raises in terms of strategic planning and institutional research.

What Is a Global University?

In defining a global university, we might start with the bundle of characteristics used by international rankings agencies to define 'internationalization.' The *Times*

World Universities Ranking uses the ratio of international staff and students and the proportion of a university's research journal publications that have at least one international co-author. The *Times* rankings reward higher volumes of international students and staff with 7.5% of its total score, and a competitor, the *QS World University Rankings*, weigh international students and staff at 10% of its total score.

At 10% or less, internationalization, per se, may not seem highly weighted in such rankings. However, increasing attention to international rankings in itself reflects the fact that reputation is now measured in global terms, and that internationalization is a driver of reputation and/or a point of differentiation—particularly for universities that may be at a disadvantage in relation to other measures. Success in the global competition for 'talent'—staff and students—will also drive reputation in more traditional indicators of institutional strength relating to research and teaching, and vice versa.

There are other powerful reasons for universities to both adopt and prioritize internationalization. It can be a positive response to change, and specifically to the mobility of people, money, and ideas and the dominance of new technologies associated with globalization.

De Wit (2014) cites Altbach's definition of globalization as "the broad economic, technological, scientific trends that directly affect higher education, and are largely inevitable in the contemporary world," and internationalization as referring to "specific policies and programs undertaken by governments, academic systems, institutions and even individual departments to support student and staff exchanges, encourage collaborative research overseas, set up joint teaching programs in other countries, or a myriad of initiatives" (quoted in de Wit, 2014, pp. 100–101; see also Altbach, Reisberg, & Rumbley, 2009).

As such, internationalization within higher education can be framed as an altruistic project with potentially positive outcomes, including the spread of knowledge to people regardless of location (Agnew, 2012; de Wit, 2014; Marginson, 2014; Tiffin & Rajasingham, 2003). It can also be seen as a positive enabler of globalization, using technologies to support the global spread of ideas and expanding access to affordable education. The relatively recent eruption of Massive Open Online Courses (MOOCs) has lent new fervor to this ideal of internationalization, with Thomas Friedman arguing that, in relation to online courses delivered across national borders and on unprecedented scale, "Nothing has more potential to lift more people out of poverty—by providing them an affordable education to get a job or improve in the job they have. Nothing has more potential to unlock a billion more brains to solve the world's biggest problems" (Friedman, 2013, p. SR1).

In Friedman's comments we find reflections of three key ideologies described by Stier (2004) as at play in higher education internationalization: idealism (the idea of internationalization as a force for improving the human condition), educationalism (the valuing of learning for its own sake), and instrumentalism (a means to maximize economic growth and productivity). Instrumentalism in relation to international higher education does not apply just to learning outcomes. It applies also to institutions, as international education in particular can be a notably lucrative activity that can contribute to the health of providers' operations. Australia, one of the earliest success stories in international education, provides a practical example of how what was once peripheral to institutions' financial sustainability is now at its core: in 1990, revenue from international students provided $139 million (Australian) or 2.9% of sectoral revenue. In 2012, it stood at $4.13 billion (Australian) or 16.4% of total revenue to universities. In some Australian universities, the proportion of revenue gained from international education approaches 40% (Australian Government, 2013). If revenue derived from research, philanthropy, and non-teaching related commercial activity is excluded from the total, the proportion is significantly higher.

Competition for the international student dollar is intensified by predictions that demand for higher education will continue to grow, but potentially at a slower rate than hitherto. Lawton et al. (2013) predicted that the balance of mobility will shift across the globe, as more students from countries that have been significant exporters of higher education (the US, the UK, and Australia, for example) travel abroad to study and other countries (particularly in Asia) develop in-country higher education capability. Add to this the as yet unrealized impact of MOOCs on student choice and mobility, and the challenge to maintain and manage an international student profile becomes potentially more intense than ever. Research funding, too, is increasingly a global game—not only in terms of industry funding, but also through national governments opening funding to international providers and rewarding international collaboration.

International activity aside, one of the determinants of a 'global university' has to be in some part the claiming of the term. While internationalization is occurring throughout higher education, not all universities identify as 'global' in scope and mission, or claim the title of 'global university.' Those that do tend to engage in international activity (especially teaching) do so on a large scale. To claim to be a 'global university' is also a positioning choice, whereby 'global' characteristics become fundamental to the university's ethos, mission, and activities. To be consciously global, therefore, is to offer more than a diverse student and staff population, or opportunities for study across borders: it implies a global orientation and places internationalization of curriculum, student and staff experience, and services and outcomes at the heart of the university's ethos and mission, and at the core of its strategy. A "global university" can also imply new organizational forms, as well as a different strategic positioning. It carries with it a set of fresh challenges in relation to institutional planning and research, some of which are considered below.

Framing Mission and Values

A significant challenge for institutional researchers and strategic planners is developing a planning process that is able to address both local and global priorities.

This is important not least because most universities are essentially products of the nation state and a 'nation-building' role is ascribed to them (Marginson, 2014). There is also an implicit connection between the mission of universities and the needs of the state, insofar as university mission statements espouse the role universities can play in creating a richer culture, a robust economy, and a more prosperous and productive populace—in short, supporting the 'public good,' as defined by the society in which they are situated.

This is hardly surprising when we consider that many universities and higher education institutions are established by the state or under state regulation. Thus, while aspiring to be global, they cannot readily dissociate their interests and activities from the requirements of the state. Apart from educating graduates, they may be sites for testing and advancing government policy and contributing to the capacity and legitimacy of the state itself (Pusser, 2014). Private or for-profit higher education providers can also be subject to state-based accreditation and local regulation, and many are recipients of some form of state funding, so they too may find themselves expected to respond to some degree to the government's economic and policy agendas.

Public or private not-for-profit universities in particular are subject to tensions between meeting the needs of the society that has shaped their evolution while engaging in teaching and research that is directed toward global imperatives and aspirations (Agnew, 2012; Marginson, 2014). To take the latter course at the expense of the former runs the risk of alienating a significant group of stakeholders, as well as risking funding.

This challenge relates not just to the perceptions of external stakeholders, but also to those within. Agnew (2012) describes a dichotomous view within institutional cultures regarding internationalization. She suggests that university staff may espouse the values and benefits of internationalization while at the same time seeing global and local needs as existing in opposition to each other. She argues that such dichotomy can impede the internationalization change process.

Overcoming such tensions in the context of planning and institutional research may require a redefinition of the community of stakeholders. What does 'region' mean to a global university, for example? Should it refer to the nation or state that invests in its activities and frames regulation, or should it be defined in terms of some transnational hinterland? Or might it refer to communities of scholars and practitioners active in key disciplines, wherever they might be located? And what does it mean for engagement with such communities? If, for example, an Australian university has at its core a commitment to lifting participation in higher education by people suffering educational disadvantage, that will obviously require specific strategies for an Australian population, but what might that mean to potential students in Beijing or Bangalore? These are among the first order of questions to consider in adopting planning frameworks and methodologies to support a global mission and purpose.

Marginson (2014) suggests that part of this project lies in the redefinition of institutional mission and the measures of its success. This includes a rethinking of the concept of 'public good' as having global as well as local ramifications. He refers to the definition in Kaul, Grunberg, and Stern (1999) of 'global public goods' as those "that have a significant element of non-rivalry and/or non-excludability and are made broadly available across populations on a global scale . . . and affect more than one group of countries'" (p. 60). Marginson (2014) offers examples of 'global public goods,' such as interuniversity scholarly collaboration and capacity building in developing nations, while noting that they are often under-recognized.

However, if universities are to set 'public good' objectives that align with an aspiration to be global, then they will also need measures by which to evaluate progress and success. Universities historically have drawn on state-based measures and data collections for planning and benchmarking purposes, as they enable comparisons over time and across institutions. However, the development of national or regional higher education data collections is predominantly rooted in national and state-based priorities and regulatory frameworks. Developing common higher education data standards allow better comparability across national and state-based systems of higher education. Such a project will go a long way in supporting the measurement of outcomes that are not only globally recognized but also comparable across borders. To do so requires institutional leaders and planners to look at meaningful measures that may exist outside national and state-based data collections and are relevant to global goals, while drawing on national systems for points of comparability and commonality.

As Borden et al. (2013) and Vorhees and Hinds (2012) argue, institutional researchers themselves can play a key role in developing such data systems, working proactively in partnership with, but with some degree of independence from, the managers of state-based systems of data collection and measurement.

The Role of Regulation

Just as constituencies and mission are often locally defined, so too is regulation. Most university regulation, and the laws underpinning it, is geared toward a national rather than a global context. Governments quite reasonably regulate to protect their own investment in the work of higher education institutions, to establish frameworks for accountability for higher education providers, and to assure their quality. This supports international recognition of qualifications and can build confidence among international student markets. Effective regulation, therefore, can act as an enabler for internationalization.

However, it also poses immediate and practical problems for universities seeking to operate transnationally. Meeting the regulatory requirements of all the states in which they operate may be difficult in practical terms and requires a detailed understanding of the law and policy intent that underpins them. The operation of privacy law across different jurisdictions is one such case. Differences in privacy laws can impede the collection and transmission of planning and performance information, for example. It may also affect the rights and obligations of staff working across jurisdictions.

At a deeper level, differences in regulation may also reflect cultural differences with which planners and administrators working transnationally must grapple. For example, in Australia, universities and higher education providers are required to demonstrate that they meet certain standards in relation to intellectual freedom in order to be registered by the Tertiary Education Quality and Standards Agency. Section 4.2 of the legislated threshold standards for registration requires that "the higher education provider promotes and protects free intellectual inquiry and expression in its higher education learning, teaching, and research activities."

Their capacity to meet these standards across all jurisdictions may be compromised in countries where such values and behaviors are defined differently or not privileged, or where compliance activity may conflict with other laws. This can be an impediment for national and international reputation as well as regulatory compliance. A number of universities operating transnationally, for example, have found that different regard for intellectual freedom in the 'host' country creates ethical and reputational problems for their academic staff and their administration.

There is no ready answer to these contradictions. However, the case for transnational policy frameworks that allow for consistency in the development of local law becomes more compelling. There is also a role for national governments in rethinking regulation to facilitate internationalization in an era when the imperative for universities to act globally is growing (Barber, Donnelly, & Rizvi, 2013). In the case of higher education, government-to-government work in developing mutual recognition and registration of providers as well as qualifications will become increasingly important, in large part because of the risks to quality and student confidence that inconsistent regulation raises. The problem, and the nature of the solutions required, suggests the need for a strong engagement by institutions with governments in seeking practical resolutions of issues relating to transnational differences in law and regulation.

Universities also need to understand and address their own role as regulators. Their own approach to internal regulation (in the form of statute, policy, and procedures and frameworks for development and implementation) can play a part in effectively meeting the requirements of a global strategy. Institutional policy and procedure frames institutional activity with a series of rules located within a framework of institutional values and behaviors. It is a reflection and a driver of institutional culture. If a university is aspiring to be truly global, it needs a framework for developing policy and procedure that encompasses the different conditions under which its transnational activity can operate, and the differences imposed by local regulation. At the same time, it must address the challenge of balancing internal diversity against the real risk of fragmentation.

One solution may be in the development of overarching policy frameworks that can accommodate local variation and interpretation while maintaining consistency. Policy frameworks (sometimes referred to as 'policies on policy' or 'metapolicy') set the rules for internal regulation, and in many cases define accountability and controls, and so can be powerful instruments in ensuring effective decision making.

However, matching policy frameworks to international activity remains a challenge for many universities. In a study of 43 Australian and eight New Zealand higher education providers, Freeman (2014) found that metapolicy—that is, the policy framework that defines and governs the making of policy itself—tends to assume a single university-wide focus without necessarily clarifying the place or relevance of location-dependent policy and instruments. She also noted that the intersection between policy development and compliance requirements was rarely addressed in the subjects of her study. This would obviously pose problems for universities operating across multiple jurisdictions, as the capacity for local compliance regimes to be at odds with university policy multiplies. There is a need, therefore, for internal processes of policy development to encompass awareness and knowledge of relevant regulation, and to engage institutional stakeholders across all sites of activity. There may also be a need for metapolicy to define circumstances and instruments that enable the development of local procedures consistent with law and regulation while remaining true to a set of institutional policy tenets. Often metapolicy is perceived (rightly) as part of an effective risk management, ensuring that institutional rules are clearly defined and understood. However, too strong a focus on the risk and 'policing' aspects of policy development may impede its effectiveness as an enabler of strategy, as the application of such rules across jurisdictions becomes important for operations and reputation transnationally.

Practical Planning—Where Is the Center?

As this discussion on regulation reflects, planning in a global university raises questions about the locus of control: where decisions are taken and enacted. If a university is truly 'global,' operating physically or virtually across borders, it may not be clear where the center resides, or whether it is even useful to think in these terms. Is a global university ideally a federation of parts, or a 'head office' with a series of 'branch campuses,' or a whole new institutional form?

In terms of practical planning, different models can be considered. To be effective, however, they must have global identity and scope at their core. The model of planning whereby international or transnational activities are treated as 'add-ons' to core institutional activities will not work in developing and implementing strategy for a global university. A planning approach that contemplates global activity but is rooted in the culture, values, and laws of the 'host' nation may reinforce the perceptions of transnational education as constituting a new form of colonialism. Lack of understanding of local cultural values or business practices can also prove to be practical impediments to universities' transnational activities (Welch, 2011;

Wilkins & Huisman, 2012). By the same token, planning that is specific to each location and that is not coordinated across all sites of activity creates the risk of fragmentation and inefficiency.

Planning and institutional research that enables some degree of integration across local/national and international requirements is called for. It may be helpful to map the governance and management structures across locations to support development of a clear set of organizational relationships. This enables some degree of decentralization of decision making and local autonomy without compromising the whole. At the same time, such an approach should be accompanied by strong consultative mechanisms to enable the input of those involved with all facets of the organization's activity. Institutional knowledge needs to flow in multidirectional channels. This is especially important in managing risk: without strong contextual knowledge of all aspects of an institution's activity, the risks associated with internationalization—for example, in relation to the student experience—may be missed or neglected.

Responding to Rankings

What Marginson (2013) describes as the "shiny bright and brittle world of university rankings" (p. 139) exerts considerable influence over the reputation and strategies of universities. He argues that the three main global university rankings "now sustain a distinctive global landscape shaped by status competition" (p. 140). Potential students and their parents refer to them as guides to institutional quality, and universities use them as marketing tools. University leaders invest significant resources in analyzing their place in the rankings and in developing strategies designed to improve performance. University performance in various rankings can in turn influence government policy, and in some cases are used as indicators of quality of the skills of the citizenry: for example, Dutch and Danish immigration laws have privileged qualifications from high-ranking universities in assessing applications for skilled migration (Hazelkorn, 2011).

However, they are also the subject of fierce critique and debate as to whether they can truly claim to be proxies for institutional quality, much of it from within universities themselves. The methodology of the three main rankings schema— the *Academic Ranking of World Universities*, the *QS World University Rankings*, and the *Times Higher Education World University Rankings*—are criticized for subjectivity, relying as they do on composite indexes that privilege research and are largely input focused (Hazelkorn, 2011; Marginson, 2013). Consequently, rankings favor older, research-intensive universities with large science and medicine faculties and so reinforce a particular institutional paradigm. For some commentators this rigidity, coupled with rankings' influence in driving institutional behavior, makes them an active deterrent to institutional innovation (Barber et al., 2013). Performance is also subject to volatility, as more institutions enter the ranking exercise and methodologies shift in ways that may not have been predicted.

For universities aspiring to be global in scope and mission, rankings pose particular challenges. As previously noted, the main university rankings afford a relatively low weight to some of the more superficial characteristics of global universities, such as diversity of staff and student populations. Not every university or higher education institution is included in rankings, which further limits their value in terms of benchmarking. Moreover, some of the activity that is broadly recognized as essential for internationalization—the development of globally relevant curricula, for example, or global employability of graduates—is not yet measured nor ranked. Even more problematically, some of the characteristics of transnational universities can actually set an institution back in global rankings. For example, students taught transnationally by a partner institution may inflate the student–staff ratios of the host institution because some of the staff who teach them are employed by partner institutions and are therefore not included in an institution's staffing profile. Such problems reflect the low value ascribed to internationalization, per se, but also the relatively static nature of rankings and the measures they draw upon in the face of a rapidly transforming sector.

However, it is difficult if not impossible for any university, particularly those aspiring to position themselves as global universities, to resist the siren call of university rankings schema, as rankings themselves are global in their reach and impact. The challenges for institutional research, therefore, go beyond lifting the performance of their own institution: they go to the challenge of influencing the rankings schema themselves to the characteristics of a global university and adapt to a sector that is changing rapidly.

Excellence in universities will always rest with the quality of education and research. Those universities that are blazing a trail in transnational education and research may also contribute to the creation of new paradigms for excellence in teaching and research, and measures that support them.

Conclusion

Several broad points can be drawn from this analysis. First, the concept of the 'global university' goes beyond the internationalization of curriculum and staff and student experience, and implies the emergence of new institutional forms to support this activity. It raises questions about the locus of institutional control, how an institution understands quality, and how services may most effectively be delivered to support mission and vision. Contemplating such questions requires a rethink of the sort of planning tools and business intelligence that are required to ensure success.

Second, the role of government, and its relationship to higher education provision, becomes more, and not less, significant in the operations of a global university. This may seem paradoxical or counterintuitive, given that international higher education and research will inevitably operate outside policy or legislative requirements of any one jurisdiction. It follows, however, that international activity requires engagement with more than one set of legislative and regulatory require-ments. This requires a different form of government relations: one that is focused on balancing the needs and interests of multiple jurisdictions with the mission and strategy of the university. Internationalization may loosen some of the traditional historic ties between the state and the university as it opens up new avenues for revenue generation, teaching, and research, but those relationships are being trans-formed by governments' strong stake in internationalization itself.

As it seeks new ways to fulfill education outcomes among its citizenry and compete in a global market for ideas and innovation, almost every government around the world is trying to encourage internationalization of higher education through facilitating education export and/or encouraging foreign providers to establish presences in-country. This creates opportunities for fresh dialogue, as gov-ernment can be an enabler for internationalization in higher education through policies that support, for example, facilitating opportunities for collaboration and student mobility. Government's development of globally relevant regulation, par-ticularly in relation to accreditation and quality assurance, can also be supportive. Conversely, policy and regulation that is blind to the implications for transnational activity will be an active constraint. Engagement with governments across borders will also require a different sort of government engagement than hitherto, and one that may support successful planning in a global university.

Such engagement, for example, can assist in the collection of data to inform business analytics, evidence-based planning, and performance benchmarking. Such engagement can also assist in regulation that supports transnational education and research activity. It can also go to a more sophisticated discussion regarding the possible forms that a partnership between institutions and the state might take in achieving mutual objectives in a world where global influence and impact is highly prized. Other industries also operating across transnational boundaries can become both exemplars and participants in such partnerships, providing examples of different governance and management forms that might inform future university planning.

Third, within the institution, attention must be paid to organizational culture if a strategic plan is to be more than an artifact. The more complex an operating environment becomes, the more interaction and engagement between decision-makers and strategists may be needed in order to achieve planning objectives (Bradley, Lowell, & Smit, 2012).

In a global university, operating across borders and potentially with a physical and virtual presence, this is a particular challenge. In one sense, it is a challenge common to all large and complex organizations with a transnational presence. For universities, which have always had a global remit in terms of the generation and transmission of knowledge, it is complicated by the fact that they are in many ways products of a particular community that defines to some extent its 'public good' role. Managing this tension in a planning sense will require a clear understanding of the locus of decision making, identification and communication with a more complex group of stakeholders, and, as always, institutional research that is relevant and accessible. There is no single path to success. However, in a global university, it will be more important than ever for planners and institutional researchers to stay close to the day-to-day operating realities of their institution while supporting far-sighted vision if they are to effectively support its mission.

References

Agnew, M. (2012). A false dichotomy of serving either the local or the global community, and its impact on the internationalization of the university, *Journal of Higher Education Policy and Management, 34*(5), 473–489.

Altbach, P., Reisberg, L., & Rumbley, L. (2009). *Trends in global higher education: Tracking an academic revolution.* Report prepared for the UNESCO 2009 World Conference on Higher Education.

Australian Government, Department of Education. (2013). *Finance 2012: Financial reports of higher education providers,* December 2013, https://education.gov.au/finance-publication.

Barber, M., Donnelly, K., & Rizvi, S. (2013). *An avalanche is coming: Higher education and the challenge ahead.* London, UK: Institute for Public Policy Research.

Borden, V., Calderon, A., Fourie, N., Lepori, B., & Bonaccorsi, A. (2013). Challenges in developing data collection systems in a rapidly evolving higher education environment. In A. Calderon & K. L. Webber (Eds.), *Global issues in institutional research, No 157,* (pp. 39–57). San Francisco, CA: Jossey Bass.

Bradley, C., Lowell, B., & Smit, S. (2012). Managing the strategic journey, *McKinsey Quarterly,* July 2012.

de Wit, H. (2014). The different phases and faces of internationalism in higher education. In A. Maldonado & R. M. Bassett (Eds.), *The forefront of higher education: A Festschrift in honor of Philip S. Altbach, Higher Education Dynamics, 42,* (pp. 95–106). Dordrecht, the Netherlands: Springer.

Freeman, B. (2014). Benchmarking Australian and New Zealand university meta-policy in an increasingly regulated tertiary environment, *Journal of Higher Education Policy and Management, 1(*14), 74–87.

Friedman, T. (2013). Revolution hits the universities, *New York Times,* January 26, 2013, published p. SR1, also retrieved from: www.nytimes.com/2013/01/27/opinion/sunday/friedman-revolution-hits-the-universities.html.

Hazelkorn, E. (2011). Questions abound as the college-rankings race goes global, *The Chronicle of Higher Education,* March 13, 2011. New York, NY: Macmillan.

Kaul, I., Grunberg, I., & Stern, M. (Eds.). (1999). *Global public goods.* New York, NY: Oxford University Press.

Lawton, W., Ahmed, M., Angulo, T., Axel-Berg, A., Burroes, A., & Katsomitros, A. (2013). *Horizon scanning: What will higher education look like in 2020?* London, UK: Observatory for Borderless Higher Education.

Marginson, S. (2013). Australia and world university rankings. In S. Marginson (Ed.), *Tertiary education policy in Australia.* Centre for the Study of Higher Education, University of Melbourne, (pp. 139–140), Melbourne, AU.

Marginson, S. (2014). Higher education and the public good. In P. Gibbs & R. Barnett (Eds.), *Thinking about higher education,* (pp. 53–70). London, UK: Springer.

Pusser, B. (2014). Forces in tension: The state, civil society and the market in the future of the university. In P. Gibbs & R. Barnett (Eds.), *Thinking about higher education,* (pp. 71–90). London, UK: Springer.

Stier, J. (2004). Taking a critical stance towards internationalization ideologies in higher education: Idealism, instrumentalism and educationalism, *Globalisation, Societies and Education, 2*(1), 1–28.

Tiffin, J., & Rajasingham, L. (2003). *The global virtual university.* London, UK: Routledge.

Vorhees, R. A., & Hinds, T. (2012). Out of the box and into the office: Institutional research for changing times. In R. D. Howard, G. W. McLaughlin, & W. E. Knight (Eds.), *The handbook of institutional research,* (pp. 73–85). San Francisco, CA: Jossey Bass/Wiley.

Welch, A. (2011). *Higher education in South East Asia: Blurring borders, changing balance.* Abingdon, UK: Routledge.

Wilkins, S., & Huisman, J. (2012). The international branch campus as transnational strategy in higher education, *Higher Education, 64*(5), 627–645.

15

IN LIGHT OF GLOBALIZATION, MASSIFICATION, AND MARKETIZATION

Some Considerations on the Uses of Data in Higher Education

Angel J. Calderon

Introduction

One of the main activities that define the nature and practice of institutional research (IR) is the systematic gathering of data, careful analysis, and subsequent reporting to assist in decisions related to institutional management and performance. Typically, offices of institutional research and planning are seen as the official sources of statistics and the keepers of performance-related information about HEIs. In countries like the US and Australia, the visibility and status of institutional research has risen as a consequence of the legislative requirement for the systematic provision of statistical information and the hunger for timely data, among many reasons. This paper invites institutional researchers, planners, policy analysts, and decision makers to think more broadly about the spectrum of policy and planning implications for each other in relation to information and data management.

There are a number of ways in which institutional data is used for decision support. For example, it is used to assess student learning as well as the effectiveness of academic programs, administrative units, and institutions themselves. Evaluative data is used to improve programs and institutions. It informs and drives institutional planning processes and supports academic-related endeavors such as course database guides, which are designed to inform students on study choices. Through these efforts, it supports decision making, and is invariably linked to having a good strategic leadership.

The sophistication of both institutional record keeping and data analysis has considerably evolved as postsecondary education has matured. According to the UNESCO Institute for Statistics (http://uis.unesco.org/), there were about 28.5 million students enrolled in tertiary education worldwide in 1970, increasing to 99.5 million by 2000. Between 2000 and 2012, tertiary education enrollments worldwide almost doubled to 196 million. This increase in enrollments has resulted in the proliferation of higher education institutions (HEIs), which, according to Webometrics (www.webometrics.info/en), numbered more than 22,000 worldwide in 2014. As a consequence of globalization and technological transformation, access to information, and innovation, the knowledge economy has exponentially increased and is contributing to competition between institutions for securing scarce financial resources, primarily from governments.

The massive explosion in the number of students and institutions cannot be seen in isolation to the changes that are occurring in other facets of human activity. In recent decades we have witnessed a series of reforms in HE that have not only accelerated institutional reform (e.g., governance and management, modes of funding, and accountability), but these reforms have opened a wave of profound change that is challenging the foundation of institutions, including the emergence of new structural models of delivery, curriculum, and financing. HE has become a focus of policy makers as HEIs play a crucial role in innovation and economic development (Dill & Van Vught, 2010; Musselin & Teixeira, 2014); Castells even described HE as "the engine of development in the new world economy" (as cited by Hazelkorn, 2012, p. 339).

These institutional changes require that institutional researchers and planners build strong and robust systems to support institutions in their strategic directions, but also to assist institutions to fulfill legislative, regulatory, and other requirements from external actors (such as governments, funding and accreditation agencies, and university rankers). In fact, it can be argued that in the ongoing massification of HE, managing copious amounts of data can be a determining factor for institutional success and thus remains a relevant issue in our globalized world (Manyika et al., 2011).

Gone Are the Days . . .

Gone are the days when HEIs officials were content with snapshots of information on a range of institutional activities at a given point in time. In the past, institutions managed records in paper form and were mechanically handled to determine, for example, how many students were enrolled, which in turn would be used to allocate space, work out a timetable for lectures and tutorials, or determine library requirements for acquisition of books, journals, and other academic resources. Over the years, institutions have embarked on self-studies with the purpose of investigating issues relevant to their circumstances, but also to identify points of distinctiveness for the communities they serve. This process has resulted in a widening of the requirements for information about students, staff, and resources of institutions. In past years, review studies conducted by institutions were focused on evaluation to assess effectiveness of programs, departments, faculties, or whole institutions. Some of these reviews may have been instigated by institution leaders themselves, but also may have been part of accreditation requirements from professional bodies and government agencies. Stuit (1960) provides a historical summary, from an American perspective, of these early evaluations of institutions and programs. A reader of those early institutional self-studies and institutional fact books (e.g., a published compendium of facts) may note that the intentionality, context, and language, among many things, are very different to the tone one observes now in similar self-studies and fact books. Today, institutional fact books are strategic tools designed to boost an institution's relative standing or a strategic tool for decision making.

Also, gone are the days when institutional fact books were diligently prepared by IR offices and proudly sent to other institutions primarily to fill the public-relations and historical-records purposes of institutional achievement (Daly & Viehland, 1996). These were the times when fact books were the statistical bibles of institutions and contained a myriad of information to support decisions for a range of internal and external stakeholders. The fact book was seen as the definitive, authoritative, and public data source for institutions, and the basis for guiding the planning and institutional research agenda. T. Elliot reports that institutional fact books most likely had their roots in publications designed by national and regional organizations whose purpose was to make statistical information available in a convenient, understandable, and accurate manner (as cited in Jones, 1996).

The origins of the institutional fact book then can be traced to around the late 1860s with the publication of *Statistics of Land-Grant Colleges and Universities*, published by the US Office of Education. In the mid-1950s, the Southern Regional Education Board started to publish a fact book on HE with the purpose of making information freely available but also to encourage uniform reporting of data (Jones, 1996). These early publications constitute the foundations for the cyclical reporting of institutional data, and for the development of the core functions that are attributed to the practice of institutional research.

Over the past few decades, the field of information management (including reporting and analysis) as an authoritative art form has changed considerably by a number of interrelated influences. Governments around the world have enacted legislation requiring greater transparency in the way institutions manage scarce public resources. Government officials have also mandated the release of information, and in many cases have developed tools to compare institutions not only in terms of student profile but also to highlight critical areas of performance. Technological transformation has exponentially increased the need for more information that is not only frequent, but also more time-sensitive and dynamic. Furthermore, the availability of analytical tools has enabled users of information to drill deeper in order to explore new dimensions and draw on unexplored relationships about the data that is collected. Because the boundaries of institutions and spheres of influence transcend local or national jurisdictions, the worldwide systematization of data collections has occurred as national systems of education have evolved, from elite to massified, and continued to embrace deregulation, marketization, and globalization. All of these developments have contributed to the availability and dissemination of information.

A Hunger for Information

Increased accountability and prestige seeking has required institutions to become savvier in the way resources are allocated and spent. The emergence of performance indicators as a tool of institutional management in HE gained significance because it has enabled the systematic measurement of institutional inputs, processes, and outcomes against objectives, either developed by institutions or governments. These efforts can be measurably helpful for institutional improvement, but they can also unwittingly tempt misinterpretations and/or create confusion among users of the data. The tomes of data readily available can be helpful in decision support, but only when used correctly.

Regimes of performance measurements have continued to evolve not only to satisfy requirements of institutions themselves but also as part of national systems of education and for being pillars for regional or national innovation. Globally, HE has become a major policy issue and is a service sector that has been heavily influenced by the New Public Management (NPM) doctrine (Hood, 1995). Musselin and Teixeira (2014) argue that this doctrine is responsible for the introduction of managerial techniques in HE borrowed from the private sector. NPM has influenced a wave of wide reforms in most industry sectors, including the public sector. NPM also influenced the use of techniques such as performance indicators, benchmarking, and total quality management, which have become an integral part of the HE discourse.

It is useful to consider the purposes of performance management. Kells (1992) describes three major uses for performance indicators within an organization: 1) to explain to others what an organization is doing; 2) to make internal management choices on an ongoing basis; and 3) to have periodic self-assessment and guide planning processes. IR practitioners need to keep in mind these major uses when reporting as these are relevant in correctly reporting institutional performance and for maintaining transparency, integrity, and consistency in the process.

Governments are a key external audience for performance management information; however they are increasingly becoming active participants in the dissemination of information and development of tools about performance of HEIs. For example, the Australian government has systematically released reports on institutional performance since 1994 (Borden et al., 2013); the Higher Education Funding Council of England published the first set of indicators in 1999 on behalf of all four UK founding councils (www.hefce.ac.uk/data/pi/). In the US, the Integrated Postsecondary Education Data Systems (IPEDS) is a collaborative effort among postsecondary institutions (http://nces.ed.gov/ipeds/), required by the US Department of Education for those institutions who wish to receive Title IV funds. Government uses of data have been used to generally fund institutions for a variety of purposes, including teaching and research activities, but data have also been used for specific or targeted purposes. As a consequence, the importance and use of information has become vital to the operations and viability of institutions. At the same time, it has exposed pitfalls or misuses in the way information is used. One could argue that there is a market orientation regarding the need for timely, accurate, reliable, and transparent information.

The fact that there has been a proliferation of performance tools reflects the willingness of institutions to seek mechanisms for improvement (whether instigated by institutions or imposed by government) and to strive for excellence. It is also a reflection that the higher education systems in countries like the US, the UK, Australia, and many others in developed nations, are mature markets.

Rankings Enter the Higher Education Arena

University rankings have not only become a force in the HE domain, but have also prompted an ongoing review cycle for institutions that seek to improve their standing or to become eligible for consideration by the various ranking schemas. However, the number of institutions that feature in the top 500 of the ranking, like QS, *Times Higher Education, Academic Ranking of World Universities,* or the *Leiden Ranking,* represent less than 5 percent of the world's total HEIs.

Rankings of colleges, universities, academic departments, disciplines, and specialized schools have been ongoing for more than a hundred years in the US (Stuart, 1995). In more recent times, the visibility of college and university rankings began when the *U.S. News & World Report* published its first ranking of institutions with undergraduate programs in 1983 (Stuart, 1995). However, global rankings as such only commenced in 2003 with the publication of the *Academic Ranking of World Universities* from Jiao Tong University in China. In contrast to performance indicators, rankings collapse a variety of indicators into a single measure (Daraio, Bonaccorsi, & Simar, 2014) and this raises a variety of issues, such as validity, reliability, and comparability of information. Performance indicators or benchmarking, for example, tend to be generally more attuned to the mission and goals of institutions, whereby a range of indicators can be selected; on the other hand, rankings are designed as tools of comparison pitting institutions against each other (Usher & Savino, 2006). This results in institutions being guarded about what these rankings are intended to measure and how these periodical results impact the short to long term on a variety of fronts, least to say the impact on financial viability. Yet, rankings are attractive in that they appear to have a degree of simplicity, creating a popular appeal (Hazelkorn, 2012).

All indications show that university rankings will remain with us, and may be seen as a performance measurement regime that is intended to not only compare institutions on dimensions that are consistent with the mission and goals of institutions, but also against objectives that are well beyond the control of institutions (or even national systems). These efforts prompt a greater need for heightened information about the institution and often are presented in a way to put the institution's best foot forward.

Intended and Unintended Uses of Data

Information gathered by HEIs is needed for multiple purposes in institutional management. The collection of information from various parts of institutions (as entities or strategic actors) is driven by the need for institutional success. In some countries, governments try to assert a form of control on the management of institutions to deliver against the intended outcomes of government contributing to national economic competiveness (Kehm, 2014). In this regard, the way information is managed from the point of collection to analysis is paramount to the success of institutions. An increased use in the information collected by institutions is helpful because it provides the basis for good decision making and autonomous strategic leadership (Hazelkorn, 2012). However, it also exposes an issue that not only hinders the work of institutional research, but may also impact the overall stability of institutions: the unintended consequences or misuses of data. In light of stakeholder demands for more evidence-based facts for decision making as well as the ongoing lure of rankings, this issue of possible data misuse becomes even more apparent and in need of focused attention.

Mentioned above, there are a variety of ways in which institutional data is used, including to assess learning, academic programs, administrative units, and institutions themselves. Evaluative data can be used to improve and support decision making, and is invariably linked to having a good strategic leadership. It informs and drives institutional planning processes and supports academic-related endeavors such as course database guides, which are designed to inform students on study choices. While there are some good examples in how data is used, there are also cases that are perplexing. To illustrate, the following are examples that resonate among institutional researchers and planners across the globe:

- *Bibliometric indicators* (such as citations and H-index) are used for a variety of purposes by institutions, governments, and university rankers. As Cameron (2005) says, measures of research impact have been used far beyond their original and intended use. The original idea of bibliometric data was to assist librarians to guide the process of journal selection and de-selection. More recently, citation data are being used as measures of performance by which scientists and faculty are ranked, promoted, and funded.
- *Quality of education or teaching*. There is no consensus about how to measure teaching, and yet it is a factor used by many university rankers, often resulting in comparing apples and oranges. One of the proxy ways in which instructional quality is measured is through the student to faculty ratio. The fundamental problem with this measure is that institutions often provide limited data to the various rankers pertaining to the number of students and the

number of academic staff. Methodologically, there are significant differences in how such ratios are calculated in institutions across national systems. For example, in Australia, the calculation of student to staff ratio includes only students who are studying in Australia during the term and excludes off-shore students as well as students who are doing research programs (such as doctorates and masters by research). On the academic staff side, research-only staff members are excluded. Across countries, there are significant differences in the way academic staff are defined and, most likely, counted. Therefore, a comparison of the Australian way of calculating faculty to staff ratio to that of the US or any other country is spurious at best.

Another proxy way in which quality of teaching is measured by ranking companies is by individual items or overall satisfaction score in student or graduate surveys. These surveys can be administered by institutions themselves or part of national survey systems to current students or graduates (the latter who are recipients of such surveys several months after completing their degree). Therefore, a comparison of scores across borders is also spurious.

- *Student feedback* has been used as a tool to evaluate teachers and whole teaching departments. It often refers to information that is collected via surveys about a number of different dimensions, for example, about academic, institutional, or campus life, learning experience, and generic skills. Often this information is only reported as a composite or part of scales, and the detailed or item responses are not reported nor used. This fine detail is often the missing element that can drive up improvement on a program or discipline basis.

- The *proportion of the institution's diversity* via race/ethnicity, economic status, and/or international status are important measures, often reported in rankings and college guides. State, local, or national definitions of diversity change over time, and some institutions may not change their reporting definitions quickly to follow national definitions, which could lead to incongruent comparisons across institutions. In addition, institutions may have differing policies on how students or staff identify themselves as international. Because indicators of diversity can be critical in institutional performance measures, it is possible that some institutions may seek to adjust relativities of what is reported rather than seeking a material improvement. In addition, the need to portray levels of diversity may have unintended consequences on hiring practices that adversely affect particular student or staff groups.

- *Misunderstood definitions*. Often, data may get misinterpreted because of inconsistent or misunderstandings of data definitions. A good example is full-time equivalence (FTE) and headcount. These are often used interchangeably when they define two different sets of data. When used incorrectly, they affect enrollment projects, budgets, and estimated staff and space allocation needs. Another example is attrition and retention rates. While these two constructs are often confused as one meaning the opposite to the other, in reality, these are very different and methodologically are designed to measure different aspects of student engagement.

- **Incorrect use of statistics.** In addition to misuses of information that comes from data, so too is the problem of using the wrong statistic. Institutional researchers frequently present information as percentages, means, medians, or other statistical measures. These can be good techniques to concisely summarize data for senior leaders. However, one must know when it is best to present data as a mean versus a median, and when to include data with a zero value. As we know, a mean salary can be quite different than a median value, and including staff who are on sabbatical or otherwise earning no salary in the reporting period can dramatically change the average salary figures.

Making Sense of the Data

Because of the driving forces for the increased use of institutional information (e.g., accountability, funding, etc.) and the diverse needs from strategic actors (i.e., the state, market forces, and civil society), there are a number of dimensions that are beneficial to ponder on the usefulness and relevance of the information that is collected. IR practitioners need to consider why the data is being used and how it impacts individuals, disciplines, institutions, and national systems of education. There is often not enough time for IR practitioners to consider the facts behind requests for information, or the intrinsic purpose for data collection. Borrowing from concepts expressed by Pusser and Marginson (2013) on rankings as an instrument for the study of power in higher education, what follows are some considerations intended to guide and frame a discourse of the uses and consequences of data in higher education.

The power of data. Institutional researchers and planners have too often heard that information is power. Performance related information provides an insight into the ways in which power shapes the web of relationships between institutions, states, civil society, and social actors (Pusser & Marginson, 2013). In this regard, information and data greatly contribute to decision making at all levels of organizations and inform government policy decisions. Having access to data and controlling the way it flows contains also an element of power, as data in an aggregated or as a value-added form can be used to allocate scarce resources, impose demands for accountability, and drive calls for improvement or reform at all levels. Therefore, information that is collected by institutions can be infused with political or power influence.

Legitimacy. Information that is collected about what an institution is and does provides legitimacy to the purpose and mission of institutions and to the set of legal instruments that fund, regulate, and assess institutional performance. For example, institutions in receipt of state funds must pursue the fulfillment of the agreed objectives for education as set by government, with the information provided by institutions to government a key mechanism to legitimize education policy and to promote institution accountability for funding. On the other hand, college and university rankings as well as college guides and other performance tools have become instruments that legitimize the role of other strategic actors in the education agenda (e.g., QS *World University Rankings*). Benchmarking and research assessment exercises as well as quality assurance mechanisms are instruments that evidence the role and influence of market forces in higher education. Institutional researchers must reflect on the purposes of the information that they are requested to provide (either as part of standard data collections or ad-hoc requests) and the purposes of these requests for information.

Ideology. In a practical or utilitarian sense, the prevailing state or local government ideology is evidenced through requirements to provide certain information, such as student performance from equity or disadvantaged groups, or performance against certain institutional targets developed in accordance with agreed objectives. Every government has a program or an agenda—or, as Pusser and Marginson (2013) call it, a *distinct ideological approach*—for the provision of higher education, and this forms the basis by the way it is funded, regulated, and assessed. Beyond the sphere of the state, there are a number of mechanisms that reinforce the prevailing ideology, including market forces that affect higher education. Consider the influence of university rankings, which are being used by governments to advance their own policy agenda (e.g., in Australia, the government proposed in May 2014 fee deregulation as means to improve the standing of Australian universities in global university rankings), and in part this explains the emergence of ranking instruments with support from governments around the world.

Transparency. Over the past twenty or so years, HEIs have been mandated to provide information to governments, external agencies, and other stakeholders to evidence how institutions are spending scarce public funds and performing on a variety of objectives. All of these changes have resulted in a greater level of accountability and transparency in institutional operations. For many years, governments of all persuasions have published reports of institutional performance, but this has been insufficient to satisfy the growing interest of a variety of stakeholders for comparative information on institutions. This has fostered the emergence of a variety of accountability and transparency instruments, such as college guides, accreditation, benchmarking, quality assurance, classification systems, and rankings (Hazelkorn, 2013). For their part, institutional researchers need to assess how they contribute and advance their institutions' efforts in being accountable and transparent.

Intentionality. Institutional researchers know that HE data collections have been organized to report against particular objectives and outcomes and these depend on the jurisdiction and the dimensions they cover. While there are a variety of purposes why institutional information is submitted to departments of education or other statutory agencies, it is also a helpful process that enables the capture, validation, reporting, and transmission of such data. Data collections aside, institutional researchers need to think about the intentionality of why certain performance indicators (or data elements) are required, what these are intended to measure, why these need to be measured, and whether or not they can propose a better measurement alternative. In this regard, institutional researchers and planners can play an effective advocacy role for developing robust and valid systems.

Relevance. Against all this background, institutional researchers are urged to consider the relevance and salience of the data and information they collect, handle, report, and analyze. As the discussion above highlights, the fact that something is counted or measured does not make it right or relevant. One needs to think on the relevance of the denominator and numerator for any given indicator and whether or not that forms part of the intended narrative against the purpose or objective of the unit of measurement. Because of time constraints, competing priorities, or other compelling reasons, we can be void of clarity and purpose in what we are intending to measure or considering valid reciprocal populations for comparison.

Enablers. Institutional researchers carry a significant weight of responsibility on accounting and explaining institutional performance in terms of quality, outcomes, and productivity. This responsibility often makes them accountable for tasks for which they were not necessarily assigned, but as highlighted throughout this book, institutional researchers are catalysts for change. Decision makers and institutional research need to strive for collaborative decision making across all levels of institutions and educational systems. One way IR practitioners can start this endeavor is by being authoritative in what performance measurement regimes (and metrics) are valid, suitable, and relevant for their institutions. On the part of decision makers, they need to invest some time in communicating their vision to institutional researchers and planners.

As a way to conclude, the uses of institutional information have evolved from being one of description, context, self-study, and record of activity to one of assessment, evaluation, and ascertaining relative performance. All the information and data points being collected are shifting progressively to being one piece in the puzzle of national systems within a global context. The unintended uses of data may also continue to occur, but in order to keep the state, civil society, and market forces informed of the vested interests of all those strategic actors involved in education, institutional researchers and planners have a duty of care to maintain a narrative that is relevant, transparent, clear, and consistent with the mission and objectives of their institutions and HE systems.

References

Borden, V., Calderon, A., Fourie, N., Lepori, B., & Bonaccorsi, A. (2013). Challenges in developing data collection systems in a rapidly evolving higher education environment. In A. Calderon & K. L. Webber (Eds.), *Global issues in institutional research, New Directions for Institutional Research*, No. 157, Spring 2013, (pp. 39–57). San Francisco, CA: Jossey-Bass.

Cameron, B. (2005). Trends in the usage of ISI biliometric data: Uses and abuses, and implications. *Libraries and the Academy*, 5(1), 105–125.

Daly, R., & Viehland, D. (1996). Electronic fact books: Turning atoms into bits. In L. G. Jones (Ed.), *Campus fact books: Keeping pace with new institutional needs and challenges. New Directions for Institutional Research*, No. 91, (pp. 63–75). San Francisco, CA: Jossey Bass.

Daraio, C., Bonaccorsi, A., & Simar, L. (2014). *Rankings and university performance: A conditional multidimensional approach.* Dipartamento di Ingegneria Informatica Automatica e Gestionale Antonio Ruperti, Sapienza Universita di Roma. Technical report No. 9.

Dill, D. D., & Van Vught, F. A. (2010). *National innovation and the academic enterprise.* Baltimore, MD: Johns Hopkins University Press.

Hazelkorn, E. (2012). European 'transparency instruments': Driving the modernisation of European higher education. In P. Scott, A. Curaj, L. Vlasceanu, & L. Wilson (Eds.), *European higher education at the crossroads: Between the Bologna Process and national reforms*, (pp. 339–360). Dordrecht, the Netherlands: Springer.

Hazelkorn, E. (2013). How rankings are reshaping higher education. In V. Climent, F. Michavila, & M. Ripollés (Eds.), *Los rankings universitarios, Mitos y Realidades.* Ed. Técnos.

Hood, C. (1995). The "new public management" in the 1980s: Variations on a theme. *Accounting, Organizations and Society*, 20(2–3), 93–109.

Jones, L. G. (1996). A brief history of the fact book as an institutional research report. In L. G. Jones (Ed.), *Campus fact books: Keeping pace with new institutional needs and challenges. New Directions for Institutional Research,* No. 91, (pp. 3–26). San Francisco, CA: Jossey Bass.

Kehm, B. (2014). Global university rankings—Impacts and unintended side effects. *European Journal of Education*, 49(1), 102–112.

Kells, H. R. (1992). *Performance indicators for higher education: A critical review with policy recommendations.* Population and Human Resources Department. Education and Employment Division background paper series, no. PHREE 92/56. Washington, DC: The World Bank.

Manyika, J., Chui, M., Brown, B., Bughin, J., Dobbs, R., Roxburgh, C., & Byers, A. H. (2011). *Big data: The next frontier for innovation, competition, and productivity.* McKinsey Global Institute. Retrieved at: www.mckinsey.com/insights/business_technology/big_data_the_next_frontier_for_innovation.

Musselin, C., & Teixeira, P. N. (2014). Introduction. Reforming higher education: Public policy design and implementation. *Higher Education Dynamics, 41,* 1–17.

Pusser, B., & Marginson, S. (2013). University rankings in critical perspective. *The Journal of Higher Education, 84* (4), 544–568.

Stuart, D. (1995). Reputational rankings: Background and development. In R. D. Walleri & M. K. Moss (Eds.), *Evaluating and responding to college guidebooks and rankings. New Directions for Institutional Research*, No. 88, (pp. 13–20). San Francisco, CA: Jossey Bass.

Stuit, D. B. (1960). Evaluation of institutions and programs. *Review of Educational Research*, 30(4), 371–384.

Usher, A., & Savino, M. (2006). *A world of difference: A global survey of university league tables.* Washington, DC: Education Policy Institute. Retrieved at: www.educationalpolicy.org.

16

TOWARD A KNOWLEDGE FOOTPRINT FRAMEWORK

Initial Baby Steps

Anand Kulkarni, Angel J. Calderon, and Amber Douglas[1]

Introduction

This chapter explores the idea of a knowledge footprint for a university, as a means of identifying and measuring the impact of a university on economy, society/community, and the environment. A knowledge footprint analysis provides a mechanism that allows for strategy development, priority setting, performance evaluation, institutional benchmarking, and trade-off analysis in the tradition of decision making under uncertainty and in situations where there are multiple courses of action. Institutional research and planning professionals can play a key role in these efforts as they have the expertise and know-how in performance measurement, as well as insight into the unique role and attributes of universities. This chapter comprises four sections. Section one is a literature review that examines the impact that universities (referred to throughout this chapter as "higher education institutions"—HEIs) have on the economy, society, and the environment. It provides a backdrop and context for section two, which explores the elements of a knowledge footprint framework as a decision making tool. Section three considers the various uses of a knowledge footprint framework for HEIs as they grapple with competing claims on resources, and changing roles and responsibilities in a dynamic environment. Section four presents some challenges in developing and implementing the knowledge footprint framework.

Higher Education's Impact on Society and the Economy

The existing literature on the impact of HEI activity canvasses many elements, including HEI impact on: a local jurisdiction; the region or regions it serves; the community or communities in which it functions or has embedded in its "third mission;" national development; and global development or engagement. The perspectives from which these studies are undertaken also vary, encompassing teaching and learning, research and development, contribution to sustainable development, and environmental impact; responses to social inclusion policies; and contribution to national innovation. To this end, it is beyond the scope of this chapter to analyze all of these studies in detail. Rather, we briefly overview key commonly identified elements of HEI impact, and include a sense of how they have been measured. It is also useful to note that we refer to the impact of HEIs to indicate the set of activities, outputs, and outcomes that institutions generate across the breadth of HEI activity.

Economic Impact Studies

Studies of the impact of HEIs on society, industry, or any other dimension, either at the local or regional or national levels, have tended to focus on the economic side (Brown & Heaney, 1997). Since the 1970s, there has been a growing interest in understanding and assessing the economic impact of HEIs on a particular geographic jurisdiction. In part, demand for such studies is a consequence of governments requiring HEIs to provide economic justification for their contribution to support HE, but it is also a consequence of the democratization and massification of HE over the past forty years that has increased competition for students, resources, and academic recognition.

One of the most widely used approaches to assess institutional impact is that developed by Caffrey and Isaacs in 1971 for the American Council of Education (as cited by Stokes & Coomes, 1998). This model is built around calculating the total local spending of an institution (e.g., students, employees, and visitors). It then applies a regional economic multiplier to determine the overall economic impact and it uses cash flow data to estimate a short-term impact. Some of the limitations of the Caffrey and Isaacs method are its failure to distinguish expenditure between resident students, employers, and employees, and its failure to separately account for the short-term economic impact of HEI expenditure on the local economy as opposed to general factors shaping the local economy (Stokes & Coomes, 1998; Ohme, 2003). Since then, there have been hundreds, if not thousands, of institution-based studies conducted that have used this model. Over the years, refinements have been made to the Caffrey and Isaacs model. Drucker and Goldstein (2007) and Garrigo-Yserte and Gallo-Rivera (2010) provide an invaluable summary of selected studies of the economic impact of HEIs.

Brown and Heaney (1997) point out that some economic impact studies have focused on the skill base of the population in a given region but such approaches can lead to an overestimation of the economic impact if the effect of migration on human resource allocation is not mediated. Other studies focus on human capital inputs (e.g., Abel & Deitz, 2011; Goldstein & Luger, 1992). There is also a growing number of studies that focus on the effect of technology transfer (e.g., Anderson,

Daim, & Lavoie, 2007), entrepreneurship activities of HEIs (e.g., Bonaccorsi et al., 2013; Carree, Malva, & Santarelli, 2012; Slaughter & Rhoades, 2009), and the effect of HEI R&D on the local economy or region. The literature also addresses the effect that HEIs have on particular geographic settings, primarily at the local level (i.e., the vicinity of the institution) and the state or regional jurisdiction, while relatively fewer studies have focused at the national level. In this regard, we observe that a number of studies coming out of the United States have focused on the impact of HEIs on the local economy (e.g., Ohme, 2003), while many studies out of Europe have emphasis on regional dimensions (Garrigo-Yserte & Gallor-Rivera, 2010; Bonaccorsi et al., 2013). This discourse may be due to the nature of geopolitical dynamics in the European region. There are some studies that have a national dimension but these tend to be sparse, and often the regional impact is added up to provide a national overview (e.g., Australian Regional Universities Network, 2012). Arbo and Benneworth (2007) provide a comprehensive review of the literature on the contribution of HEIs to regional development.

Over the years, variations in microeconomic approaches to assess the impact of HEIs have been developed, and some of these focus on knowledge production functions. Florax (1992) developed a model that emphasizes the effects of HEI activity on local expenses and the development and diffusion of knowledge. Florax identified a number of dimensions by which the regional effects of HEIs can be analyzed (such as politics, demography, infrastructure, and the economy). Florax's typology is useful because it is similar to the "Political, Economic, Social and Technological analysis" (PEST—or our alternative "SPEEDI" analysis that we outline below) as used in the environmental scanning component of strategic management.

Community Engagement

Another stream in the literature on impact studies focuses on community engagement. A number of approaches have been employed to assess institutional impact. These studies assess the impact on the community (or communities) that institutions serve. Jongbloed and Benneworth (2013) provide a comprehensive review of the attempts to measure HEI impact on communities, including approaches such as the Russell Group indicators for measuring third-stream activities in the United Kingdom. Jongbloed and Benneworth argue that there are a variety of purposes underlying efforts to measure university–community engagement and that such engagement is very difficult to measure, particularly as it is a subjective task and it is difficult to identify a singular definition of what matters in HEI engagement. Further, we observe that due to differences in institutional missions, comparability of institution-based studies is difficult. No one approach will stand out because HEIs form part of a system of institutions embedded in a geographical setting that operate, function, and serve a variety of communities. These communities and their stakeholders are diverse, often spread across multiple jurisdictions, and represent diverse interests. Thus, while we observe that there is richness and depth in such studies, there is no consensus on what approach or method should be used to measure it meaningfully.

International Engagement Studies

While we believe this topic will become a focal point in the near future, presently, there are very few studies that focus on the impact of HEIs operating across national borders. While many of the economic impact studies take into account the activity generated as a result of the presence of students from abroad in university campuses (and as a consequence of residing during term in the community), the inherent international footprint or the institutional impact across borders has not yet been fully considered. Lane and Owens (2012) ponder the role of colleges and universities as economic drivers for development, with limited coverage on the international dimension. In part, this occurs because there is not a substantive body of work that has covered the footprint of institutions in the countries where they have an impact. Lane and Owens (2012) do consider however the role of HE in international trade and investment as well as training a globally competitive workforce. In light of the internationalization of institutions and integration of national systems of education with the global economy, an understanding of the exact nature and extent of a university's global footprint (or at least in the countries where they are engaged) is an important part of strategic deliberations. We see the need to develop an international engagement approach that encompasses the sum of all institutional activities across borders and how these impact outside home countries, rather than institutions simply focusing on student and staff mobility, commercial presence, and cross-border supply. In this regard, we see that the Triple Helix framework (Etzkowitz, 2003) provides a useful framework to guide knowledge-based economic and social development.

Sustainability Impact Studies

Since the 1990s, the concept of sustainability has gained prominence in understanding and measuring the impact of HEIs on the local, regional, and national jurisdictions in which they operate. While it was originally conceived to address specific environmental problems and to maintain sustainable conditions for human development, analysis has widened over time to address issues of sustainability in the way HEIs operate and manage resources (Peer & Stoneglehner, 2013) and their overall impact on the environment. These broad two applications of the concept of sustainability in HEIs have cemented the role of HEIs in the sustainability, regional development, and community engagement debate. The application of sustainability and environmental reporting has been embedded through a variety of tools such as triple bottom line reporting, institutional key performance indicators, and benchmarking against peer institutions.

University Rankings

Over the past ten years, university rankings have gained a foothold in the management of HEIs and when these are released, their results are widely debated in terms of their usefulness and worthiness. We observe that while the existing university ranking schemas aim to measure institutional performance against a range of indicators, these are generally limited with a strong focus on measuring research impact. Little attention has been paid to measuring the impact of HEIs on community, regions, or across borders. University rankings tend to focus on output and input measures rather than the outcomes that affect the way in which universities influence real economic and other activity of locations, regions, and across national borders.

The emergence of strategic tools (such as U-Map and U-Multirank), which are in response to the rise of university rankings, are enabling HEIs to develop profiling or mapping of peer or competing institutions based on a range of indicators, including against activities directed at knowledge transfer. Both U-Map and U-Multirank have a dimension that is intended to measure HEIs' efforts in regional and community engagement. However, institutions tend not to gather this information in a way that enables spatial disaggregation (i.e., distinguish activity, outcomes, and impact between a local community, region, or across borders) and there is lack of agreed definitions of indicators and metrics to use (van Vught & Ziegele, 2011).

Summary—HEI Impact Measurement

What we have observed in the available literature is a degree of agreement on the relative contribution that HEIs make to economic development (locally or regionally), but there is less consensus on social and community impacts (Bonaccorsi et al., 2013). In part this occurs because there is not a uniform approach or framework that enables an authoritative analysis (Jongbloed & Benneworth, 2013). We believe it is unrealistic to expect that there will be a model that is suitable for all HEIs but we believe that a framework is possible that provides pointers to a more comprehensive impact analysis that could be modified to reflect particular institutional characteristics. Similarly, an approach is required that captures the full global impact of HE activities, recognizing that institutions increasingly operate across borders or recruit students from abroad.

We see this as a key area for future practice, as institutional researchers continue to find ways to measure the full and interdependent institutional impact on economy, society, and environment, and seek new and better ways to present information that is meaningful. Institutional researchers can drive the development and adoption of the framework, and adapt it to suit different strategic settings, as institutions will vary in size, strategic intent, and capability, and operate in different policy contexts.

Knowledge Footprint: Toward a Framework

To address the needs we identify above, we see the need for a comprehensive approach and set of tools to capture the full and interdependent impact of HEIs, both at home and abroad. We therefore argue for something akin to a knowledge footprint framework to measure the extent and magnitude of an HEI's impact on economy, society, and the environment.

We argue that for an HEI, the size and quality of its knowledge footprint is important to develop and maintain competitive advantage. This is in the context of:

a)   Growing importance of innovation and the knowledge economy for nations;
b)   The role of HEIs as innovative hubs[2];
c)   Growing expectations on HEIs to be key players in solving critical challenges such as environmental issues and health solutions; and
d)   Reputational effects associated with the institutional profile.

As noted above, there has been increasing recognition of an HEI's contribution to sustainability. This mirrors broader trends toward identifying environmental impact, with the recognition of an organization's and nation's environmental footprint, i.e., the use of physical resources (land, physical inputs) relative to availability of resources, now a well-known concept (Dill & Van Vught, 2010). While we recognize a separate body of literature linked to innovation and the role of HEIs, we contend that the concept of a knowledge footprint, i.e., the application and diffusion of an institution's intellectual capital relative to resourcing and contextual factors, is less well-known.

Whereas the objective of an institution and nation is generally to *reduce* its environmental footprint as far as is feasible, having regard to economic, social, and, obviously, environmental factors, the knowledge footprint is to be *enlarged* to allow for wider and deeper knowledge application and diffusion and solutions sought for complex problems, subject, of course, to resource constraints.

A knowledge footprint approach would assess to what extent, and in what manner, an HEI's teaching, research, and other "offers" were developed, applied, and diffused. A knowledge footprint extends beyond the traditional concepts of university success in research and teaching to consider factors such as community engagement and community impact, influence on society, urban/city character and tradition, and the capacity to address economic and social need. As such, the knowledge footprint of an institution is becoming more complex and multifaceted due to changing roles, expectations, and challenges facing HEIs.

Challenges facing HEIs include pressures to become more commercially oriented, with attendant competition from other sources of knowledge provision, e.g., other research and educational institutions; growing expectations and evidence that HEIs are and will play a stronger role in economic and social matters in particular locations; and increased knowledge flows across institutional and spatial boundaries, aided by student and staff/researcher mobility, and online communication.

A Framework for the Knowledge Footprint

In the framework presented in Figure 16.1, the knowledge footprint is a complex interplay of a number of elements. First, we consider our SPEEDI (Social, Political/Policy, Economic, Environmental, Demographic, and Innovation) sub-framework, which represents the context or broader operating environment facing HEIs. This environment shapes what HEIs realistically can and cannot do. SPEEDI therefore represents the *conditioning factors* that influence the possibility for enlargement (or otherwise) of the knowledge footprint.

The SPEEDI dimensions that shape HEIs can be described as follows:

- *Social*—cultural, community, and civic values, norms, ways of doing things, history, and tradition associated with distinctive features of locations that both influence (and are the outcomes of) a university's capacity to address community and social needs and build and maintain social capital;
- *Political/policy*—civic, political, and policy considerations at the international, national, and local level, including systems of government, legal and regulatory frameworks, and sovereign risk;
- *Economic*—the broad macroeconomic environment within which HEIs operate, including the overall strength (and weakness) of the economy such as growth, business-friendly economic environment, etc.;
- *Environmental*—refers to the natural environment that is increasingly shaping HEI strategies, including effort to reduce environmental footprint, conserve energy, utilize alternative energy sources, and capitalize on opportunities in sustainable practices;
- *Demographic trends*—changes in population size and composition at home and abroad that shape an HEI's offerings, student cohorts, and modes of delivery;
- *Innovation*—refers to the "state of the art" knowledge in terms of the growth and development of new technologies, knowledge-based industries, advanced production techniques, and the like. It should be noted that HEIs are influenced by and shape this factor.

While SPEEDI provides the *context* or *operating* environment (conditioning factors) for an HEI's strategic intent, we contend that there are three *mechanisms* that drive knowledge footprint: knowledge transfer, knowledge transformation, and knowledge translation.[3]

Knowledge transfer is the application and diffusion largely of existing (or incrementally different) sets of knowledge and capability, either specific to an HEI (proprietary knowledge) or that which is generally available and known. It refers to the capacity of an HEI to harness its knowledge base, be it research, teaching,

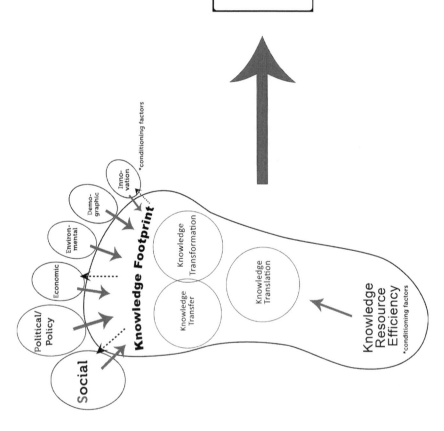

FIGURE 16.1 Knowledge Footprint Framework

technological, or entrepreneurial knowledge, and transfer this to the wider economy and society. This transfer process occurs through a multiple series of channels including: (a) teaching; (b) spinoff enterprises; (c) licensing/contract/consulting activity; (d) collaborative solutions to industry and community challenges; (e) graduates in employment; and (f) active engagement of alumni, students, and staff in civic and economic roles.

Knowledge transformation, while relying on many of the same channels for diffusion, e.g., spinoffs, is less about transfer of existing knowledge but more fundamentally altering the economic and social landscape through the development, application, and diffusion of new technologies, contributing to significant industrial structural change, community renewal, and solving of "wicked problems." In reality, the exact boundaries between knowledge transfer and knowledge transformation are difficult to pinpoint precisely without far greater examination, but the purpose of this chapter is to highlight and describe broad parameters of knowledge activity. The defining differences in characteristics relate to scale of change and impact, time frames (knowledge transformation arguably would operate over a longer time frame than knowledge transfer), and the greater emphasis on fundamental knowledge breakthroughs and discovery that resides in knowledge transformation.

Knowledge translation we regard as a key input to the process of knowledge transfer and knowledge transformation, and a key capability in its own right. We posit that in an increasingly global environment, in which mobility of academics, students, and institutions is growing, and ideas move relatively freely across the globe, that the capacity of HEIs to identify, access, absorb, and utilize ideas and knowhow from elsewhere and mesh with its own capability will be increasingly important in its own strategy development and in contributing to economic and social need, including in local areas.[4] Given the complexity of challenges faced by HEIs, it is unrealistic to contend that any one institution (or, indeed, nation) will have a mortgage on all elements of knowledge. Thus the challenge to efficiently and effectively manage knowledge flows from elsewhere and translate this into workable outcomes with impact, including contextualizing it for local circumstances, is a key one for HEIs.

Our second conditioning factor is knowledge resource efficiency. Ultimately HEIs are constrained by available resources, be they financial, human, or physical capacity. This in turn places a premium on HEIs to carefully and efficiently balance expansion paths and other investments against these constraints.

Taken together, SPEEDI, the three knowledge mechanisms, and the other conditioning factor of knowledge resource efficiency represents the elements of the footprint. When considered as a whole they represent what is feasible in terms of enlargement of HEI's knowledge remit, the mechanisms through which it occurs, and the constraints.

Framework Outcomes and Impacts

Having considered briefly the elements of the framework, it is useful to touch upon the reach and impact of the framework. Reach refers to the extent to which an HEI's activity occurs over a narrower or wider spatial basis, in both the physical and virtual domains. The impact refers to the extent to which an HEI's activity shapes economic and social change. Impact itself has two dimensions: quantity and quality aspects. Quantity refers to volume impacts such as the number of students graduated in employment, number of spinoff enterprises created, and number of patents generated. Quality refers to, for example, the number of jobs created in high growth knowledge sectors as a result of HEI activity. It is quite possible for an HEI to have a large reach in terms of the distance to which it extends influence, but have a low impact level either in quantity or quality sense, and vice-versa.

Table 16.1 below reflects the various strategic implications of reach and impact aspect for a hypothetical HEI. At the conceptual level, it specifies four possible states of the world: "high reach, low impact," "low reach, high impact," "low reach, low impact," and "high impact, high reach."

Understanding the relative balance between reach and impact allows for the possible identification of key strengths and weaknesses in an HEI overall mix of activity and priorities.

Framework Indicators and Metrics

While the development of metrics and indicators is beyond the scope of this chapter, the table below identifies the impact elements of knowledge footprint and example indicators.

TABLE 16.1 Impact and Reach Matrix

High Reach, Low Impact	High Reach, High Impact
• "Scattered" approach lacking scale, focus and critical mass, relationship building, and therefore real influence.	• HEI activities having a large footprint, potentially both local and global with major impacts on economy and society • Possible danger of "over-reach" relative to resource base
Low Reach, Low Impact	**Low Reach, High Impact**
• Struggling for viability	• Likely to be very strongly locally focused and very strongly anchored to local community, economically and socially. However, sustainability of this approach is open to question in the context of changes to external environment, including competition and structural change.

TABLE 16.2 Indicators of Impact

	Quantity Indicators	*Quality Indicators*
Knowledge Transfer	• Number of spinoffs • Graduates in employment	• Spinoffs that are growing by more than 10% per year in turnover • Employment of graduates in knowledge intensive occupations
Knowledge Transformation	• Number of patents in emerging technologies	• Rate of commercialization of patents
Knowledge Translation	• Number of international staff • Number of (national and international) research collaborations	• International staff with major international awards • Collaborations leading to technological breakthroughs
Knowledge Resource Efficiency	• Realization of budget targets	• Triple bottom line measures associated with budget targets

Table 16.2 shows possible "quantity" and "quality" impact indicators for the elements of the footprint. To these impact measures, we would add "reach" indicators to measure the spatial dimensions. For example, knowledge transfer indicators such as number of spinoffs could include number of spinoffs over a specified area to provide insight into the spread of an HEI influence.

Uses of the Framework

Section two presented the methodological approach to the footprint framework. Here, we seek to highlight the potential uses of the framework, which could be used flexibly to inform strategic decisions both internal and external to the institution. Broadly, we see the framework as moving toward a holistic and integrated approach to understanding and appraising possibilities, constraints, and strategic priorities, and one that leverages a broader range of indicators that can better reflect the diverse activities of institutions. Of course, if adopted by an institution, implementation decisions such as the main use and the audience for the framework (for example, whether it is internal or external, or whether information is confidential) will all bear on its use and purpose.

Primarily, we see the framework as a strategic planning tool that can have retrospective and prospective application. Retrospectively, the footprint framework can enable institutions to measure performance against the indicators encompassed by the framework. More specifically, the framework also provides scope for an institution to evaluate its progress toward particular strategic priorities such as global reach or a particular specialization. An HEI could identify a set of indicators linked to a technology specialization to identify and evaluate its local and global "technology knowledge footprint." Prospectively, the framework can support institutional decision making and foresighting, to highlight the potential implications of institutional action and projecting possible "future footprints." These "future footprints" could be used to inform trade-off analysis and institutional strategies to maximize impact within constraints. To illustrate, it is useful to again consider Table 16.1—whereas an institution may aspire to a "high reach, high impact" model, pursuing new global points of presence could potentially risk "over reach" and (at the risk of over-playing the pun) an unstable institutional footprint. This analysis could in turn support institutions to refine their strategies, including by identifying whether an institution can or should move from knowledge transfer through to knowledge transformation, and/or whether effort to progress in one area could affect other dimensions of the footprint.

Similarly, if such an approach were adopted by institutions, the footprint framework could present an alternative means of international benchmarking and potentially enable a more nuanced approach to understanding institutional performance. For example, the framework will seek to incorporate a broader array of indicators beyond the traditional research-output focus of many rankings schemas. This could enable comparison against "community" impact and social indicators, along with a comparison of institutional performance relative to resourcing. Such an approach could have the benefit of identifying institutions that may be "punching above their weight" in terms of impact relative to resourcing, or relative to specific funding sources such as government research grants. Further, the footprint framework has obvious marketing potential and we suggest that there may be simple appeal in something like a footprint to help illustrate some of these concepts to a broader audience.

Further, looking more widely, a more nuanced approach to HEI performance presented in a more accessible format could usefully inform the relationship between policy-makers and institutions. For example, a local government may be able to draw on the footprint framework to identify which particular institutions in their region are more focused on making an impact in the local area or activities abroad, and/or to highlight the impacts of institutions in their region to support inward investment and industry policy.

There is also potential scope for the footprint framework to inform a new reporting and performance management framework to government, and a more accessible and informative footprint could also underpin institutional advocacy and potentially inform grant applications.

We also argue that the value of this framework is heightened by explicitly identifying the key conditioning factors that bear on institutional performance and strategy. After all, institutional impact and reach within a particular location is logically affected by the "SPEEDI" factors that bear on organizations and individuals within that environment, such as political or demographic constraints. Similarly, the framework helps to highlight that institutional resourcing is not limitless and that it is useful to consider institutional performance relative to resourcing. Both environmental scanning and financial sustainability analyses will already occur to varying degrees within all institutions: the framework emphasizes these factors as a mediator to understanding past success or projecting institutional impact into the future.

Results could in turn inform future strategic action, such as by highlighting areas that may be resource-intensive relative to outcomes. Further, the framework seeks to bring together in a coordinated, overarching manner—as far as possible— the key elements that underpin current strategies and impacts on community, economic, and international measures.

Challenges for the Knowledge Footprint Framework

This chapter has provided a broad framework, a "knowledge footprint," as a way of thinking about, understanding, and measuring an HEI's economic, social, and environmental impact, recognizing that increasingly institutions operate on a global scale and across borders. However, there is more to be done before this concept can be embedded into institutional thinking and into performance/planning frameworks. In this section we identify select challenges to implementation.

First, while it was beyond the scope of the chapter to present a detailed list of indicators that could or should underpin the framework, it is well recognized that agreeing and implementing a set of meaningful indicators is challenging. This is quite apart from whether the requisite data is available. The large and growing body of literature related to measuring HEI impact (e.g., as touched on above) is evidence that goes to such challenges. To this end, we acknowledge that a critical challenge for the framework will be to develop robust, defensible, verifiable, and measurable indicators to ascertain the extent and magnitude of a knowledge footprint. Further, indicators should enable HEIs to compare their current performance to past performance, and against national or international comparisons, as a basis for developing strategy and planning future investments. Here we identify opportunity to leverage new technologies and data systems (e.g., as discussed in chapter 1, technology is increasing access to timely data and the capacity for analysis to support decision making). For example, we believe that tools can be developed to visually indicate knowledge footprint sizes and patterns as a "ready reckoner" for university planners and researchers. This could involve the capacity to alter weightings in variables to obtain a sense of the impact on size and direction of the footprint.

Second, given the variety of potential uses for the framework, agreeing its key purpose/s and its audience in an institutional setting is important, as this may drive the particular approach and indicators adopted. These decisions will be intrinsically linked to identifying the best means to link footprint analysis into institutional planning cycles. For example, at the start of a planning cycle, some preliminary indication of the size of the footprint that an HEI wishes to develop (or maintain) could be made, informed by institutional objectives and the conditioning factors outlined above. This could then inform the various elements of institutional activity to align with those goals. In a sense, this is analogous to broad "budget envelopes" that government policy-makers manage with regard to key objectives and competing claims on scarce resources. That is, the footprint thus provides an important frame of reference for planning by linking HEI objectives and constraints (financial, physical, human capital). It allows for key tradeoffs to be assessed and judgments to be made in planning about the relative benefits and costs of expanding a footprint or altering its parameters.

Given there are existing and evolving means to measure and report against HEI performance, it will also be important for institutional researchers and planners to consider how to leverage existing thinking, including whether to develop (or augment) an institutional ranking scheme based on footprint analysis. Such a rankings system would examine in totality the impact of an institution on economy and society, and mark a departure from current arrangements that do not consider "whole of institutional" arrangements in that they tend to focus on a narrow range of HEI inputs/outputs. Similarly, in suggesting a new measurement system, it will be important not to further burden HEIs with resource-intensive reporting systems, either internally or externally.

Finally, we accept that there will be considerable debate about whether the elements of the framework best represent the activities and priorities of HEIs in the second decade (and beyond) of the twenty-first century. For example, as per our discussion above on community engagement, there are significant challenges to measure university impacts in the community domain alone.

Nonetheless, we consider that the knowledge footprint framework is an idea worth further debate and exploration in HEIs and government policy circles. It can guide institutional researchers, planners, and decision makers to assess institutional performance against agreed objectives and inform the development of strategic directions. Indeed, this potential prospective application is a key strength of the framework through its capacity to support strategic decision making—which, as noted in chapter 1, is an intrinsic measure of relevance and success of IR. That there is a rich and growing literature regarding HEI impact and performance measurement goes to demonstrate that there is considerable and ongoing interest in developing new and more effective tools. Certainly, leveraging previous thinking, identifying the changing role and impact of HEIs—particularly across borders—and co-opting new technologies will present challenges and will require creativity. This chapter provides some baby steps toward that debate.

Notes

1. The authors are affiliated with RMIT University. The views expressed here are those of the authors.
2. For further consideration of the role of the HEI in hubs, see e.g., Gais and Wright, 2012.
3. Such an approach is consistent with previous work, including a focus on the knowledge activities of HEIs (see e.g., Gais and Wright, 2012) and identifying a knowledge typology across progressively complex boundaries (Carlile, 2004).

4. This approach builds on work that considers the value of absorptive capacity (e.g., importing technology from abroad) for companies, industries, and countries, see e.g., Kneller and Stevens, 2006.

References

Abel, J. R., & Deitz, R. (2011). *Do colleges and universities increase their region's human capital?* Federal Reserve Bank of New York. Staff Report #401. New York, NY: Federal Reserve Bank.

Anderson, T. R., Daim, T. U., & Lavoie, F. F. (2007). Measuring the efficiency of university technology transfer. *Technovation, 27*(5), 306–318.

Arbo, P., & Benneworth, P. (2007). *Understanding the regional contribution of higher education institutions: A literature review.* OECD education working paper 2007/09. Paris, France: OECD.

Australian Regional Universities Network. (2012). *Economic Impact.* Retrieved from: www.run.edu.au/resources/Economic_Impact_Study.pdf.

Bonaccorsi, A., Massimo, G., Colombo, M. G., Guerini, M., & Rossi-Lamastra, C. (2013). The impact of local and external university knowledge on the creation of knowledge-intensive firms: Evidence from the Italian case. *Small Business Economics.* DOI 10.1007/s11187-013-9536-2.

Brown, K. H., & Heaney, M. T. (1997). A note on measuring the economic impact of Institutions of Higher Education. *Research in Higher Education, 38*(2), 229–240.

Carlile, R. R. (2004). Transferring, translating, and transforming: An integrative framework for managing knowledge across boundaries. *Organization Science, 15*(5), 555–568. DOI 10.1287/orsc.1040.0094.

Carree, M., Malva, A. D., & Santarelli, E. (2012). The contribution of universities to growth: Empirical evidence for Italy. *Journal of Technological Transfer, 35*(1), 141–180. DOI 10.1007/s10961-012-9282-7.

Dill, D. D., & Van Vught, F. A. (2010). *National innovation and the academic enterprise.* Baltimore, MD: Johns Hopkins University Press.

Drucker, J., & Goldstein, H. (2007). Assessing the regional economic development impacts of universities: A review of current approaches. *International Regional Science Review, 30*(1), 20–46. DOI 10.1177/0160017606296731.

Etzkowitz, H. (2003). Innovation in innovation: The triple helix of university-industry-government relations. *Social Science Information, 42*(3), 293–338. DOI 10.1177/05390184030423002.

Florax, R.G.M. (1992). *The university: A regional booster? Economic impacts of academic knowledge infrastructure.* Aldershot, UK: Avebury.

Gais, T., & Wright, D. (2012). The diversity of university economic development. In J. E. Lane & B. D. Johnstone (Eds.), *Universities and colleges as economic drivers: Measuring and building success* (pp. 31–60). Albany, NY: SUNY Press.

Garrigo-Yserte, R., & Gallo-Rivera, M. T. (2010). The impact of the university upon local economy: Three methods to estimate demand-side effects. *The Annals of Regional Science, 44*(1), 39–67.

Goldstein, H. A., & Luger, M. L. (1992). *Assessing the regional economic development impacts of universities: A review of current approaches.* Carolina: The University of North Carolina at Chapel Hill and the state's economy. Final report prepared for the University of North Carolina at Chapel Hill Bicentennial Observance. Chapel Hill, NC: University System of North Carolina.

Jongbloed, B., & Benneworth, P. (2013). Learning from history: Previous attempts to measure universities' community impacts. In P. Benneworth (Ed.), *University engagement with socially excluded communities* (pp. 263–283). Dordrecht, the Netherlands: Springer. DOI 10.1007/978-94-007-4875-0_14.

Kneller, R., & Stevens, P. (2006). Frontier technology and absorptive capacity: Evidence from OECD manufacturing industries. *Oxford Bulletin of Economics and Statistics, 68*(1), 1–21.

Lane, J. E., & Owens, T. (2012). The international dimensions of economic development. In J. E. Lane & B. D. Johnstone (Eds.), *Universities and colleges as economic drivers: Measuring and building success* (pp. 205–238). Albany, NY: SUNY Press.

Ohme, A. (2003). *The economic impact of a university on its community and state: Examining trends four years later.* The University of Delaware. Retrieved from: www.udel.edu/IR/ presentations/EconImpact.doc.

Peer, V., & Stoneglehner, G. (2013). Universities as change agents for sustainability—framing the role of knowledge transfer and generation in regional development processes. *Journal of Cleaner Production, 44*, 85–95. Retrieved from: http://dx.doi.org/10.1016/ j.jclepro.2012.12.003.

Slaughter, S., & Rhoades, G. (2009). *Academic capitalism and the new economy: Markets, state, and higher education.* Baltimore, MD: Johns Hopkins University Press.

Stokes, K., & Coomes, P. (1998). *The local economic impact of higher education: An overview of methods and practice.* Number 67, Spring, 1998. The Association for Institutional Research. AIR Professional File.

van Vught, F., & Ziegele, F. (Eds.). (2011). *Design and testing the feasibility of a multidimensional global university ranking. Final report.* Consortium for Higher Education and Research Performance Assessment. CHERPA-Network.

17

THE EVOLUTION OF INSTITUTIONAL RESEARCH

Maturity Models of Institutional Research and Decision Support and Possible Directions for the Future

John Taylor

Introduction

As discussed in chapter 1 of this book, those who undertake the tasks related to institutional research (IR) may use different terminology and may experience a stronger or weaker focus on one or more of the activities that comprise the larger scope of IR. There are a number of definitions, but, at the heart of all, IR may be seen as a set of activities that provides information to support institutional planning, policy formulation, and decision making. This chapter considers the evolution of institutional research and, in particular, its role within institutional decision making processes in higher education. In so doing, it will discuss models of maturity in business processes and thereby provide a new approach to the international comparison of IR and to the understanding of the development of institutional research over time.

The Development of Institutional Research

Earlier chapters of this book have discussed the development of IR in various parts of the world. While the origins of institutional research in the US have been traced back to the early eighteenth century and the foundation of Yale University (Cowley, 1960), the modern use and description of institutional research dates from the first half of the twentieth century with the increasing use of self-surveys to inform institutional management on issues such as cost and efficiency and to meet the needs of external agencies. Rourke and Brooks (1966) estimated that, in 1955, there were 10 offices of institutional research in US universities and colleges; by 1964, this figure had increased to 115 and 21 offices were established in 1966 alone (pp. 45–46). The main driver was the increasing demand for accountability within the publicly funded sector, rather than aspirations toward organizational self-improvement. However, in the 1960s, the view of institutional research began to broaden, stimulated, in particular, by two key publications: *Research Designed to Improve Institutions of Higher Learning* (Brumbaugh, 1960) and *The Managerial Revolution in Higher Education* (Rourke & Brooks, 1966). These works emphasized the importance of self-evaluation and self-motivated quality assurance and improvement. In this way, the importance of institutional research as an activity within university management became more established. More recently, as discussed in more detail elsewhere in this book, Terenzini's three tiers of intelligence (1993), Volkwein's Four Faces of IR (1999), Serban's addition of a fifth face for IR (2002), Terkla's (2008) discussion on the importance of "decision-making based on evidence" (p. 1), and Volkwein, Liu, and Woodell's (2012) designations of IR maturity have extended the understanding of IR. These, and other publications, document the growing value of IR as a form of decision support that can assist higher education leaders in policy, planning, and decision making.

What is clear from the existing literature is how, over the years, institutional research has moved from an independent service function to a central activity influential within policy formation and decision-making. This role will be explored further in this chapter. The term "institutional research" is unrecognized in many countries; elsewhere, it is understood only by members of a very small professional community. It can also be argued that many aspects of institutional research are present in these settings, but have taken different forms, commonly existing within admissions, planning, quality assurance, finance, human resources, and marketing departments. In that sense, it is the idea of institutional research as an "umbrella" for certain aspects of these functions that is absent rather than the functions themselves. Nevertheless significant changes began to appear in the 1980s. With the emergence of ideas of "the evaluative state" (Neave, 1988) and "the audit society" (Power, 1997), new expectations of accountability began to impact higher education institutions. Similarly, with the spread of more market-based mechanisms, often associated with "new public management" and "new managerialism," a new impetus was created for universities to understand their own activities, not least to seek out competitive advantage or to respond to competitors.

At the same time, a new emphasis on quality, and especially on quality enhancement and on the public assurance of quality, raised new demands for information and for informed analysis. Thus, institutional research, although still not recognized by that name, began to emerge more strongly in the 1990s, especially in the UK and in some other European countries, and in Australasia. Other chapters in this book show that this trend has continued and illustrate how universities all over the world are now developing forms of institutional research, driven by pressures from government and/or increasing marketization. Beyond the US, a rather different functional typology is associated with institutional research, including routine institutional management, strategy formation, quality assurance and quality enhancement, and marketing and competitive data analysis (Taylor, Hanlon, & Yorke, 2013).

Institutional Research and Decision Support Systems

It is significant that both the two "traditions" of institutional research have converged in the present emphasis on the provision of information to support decision making. Institutional research is therefore closely associated with the formation of information systems and with decision support systems. An information system seeks to convert data into information; a decision support system will use such information, with other inputs, to identify and analyze problems that lead to decisions. Institutional research can be seen to span this whole process, from initial data collection to final decision making.

Schultheis and Sumner (1995) refer to information as "data with meaning" (pp. 35–36). They present a model of an information system to describe the process by which data is converted into information, based upon technological, organizational, and human factors. At the heart of this model are people. Here, it is possible to identify one of the key functions of institutional research. Human intervention is needed to decide what data is actually useful and how it needs to be manipulated in order to form information. This introduces a formative and subjective element within the process. In practice, the institutional researcher is using their own perspectives to shape the process; in other words, they are applying their own professional judgment.

The role of the information system may also be understood from different perspectives (Mano, 2007). As a social phenomenon, "*Information systems are a*

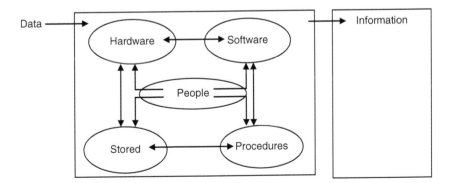

FIGURE 17.1 Model of an Information System

Source: Schultheis & Sumner (1995)

multidisciplinary discipline and a social science, and should not be analysed in a purely technological perspective" (Galliers, 1992, p. 3). From an organizational perspective, *"The information system is a system that creates, transforms, transmits and memorizes information, whose function is to provide the decision system with information regarding the organizational system"* (Le Moign, 1978, p. 40). And from the human perspective: *"Regardless of the technologies used in the 'informatization' of organizations, it is the human component of the information systems that is normally responsible for its complexities and which makes its study interesting"* (Caldeira & Romao, 2002, p. 78).

The information system may also be seen as a sub-section within a broad decision support system (Mano, 2007). Keen (1987) defined a decision support system with reference to its constituent words:

- **Decision**–centered on the modeling, analysis, and decision maker selection processes;
- **Support**–centered on the idea of providing help and guidance (utility) for those involved in making decisions; and
- **System**–centered on technological characteristics and the idea of interaction between distinct elements to a common objective.

The concept of a "system" often implies formality and rigidity. However, Costa (2000) sees the decision support system as flexible, adaptable, and easy to use; most important, the system should act as a tool for leaders, managers, and decision-makers, but does not replace them or reduce their ultimate responsibility. The interaction between the decision support system should be strong and dialectic, but flexible. The system should reflect the character and culture of the organization, not *vice versa*. However, the system will also have implications for the organization.

We know that information is central to decision making and decision support systems within higher education, and is at the heart of institutional research. Information should be **relevant, timely, accurate, and understandable**. A further critical aspect of the use of information within a decision support system is that such information needs to be **effectively integrated**. Of particular importance is that information should be consistent across the institution such that, for example, information on staffing and on students can be used together, and that, when a specific question is asked at a particular point in time, there is a single, authoritative response. Information should also be integrated in another sense. Since decision-makers often need both quantitative (countable) and qualitative (uncountable and based on subjective analysis) information, effective integration of interpretation is important.

Within a classical organizational structure, the decision support structure will support the three levels of management (strategic, executive, and operational). Table 17.1 shows how levels of decision making and information systems can interact and thereby shape the nature of institutional research within an institution.

TABLE 17.1 Higher Education Decision Making and Information Systems

Higher Education Decisions			Information Systems		
Management Levels	Activity	Work structure	Objectives	Relevance (a)	Other characteristics (b)
Top-Strategic Planning	Long-Term Planning	Politics Program	Decision Support	1. Ad-hoc basis 2. Summaries of data 3. Highly subjective data	a) Results often contain surprises b) Predictive of the future c) Mostly external d) Highly unstructured e) Top manager f) Goal oriented
Middle-Tactical	Budget Plans	Procedures Processes	Demand Report	1. Regular 2. Summaries of data 3. Some subjective data	a) Some surprises may occur b) Comparative nature c) Internal and external d) Some unstructured data e) Middle manager f) Oriented toward control and resource allocation
Base-Operational	Daily Transactions	Tasks Operations	Schedule Report	1. Regular, repetitive 2. Very detailed 3. Highly accurate data	a) Expected results b) The past c) Internal d) Highly structured e) First line supervisors f) Task oriented

a) Relevance: 1) frequency; 2) detail level; 3) accuracy.
b) Other Characteristics: a) results dependability; b) time period covered; c) data source; d) data nature; e) typical user; f) decision level.
Source: adapted from Schultheis (1995) and Mano (2007)

Business Process Maturity

Maturity models provide organizations with an evaluative methodology for assessing the scope for improvement, additional efficiency, or increased capability within business processes. The concept of measuring maturity was first developed by the Software Engineering Institute, Carnegie Mellon (the Capability Maturity Model Integration [CMMI]; Paulk, Weber, Garcia-Miller, Chrissis, & Bush, 1993). Further models relevant to institutional research were developed in the early 1990s, including the European Foundation for Quality Management (EFQM) Excellence

Model, which centered on business management; the Process Maturity Model, which was more concerned with process management; and the Project Management Maturity Model, that focused on managing the scope of a project. De Bruin, Freeze, Kaulkarni, and Rosemann (2005) noted that "more than 150 maturity models have been developed to measure, among others, the maturity of IT service capacity, strategic alignment, innovation management, program management, enterprise architecture and knowledge management maturity . . .[and that] most of these models simply provide a means for positioning the selected unit of analysis on a pre-defined scale" (p. 2). Underlying the use of maturity models is the assumption that, as a process increases in maturity, the strategic objectives of the organization are more likely to be achieved. The optimum level of maturity is that which delivers the strategic objectives of the organization in the most effective and efficient way, which is not necessarily the highest level (Taylor et al., 2013).

As the institutional research activity and profession evolved, it became a central function within both information systems and decision support systems. IR's current level of development enables us to apply ideas of business process maturity to institutional research. An important starting point is the concept of business process orientation (BPO). Based on the work of Porter (1985), organizations began to adopt a "process view" based on better internal connectivity and reduced internal competition between different functions and organizational units. Within higher education, it is possible to view the development of institutional research as a service function, operating across the organization and informing the establishment and implementation of corporate strategy, as part of this increasing process view. Central to the development of institutional research within a BPO environment are:

- **Process management and measurement**—measures for the effectiveness of institutional research including output quality, timeliness and relevance of research outputs, and activity cost;
- **Process people**—jobs that focus on processes rather than functions, and are cross-functional and cross-institutional in responsibility; and
- **Process view**—a cross-functional, horizontal view of the higher education institution, including structure, focus, measurement, and service users (adapted from Lockamy & McCormack, 2004).

Using the principles of BPO, it is possible to develop a maturity model for institutional research, as follows:

Stage 1: **Ad Hoc**—The role of institutional research is ill-defined and unstructured. Measures of performance are not in place. Tasks and organizational structures are based on traditional processes and horizontal processes. Individual interests and efforts dominate; individuals try to work "around the system," not for it.

Stage 2: **Defined**—Basic processes are defined and documented. The work of institutional research follows clear procedures. Jobs and organizational structure include a process aspect, but remain essentially disconnected and individually motivated. Meetings within institutional research and with users occur, but predominantly as representatives of different functions.

Stage 3: **Linked**—The breakthrough level. Leaders and managers use process management with strategic intent. Institutional research operates within broad processes and structures. Cooperation with other functions takes the form of teams that share common process measures and goals.

Stage 4: **Integrated**—The institution operates at a process level, and institutional research within it. Organizational structures are based around processes. Advanced process management is dominant. Institutional research as an identifiable, independent function begins to disappear.

Stage 5: **Extended**—A horizontal structure is in place. Institutional research is undertaken across the institution, embedded with other functions.

This model assumes that, as a process such as institutional research matures, it moves from an internally focused perspective to an externally focused perspective. A maturity level represents a threshold that, when reached, will institutionalize a total systems view; each level of maturity establishes a higher level of process capability for an organization (Dorfman & Thayer, 1997). This capability can be defined by:

- **Control**—the difference between targets and actual results;
- **Predictability**—the variability between cost and performance objectives; and
- **Effectiveness**—the achievement of targeted results and the ability to raise targets (Lockamy & McCormack, 2004).

Following these guidelines, it is suggested that, over an extended period, the specialized, independent function of institutional research might be transformed from a distinct unit within the organization to a more distributed activity (not unlike the approach to institutional research in some institutions outside the US). Taken to its ultimate point, institutional research becomes more dispersed, but integrated across the institution. While this might have the advantage of spreading professional skills and insights, it might also be seen as an erosion of the institution-wide, multi-functional expertise and knowledge available within a more centralized structure. In this sense, institutional research provides a focus for tacit as well as implicit knowledge, and needs to serve the institution accordingly.

Another approach to developing a maturity model for institutional research, centered on the development of institutional research, was set out by Taylor et al. in 2013. This model draws on the functional typologies discussed above and focuses on five main areas of activity: routine management, strategy formation, quality assurance and enhancement, marketing and competitive analysis, and independent research. This is shown in Table 17.2.

TABLE 17.2 Maturity Model for Institutional Research and the Development of a Profession

	Routine Institutional Management	Strategy Formulation	Quality Assurance and Enhancement	Marketing and Competitive Analysis	Independent Research and Study	Areas of Interest
Level 5: Mature	Academic management processes monitored Mature predictive analytics Extensive dashboarding and visualization	Collaborative international process benchmarking	Institutional QM Framework adopted (e.g., Baldrige, TQM EFQM)	Staff, alumni, stakeholders contribute to CI Systematic customer experience marketing	Broadly based, integrated, self-directed research program	IR embraces analysis of all functions and outputs (not necessarily with direct responsibility)
Level 4:	Interactive online reports Strong data governance Ongoing investment in BI	Outcome benchmarking Scenario planning refines formative strategy	Feedback loops between institution, students, and staff Evidence repository for profession and regulator accreditation	International competitors' analyzed	Integrated research program, leading to publications	Includes detailed financial analysis, estates management, and overall management performance
Level 3: Semi-mature	Integrated data-warehouse and BI Competency Centre Analytical reporting calendar Longitudinal studies	First generation predictive analytics Institutional performance analysis drives strategy choices/review	Lifecycle approach to student and stakeholder feedback Multi-dimensional reporting of course/program quality	Global rankings analyzed and modeled Some customer experience marketing	Occasional self-directed, integrated research	Broad range of areas, including staff and students, teaching, research, management, and service
Level 2:	External/internal reporting from discrete functions and systems	Institutional KPIs defined and tracked	Some student feedback mechanisms Staff and student satisfaction surveys Limited course quality measures	Competitor student market share analysis Global rankings monitoring	Occasional function-specific independent research Occasional papers for conferences and meetings	Primarily student and staff based
Level 1: Immature	Static ad hoc reporting Non-integrated data	Strategy unquantified and/or indistinctive	Nil	National rankings monitored	Nil	Primarily student based

Source: Taylor, Hanlon, & Yorke (2013). © Wiley Periodicals, Inc.

However, alternative approaches can also be considered that may be used to examine the position of institutional research within the context of wider institutional business processes and decision making. One approach is based on the work of Fisher (2004) that aims to analyze business process maturity in a way that is both multi-dimensional and non-linear. The first stage is to consider the extent to which an activity is aligned with organizational objectives according to five "levers of change":

- **Strategy**—Understanding the role, positioning, responsibilities, and priorities for institutional research in decision making in support of overall institutional objectives;
- **Controls**—The governance model for the management, administration, and evaluation of the contribution made by institutional research within the institution;
- **People**—The human resource environment for undertaking institutional research, including skills, organizational culture, and organizational structure;
- **Technology**—Enabling information systems, applications, tools, and infrastructure for institutional research;
- **Process**—Operating methods and practices, including policies and procedures that determine how institutional research is undertaken.

All five levers can be observed in the practice of institutional research. However, Fisher (2004) suggests that most organizations are concerned only with people, process, and technology. If these three factors are out of alignment with institutional strategy and objectives, the result may be very efficient processes that fail to produce the desired outcomes. If these three factors are not considered within the context of institutional governance, the institution will lack the internal cohesion and cohesiveness to ensure that strategy is delivered. Fisher concludes that: "The key to the Five Levers is the ability to achieve consistent alignment across all five. When that is achieved, then the organization is operating at a level where it can achieve optimal results" (Fisher, 2004, pp. 1–2).

As far as the development and maturity of institutional research is concerned, the key point here is that, as a management function, it cannot be seen in isolation; maturity is a reflection of a series of interactions within the institution. Of particular importance is recognition of the significance of organizational culture in shaping the contribution to be played by institutional research. If the prevailing culture does not favor the open sharing of information and its use within the decision-making process, it will always be difficult for institutional research to have an optimal impact.

However, Fisher's model goes further and introduces a dynamic element to the model, referred to as "States of Process Maturity." Five "states" are identified, representing a progression, but not in a consistent, linear fashion; moving from one level to another may take longer or be more problematic than others, and reverse movement may also be possible. All five levels can be applied to institutional research:

- **Siloed**—In this case, institutional research exists in isolation from the rest of the institution, pursuing its own ends, setting its own objectives, and engaged in self-evaluation. Goals are commonly related to operational efficiency rather than institutional strategy. Few links are maintained with other aspects of institutional management. This is a functional silo.
- **Tactically Integrated**—This is the first stage in the integration of institutional research within the overall strategy of the organization. Integration often takes the form of discrete projects or specific initiatives, and is often narrowly defined. Links with other management functions are based on information systems rather than human interaction, and will be mainly horizontal in nature. Again, operational efficiency and the achievement of detailed objectives are the main drivers. This level still falls well short of cultural integration or alignment with institutional strategy.
- **Process Driven**—This is arguably the most important and most difficult step within the model. Here, institutional research moves from being primarily inward looking to effective integration with other management functions and working to support strategic decision making across the institution; in effect, this is a change in the mind-set for those working in institutional research. Institutional research responds to a top-down mandate and meets the needs of institutional leadership; the need to support institutional strategy and objectives become dominant. At this stage, information systems become less important, used more flexibly to provide key management information rather than dictating the range of data available. The emphasis at this level is on institutional research as part of a holistic model, working both vertically and horizontally within the organization; the primary concern is less narrow efficiency and more the successful achievement of "end-to-end processes."
- **Optimized Enterprise**—This step marks a move from developing a process-driven mentality to a position where the role of institutional research is fully embedded, optimized, and integrated across the institution. The work of institutional research may be self-initiated or requested from above or below, but is always undertaken with a view to ensuring that institutional strategic objectives are met.
- **Intelligent Operating Network**—This is the final stage in Fisher's model, where all the actions in the first four stages are working to the maximum across the whole institution resulting in optimal effectiveness. However, this ultimate stage goes further by predicting changes in the operating environment and making decisions that ensure that negative effects can be avoided or minimized.

The overall model, adapted to institutional research, is set out in Table 17.3.

TABLE 17.3 A Maturity Model for Institutional Research Based on Business Process Maturity

	Siloed	Tactically Integrated	Process Driven	Optimized Enterprise	Intelligent Operating Network
Strategy	• Reactive to higher education environment within 1–2 years, typically chasing a competitor • Internal integration within functions • Primary focus on quality, cost, and efficiency	• Adapt/react to changing environment and market dynamics within 12 months • Some cross-functional integration to solve problems and inform planning • Initial entry into point-to-point integration with partners	• Adapt/react to higher education context and market dynamics within 3–6 months • Enterprise-wide process leadership is established • The business element of the enterprise • Effective integration across the institution	• IR adaptive to market dynamics/changing requirements within weeks • Enterprise organized completely around processes • Optimized processes and execution yield competitive advantage/quality enhancement	• Predictive capabilities and market leadership • Continuously adaptive to market dynamics and changing environment in near real-time • Institution is organized around processes • Competitive advantage is driven across institution
Controls	• Local and functional level authority/autonomy for IR • No institution-wide standards or governance • No formal value/performance measurement program across the institution	• Hierarchical management structure • Independent functional department decisions • Limited enterprise-wide standards or governance/performance measurement	• Formal process leadership establishes priorities for IR • Business cases/market information drive projects • Process metrics tied to individual, organizational unit and institutional performance	• Process teams responsible for overall performance • Relevant process metrics institutionalized as main performance measures	• Inter-enterprise process teams own performance • Relevant process metrics are used to measure actual and directional performance

(Continued)

TABLE 17.3 (Continued)

	Siloed	Tactically Integrated	Process Driven	Optimized Enterprise	Intelligent Operating Network
Process	• Static business processes • Functional silos • Geographic silos • Department focused • Informal communications within departments • No overall responsibilities	• Limited process re-engineering and cross-functional/process coordination • Systems drive baseline process definitions.	• Fully transitional from functional to process focus, including management structure, execution teams, and performance evaluation • Targeted IR	• Total process integration across the enterprise • Commitment to continuous process improvement program • Outsource non-core business processes (reduce costs *and* increase quality)	• Total process integration across the institution (eco–system) • Key processes flow seamlessly across firewalls
People	• Subject matter experts • Adversarial interaction within the institution; mutual distrust • No formal change management procedures • "I'll do my job, you do yours"	• Cross functional/process team members (usually led by IT) • Limited understanding of cross-departmental process needs and dependencies	• IR leaders define, deploy, enhance, and maintain core processes • Functional teams focus on quality execution	• Lean organization focus on optimizing process definitions and execution • Ongoing process training for employees	• All staff pursue process and cultural attributes • Ongoing process training for employees and partners
IT	• Independent systems • Duplication of systems across the institution • "Islands" of automation • Limited integration, only within functions	• Initial development of systems for cross-functional integration • Point-to-point partner integration • IT leads cross-functional initiatives (systems focused)	• IR works with IT support process leadership team in specific initiatives • System and instance consolidation to streamline processes and information management	• Utilize business process management (BPM) solutions to automate process execution, monitoring, and control across the institution	• Utilize business process management (BPM) solutions to automate and monitor process execution throughout the institution/ecosystem

Source: adapted from Fisher (2004)

Each of the maturity models described thus far emphasize the role of institutional research within the context of the overall institution of higher education and views institutional research as contributing to overall strategy and policy, rather than as an end in itself. The models represent stages in the development of institutional research in this role. However, it is also necessary to consider the mechanisms that may encourage or discourage such evolution. Luftman's (2000) business alignment maturity suggests that there is a range of factors that influence the relationship between institutional research and the wider institution. First, it is important to identify a series of "enablers" and "inhibitors." Enablers are the processes and individuals in senior leadership who support institutional research staff and function by ensuring they have well-prioritized research projects that are seen as essential, and that enable them to be involved in strategy development. These senior managers enable institutional researchers to show leadership and initiative, working in partnership with others in the decision support process. On the other hand, inhibitors keep institutional research detached from senior leadership and limit IR's involvement in decision support. The detached nature of their position distances institutional researchers from senior leaders, inhibits them from being actively involved in fulfilling core institutional objectives, and prompts others to see IR as lacking in leadership and talent.

Second, Luftman (2000) suggests that building blocks underpin the process of strategic alignment. These building blocks include: 1) a focus on the scope, distinctive competencies, and the organization's governance; 2) consideration of the administrative structure and organization's culture; 3) strategies that ensure success including access to technology, access to information across the institution, clarity of project prioritization, and how to clarify discrepancies; 4) understanding the organization's infrastructure, priorities, and polices for data collection and analysis, a clear process to develop and maintain applications, and support to recruit and retain appropriate staff. When these processes are in place and done so with clarity and precision, organizations, including institutional research, can perform the decision support process from a point of strength, and in ways that assist in strategy and policy development.

Conclusions

Colleges and universities today face many different pressures for change. In particular, global competition and marketization are affecting higher education at all levels and in all countries. The practice of institutional research is, inevitably, changing as part of this wider process. Increasingly, competition in higher education is based on capabilities or "complex bundles of skills and accumulated knowledge" (Day, 1994). Herein, perhaps, lies the present and future role of institutional research, functioning less as an independent source of self-motivated, "academic" research and more as a service, tasked to help the institution to achieve its core objectives. Specific areas of activity, such as quality enhancement and student achievement or the analysis of trends in staffing, are increasingly seen as significant, not simply for their own intrinsic importance, but, rather, within the context of wider strategy, as a means to an end. In this context, institutional research may, indeed, be viewed as a strategic asset. Universities, like many other organizations, now operate less as a rather chaotic, disconnected collection of functional areas and increasingly as a combination of closely integrated processes (Hammer, 1996). Within the organization, therefore, different processes require investment and development as they mature, and the idea of process evolution and process maturity become more important. Institutional research may be seen as one of these processes within the higher education institution. The idea of process maturity assumes that a process has a lifecycle that is explicitly defined, managed, measured, and controlled, and evolves in developmental stages. The concept also suggests the extension of process capability, understanding, and application across the whole organization (Dorfman & Thayer, 1997). The boundaries between these stages in the evolution of institutional research may be "fuzzy;" similarly, evolution may not be linear, moving in one direction; change may occur in different directions or in reverse. However, it is suggested that some understanding of the role of institutional research as a business process can strengthen the development of institutional research within an institution and enhance both the activity itself and its contribution within the organization.

Although institutional research has grown to a greater degree and/or includes different traditions in certain parts of the world, it can be argued that the collection, analysis, and presentation of information for decision support is central to institutional research. It is by understanding further the link between information and decision making that additional insights can be gained into the evolution of institutional research and its role within the management of higher education institutions. Similarly, the use of business maturity models can provide some further understanding of the stages of the evolution of institutional research within any institution. This can help to maximize the useful impact of institutional research and enhance the efficiency of operation; it can also provide a yardstick by which the contribution of institutional research can be measured. In this chapter, three different models have been presented, one guided by ideas of business process orientation, one focused on the development of institutional research as a professional activity, and the third centered upon business process maturity. There are no "rights" and "wrongs" in these models—instead, they may be tailored to reflect local circumstances and priorities. Similarly, within the world of higher education, business models of this kind should not be used in a slavish or formulaic way—instead, they can provide a helpful tool to be used to inform, to guide, and to stimulate thought. They do not offer a definitive route-map for the evolution of institutional research, but, given the changes that have already occurred in the practice of institutional research, they can help higher education institutions to take stock of both the present position and possible future trajectories.

Acknowledgments

The author wishes to acknowledge the contribution of Margarida Mano in the preparation of this chapter.

References

Brumbaugh, A. J. (1960). *Research designed to improve institutions of higher learning*, Washington, DC: The American Council on Higher Education.

Caldeira, M. M., & Romão, M. J. (2002). Estratégias de investigação em sistemas de informação organizacionais–a utilização de métodos qualitativos. *Portuguese Journal of Management Studies, 7*(1), 77–97.

Costa, J. (2000). *Sistemas de Apoio à Decisão*, FEUC, University of Coimbra, Portugal.

Cowley, W. H. (1960). Two and a half centuries of institutional research. In R. G. Axt & H. T. Sprague (Eds.), *College self studies: Lectures on institutional research* (pp. 1–16), Boulder, CO: Western Interstate Commission on Higher Education

Day, G. S. (1994). The capabilities of market-driven organizations. *Journal of Marketing*, October, *58*(4), 37–52.

De Bruin, T., Freeze, R., Kaulkarni, U., & Rosemann, M. (2005). Understanding the main phases of developing a maturity assessment model. In B. Campbell, J. Underwood, & D. Bunker (Eds.), *Australasian Conference on Information Systems, 2005*, Sydney, AU.

Dorfman, M., & Thayer, R. H. (1997). The capability maturity model for software. In M. Dorfman & R. H. Thayer (Eds.), *Software engineering* (pp. 427–438), Los Alamos, CA: IEEE Computer Society.

Fisher, D. M., (2004). *The business process maturity model: A practical approach for identifying opportunities for optimization*, BP Trends: BearingPoint Inc.

Galliers, R. (1992). *Information systems research: Issues, methods and practical guidelines*, Oxford, UK: Blackwell Scientific Publications.

Hammer, M., (1996). *Beyond reengineering: How the process-centered organization is changing our lives*, New York, NY: Harper Business.

Keen, P. (1987). Decision support systems: The next decade. *Decision Support Systems, 3*, 253–265.

Le Moign, J. (1978). La Theorie du systeme d'information organizational. *Informatique et Gestion, 101*, 25–31, 39–42, & 102.

Lockamy III, A., & McCormack, K. (2004). The development of a supply chain management process maturity model using the concepts of business process orientation. *Supply Chain Management, 9*(4), 272–278.

Luftman, J. (2000). Assessing business-IT alignment maturity. *Communications of the Association for Information Systems, 4*(14), 99.

Mano, M. (2007). *Proposal for a governance decision-making model in a Portuguese Public University*. Unpublished thesis for the degree of PhD, University of Southampton, UK.

Neave, G. (1988). On the cultivation of quality, efficiency and enterprise: An overview of recent trends in higher education in Western Europe, 1986–1988. *European Journal of Education, 23*, 7–23.

Paulk, M., Weber, C., Garcia-Miller, S., Chrissis, M., & Bush, M. (1993). Key practices of the Capability Maturity Model version 1.1 (CMU/SEI-93-TR-025), Software Engineering Institute, Carnegie Mellon University, retrieved from www.sei.cmu.edu/library/abstracts/reports/93tr025.cfm.

Porter, M. E. (1985). *Competitive advantage: Creating and sustaining superior performance*, New York, NY: Free Press.

Power, M. (1997). *The audit society*, Oxford, UK: Oxford University Press.

Rourke, F. E., & Brooks, G. E. (1966). *The managerial revolution in higher education*, Baltimore, MD: Johns Hopkins University Press.

Schultheis, R., & Sumner, M. (1995). *Management information systems—The manager's view*, New York, NY: Richard D. Irwin Publishing.

Serban, A. M. (2002). Knowledge management: The fifth face of institutional research. In A. M. Serban & J. Luan (Eds.), *Knowledge management: Building a competitive advantage in higher education. New Directions for Institutional Research, No. 113* (pp. 105–111), San Francisco, CA: Jossey-Bass.

Taylor, J., Hanlon, M., & Yorke, M. (2013). *The evolution and practice of institutional research*. In A. Calderon & K. L. Webber (Eds.), *Global issues of institutional research, New Directions in Institutional Research, No. 157* (pp. 59–75), San Francisco, CA: Jossey Bass.

Terenzini, P. T. (1993). On the nature of institutional research and the knowledge skills it requires. *Research in Higher Education, 34*(1), 1–10.

Terkla, D. G. (2008). Editor's notes. In D. G. Terkla (Ed.), *Institutional research: More than just data, New Directions for Higher Education, No. 104* (pp. 9–19), San Francisco, CA: Jossey-Bass.

Volkwein, J. F. (1999). The four faces of institutional research. In J. F. Volkwein (Ed.), *What is institutional research all about? A critical and comprehensive assessment of the profession. New Directions for Institutional Research, No. 104* (pp. 9–19), San Francisco, CA: Jossey-Bass.

Volkwein, J. F., Liu, Y., & Woodell, J. (2012). The structure and functions of institutional research offices. In R. Howard, G. McLaughlin, & W. Knight (Eds.), *The handbook of institutional research* (pp. 22–39), San Francisco, CA: Jossey Bass.

18

EYES TO THE FUTURE

Challenges Ahead for Institutional Research and Planning

Karen L. Webber

Concluding Thoughts

In the proceeding chapters, colleagues around the world who have been instrumental in establishing or strengthening tasks related to institutional research (IR), planning, and decision support have discussed a number of important issues. They provide thoughtful comments, documentation on the current status of IR and planning in regions around the world, and they offer sage advice for the future.

We know that the tasks related to institutional research vary by region of the world and take on a variety of names. As mentioned in chapter 1 of this book, there are vast differences in the composition, governance structure, and funding arrangements of higher education institutions (HEIs) and that makes a single IR typology rather impossible. Yet the tasks related to IR are increasingly important to senior administrative officials and we see a subsequent increase in recognition of the IR function across many parts of the world.

Common titles for a college or university administrative unit that has responsibility for some IR issues include 'institutional research,' 'planning,' 'academic management support,' 'quality assurance,' 'assessment,' and/or 'institutional effectiveness.' IR professionals may be charged with responsibility for a limited number of related tasks, or they may be responsible for the full range. Shown in Figure 18.1, Volkwein's (2008) Golden Triangle seems to fit many instances of IR around the world. Even if there are not formal organizational relationships articulated, individuals in (1) institutional research and analysis, (2) planning and budgeting, and (3) assessment, effectiveness, and accreditation find value and economy in working together to provide information for all three of these very important areas.

Institutional Reporting
& Policy Analysis

IR
Golden
Triangle

Planning, Enrollment
& Financial
Management

Quality Assurance, Outcomes
Assessment, Program Review,
Effectiveness, Accreditation

FIGURE 18.1 The Golden Triangle of Institutional Research Analysis

Source: Volkwein, 2008. © Wiley Periodicals, Inc.

IR has evolved in different parts of the world at different rates. While the US and parts of Europe have longer and more formally established roles in IR, other regions of the world such as Latin America, Asia, and the Middle East and Northern Africa (MENA) are in the early stages of growing the IR function. Some, like the MENA region, have quickly acknowledged the value of IR and planning and have enthusiastically grown its roles, responsibilities, and need for knowledgeable professionals. From massification experienced in many regions, considerations of access, diminished funds, and the growing needs for accountability, senior leaders at colleges and universities around the world have come to see clearly the value and need for skilled individuals who can provide the array of decision support tasks.

Contemporary higher education institutions are faced with new challenges including economic reductions; debates on the public versus private good or value of higher education; rapidly changing technologies that require substantial funds for the purchase of new equipment and for personnel training; how to balance the missions of teaching, research, and service; increasing requirements for quality assurance and institutional rankings; and the role of online education and MOOCs. Happily, IR officials have the knowledge and skills to strongly assist in providing support information to many of these issues faced today.

Regardless of the range of tasks that one endeavors, all roles related to IR require staff members to strive toward mastery of the three tiers of intelligence (Terenzini, 2013). These skills and knowledge resonate so well with many IR professionals: thus why the three tiers are mentioned in several chapters of this book. Terenzini (2013) reminds us of the value in understanding and mastering the **technical and analytic skills**. He reminds us that it is equally important to understand the **issues** that are fundamental to higher education. And it is critical that all who wish to be or become effective IR professionals deeply understand the specifics of higher education in the particular location and institution to integrate the issues within the **context**. As we discussed in chapter 1 of this volume, contextual intelligence remains valid and it requires a much broader focus and a stronger emphasis on the awareness and analysis of an institution's state, national, and international environments. Also as mentioned, we believe the ability for IR practitioners to interpret, adapt, and influence policy makers is vital for their ongoing professional success. This comes through mastery of skills, knowledge of issues related to higher education in general, and the specific context of one's institution.

While the needs for general knowledge about higher education remain the foundational dimension for the work IR practitioners and planners perform, the need for attention to detail and technical expertise is often underestimated. The more information that is collected, the greater the complexities in managing it; and yet it exponentially widens the scope for analysis and it provides an opportunity for exploring new possibilities and for fostering institutional innovation. We are of the view that for this innovation to occur requires IR practitioners to have a very good understanding of the data as well as the ability to interpret and draw inferences about a variety of internal and external data sources. Furthermore, it also requires that decision makers provide support, vision, and commitment in resources for the objectives institutions seek to achieve. IR practitioners need to develop and enhance their skills so they are effective in combining qualitative and quantitative approaches in the fulfillment of their professional duties. As mentioned in the NASH report (Gagliardi & Wellman, 2014), good IR also requires practitioners to have a good understanding of public policy and the forces of change that impact HE.

As mentioned in chapter 1, the roles assumed by IR depend on the environment and boundaries that prevail within the HEI. Generally, governments have enacted legislation for institutions to provide information about how institutions spend public funds and how HEIs are transforming the lives of those people who benefit. In some regions, the central role of IR has been cemented through these legislated requirements for institutions to provide statistical information. Historically, IR and planning offices have been charged with responsibility in extracting, validating, and reporting institutional data that has been transformed into usable information. Having access to information, tools, and methods for analysis has underpinned the foundation for IR. It provides the avenue to endeavor a range of studies related to institutional performance and effectiveness as well as a foundation for institutional repositioning and setting strategic directions. These are indeed the common threads that define the practice of IR and planning whether it is undertaken in an institution based in North America, Europe, Latin America, South Africa, or Asia.

It seems that each day brings a new discussion on electronic listservs, higher education news publications, or books on globalization of higher education. Notable recent publications include:

- *Globalization of Higher Education* by Joel Spring (2014);
- *The Future of a Post-Massified University System at the Crossroads* by Jung Shin and Ulrich Teichler (2014);

- *Higher Education in America* by Derek Bok (2014);
- *Globalization and Education: Integration and Contestation across Cultures* by Nelly P. Stromquist and Karen Monkman (2014);
- *Higher Education in the Global Age: Policy, Practice and Promise in Emerging Societies* by Daniel Araya and Peter Marber (2014); and
- *The International Imperative in Higher Education* by Phillip Altbach (2013).

Previous chapters in this book detail the roles and status of IR, planning, and quality assurance around the world. Clearly, the set of tasks related to IR have grown and continue to increase in importance. Knowledgeable, skilled, and enthusiastic IR practitioners are needed in all sectors of higher education across the world. Global higher education is requiring us to reconsider some of the missions, goals, and traditions that have occurred in local higher education in previous decades and centuries. IR officials can provide valuable assistance in using information about today's higher education to consider our future. Shin and Teichler (2014) remind us that, "the complexities of contemporary higher education cannot be reduced to a single theoretical framework. University development is the result of continuous interactions between new ideas, environments, and historical institutional forms. Policymakers tend to emphasize new ideas and environmental changes as the logical grounds for their reform policy" (p. 4).

Shin and Teichler (2014) further believe that looking to the future in higher education means developing scenarios for a "post world-class university" higher education system and a "post-massified" higher education system. They also ponder the possibility of a future higher education system that is not the servant of the most powerful current political ideology but, rather, can serve a multitude of approaches through a creative balance. They suggest that this requires both a realistic and an idealistic discourse, and more projects like HELF (Higher Education Looking Forward), sponsored by the European Science Foundation (ESF). This project concluded that "forward-look" projects are a promising way to explore the possible futures of technology and society, as well as possible futures of research in the respective areas (Shin & Teichler, 2014).

Researchers in the European higher education community (e.g., Brennan, Enders, Musselin, Teichler, & Valimaa, 2008; Brennan & Teichler, 2008) raised the following salient future issues: What concepts of "knowledge society" will shape the future discussions, and what kind of developments are to be expected in society with respect to the utilization of knowledge as compared to internal knowledge developments in the system of higher education and research?

- In light of expansion, how will higher education change its role in relation to social equity, social justice, social cohesion, and meritocracy? Will there be an increasing divide between winners and losers of higher education expansion, or will efforts succeed in reducing social inequities with the help of education?

- Will higher education move toward more comprehensive functions both by widening the activities beyond knowledge production and dissemination, as the discussions about the "third mission" of higher education suggest, and by including more "stakeholders" into the decision-making processes, or will higher education consider such movements as a "mission overload?"
- How will management of the higher education system change as the consequence of future challenges: will governments play an even stronger role than in the past, will there be a coexistence of strong governmental and university strategies, will market forces play a stronger role, will autonomy of institutions of higher education increase, or will another mix of steering occur?
- What will the future structure of the higher education system look like? Will national higher education systems in the process of expansion become extremely stratified, as, for example, the discussion about "world-class universities" and rankings suggest, or do we note moves toward a relatively "flat hierarchy" and toward a variety of "profiles" of the individual universities?

Indeed, our colleagues who spend their days in more focused educational research will contemplate these questions more deeply than most practitioners in IR, but there is a need and an available synergy that can occur between IR and education research colleagues. When possible, IR practitioners should take advantage of opportunities to partner with educational researchers.

The Future of Institutional Research and Its Practitioners

Again, we emphasize the IR practitioner's need for attention to detail, statistical and technical expertise, and an understanding of the issues that is embedded in the HEI specific context. The more information that is collected, the greater the complexities in managing it; and yet it exponentially widens the scope for analysis and it provides an opportunity for exploring new possibilities and for fostering institutional innovation. Good analytic work such as this requires IR practitioners to have a very good understanding of the data as well as the ability to interpret and draw inferences about the data, synthesizing information from a variety of internal and external data sources. It also requires that decision makers provide support, vision, and commitment in resources for the objectives institutions seek to achieve. IR practitioners need to develop and enhance their skills so they are effective in combining qualitative and quantitative approaches in the fulfillment of their professional duties. It also requires them to have a good understanding of public policy, and the forces of change that have an impact on higher education. This is the future of institutional research in higher education, and this enhanced role will enable senior academic leaders to further increase the positive perceptions they hold about IR and planning.

Broadening the Practice of IR

Although some individuals in state and national government systems may perform IR tasks, the broad scope of IR has generally been confined to the boundaries of an institution (Maasen & Sharma, 1985). The focus of IR has been to complete self-studies for institutional improvement and effectiveness and to undertake some specialized research to investigate relevant issues that have an impact on the institution. However, this scope is being further broadened as there is a growing number of institutions globally that operate beyond and across multiple national borders. Additionally, institutions are part of national systems of education and respond to varying national policy imperatives, plus institutions have formal strategic alliances with like institutions (either within a region or within national borders or even internationally).

There is also a growing trend for IR practitioners to undertake studies within and across industry sectors (and in other domains) that require specialized knowledge residing outside IR and planning offices. In this regard, the decision-making process at the institutional level is not only multi-layered across these various entities (some which may also respond to different legislative, accreditation, and reporting requirements, among many other things), but it is also dispersed across stakeholders within and outside the institution. In turn, this requires that IR practitioners be aware of the wider spectrum of institutional activities, strategic intent, and policy within the education industry and across industries over multiple jurisdictions. Further, traditional models of university governance are progressively being transformed so that universities are becoming not only strategic actors competing in decentralized markets in a comparable manner to private companies, but are also knowledge production actors supporting public policy goals of government, with an ever increased public accountability, but with shrinking government financial support. These profound reforms in HE are changing the nature and characteristics of institutional management and the way activities are planned, developed, and assessed. These changes are having an impact on the roles, functions, service, and purpose of IR. Dedicated IR practitioners are not only required to adapt and embrace not only new forms of day-to-day operations, but need to respond by broadening and deepening their skills so they can be effective in the emerging workplace models resulting out of ongoing reforms taking place worldwide.

IR practitioners can operate across several functional units and perform various roles within the university, including admissions, marketing, registration, quality, assessment, and strategic planning. While this can be positive, it may hinder professional progress, as it is reliant on knowledge expertise as opposed to management expertise. IR practitioners are not alone in this dilemma of the roles and functions performed by most blended professionals as described by Whitchurch (2009). Blended professionals, like those who perform IR functions, can be characterized by not having a defined identity within the realm of institutions. In some respects, perhaps this broader identity can be advantageous to the practice of IR, as it can be an incentive for innovative work practices and for pursuing exploratory and speculative research to advance the institution's mission, and play an active role in shaping HE policy generally.

Reflecting on the current status of IR and planning gives one pause to consider our role and where we are heading. Often, IR practitioners wear many hats and generally own none. They are active in shaping strategic directions for the institutions but are behind the scenes (some even call it 'back room' workers); often they are agents of change but are not directly involved when the crunch comes to making a decision. IR practitioners are, unlike those who perform defined roles and functions within the institution (e.g., marketing; student services or career counselors), at the mercy of decision makers.

While it is an identity issue, it is most important to consider how IR practitioners define their role for the future. Given the hierarchical structure of institutions, many IR practitioners are, in the formal sense, one, two, or more layers removed from the inner sanctum of institutional decision making. In the informal sense, IR practitioners are closer to the formal decision making or influential in the shaping of policies, but are often seen as simply data providers. The reality is that there are many data gatherers across the institutions but IR practitioners tend to be distillers, weavers, interpreters, and policy builders. Perhaps, however, IR practitioners are closer to, or should strive to be positioned closer to, the core of decision making.

Expand the Footprint

In chapter 17 of this volume, Kalkarni, Calderon, and Douglas discuss how the decision support functions in IR can contribute to the existing and growing educational footprint. Current roles call for the IR practitioner to develop robust, defensible, verifiable, and measurable indicators to ascertain the extent and magnitude of institutional goal completion, and, thus success. Comprehensively, these indicators of success identify for the institution—and, collectively, the higher education sector—its knowledge footprint. Indicators also enable HEIs to compare their current performance to past performance, and against national or international comparisons, as a basis for developing strategy and planning future investments. There are opportunities to leverage new technologies and data systems to ensure timely data collection and analysis to support decision making.

The Kalkarni et al. framework has good potential use. Decisions on how it is used and its ultimate purpose can link the footprint analysis into institutional planning cycles. For example, at the start of a planning cycle, some preliminary indication of the size of the footprint that an institution wishes to develop (or maintain) could be made, informed by institutional objectives and the conditioning factors outlined above. This could then inform the various elements of institutional activity to align with those goals. In a sense, this is analogous to broad "budget envelopes" that government policy makers manage with regard to key objectives and competing claims on scarce resources. That is, the footprint thus provides an important frame of reference for planning by linking institutional objectives and constraints (financial, physical, human capital). It allows for key trade-offs to be assessed and judgments to be made in planning about the relative benefits and costs of expanding a footprint or altering its parameters.

Given there are existing and evolving means to measure and report HEI performance, it will also be important for institutional researchers and planners to consider how to leverage existing thinking, and this could include development (or augment) of an institutional ranking scheme based on footprint analysis. Such a rankings system would examine the broad impact of an institution on the economy and society, and mark a departure from current arrangements that tend to focus on a narrow range of HEI inputs/outputs.

Strive for Tier 3 Intelligence

Contributing to a greater knowledge footprint also produces higher contextual intelligence (Terenzini, 2013). Proficient performance at this level requires mastery of skills and knowledge in the techniques and institutional issues, but is also requires one to "blend those two intelligence sets in a detailed and nuanced grasp of the context and culture of a particular IR operation—the institution where IR professionals practice their craft" (p. 143). Mastery of Tier 3 requires the knowledge of the institution's past and consideration of where it is heading in the future, it requires one to understand formal and informal organizational structures and cultures, and it requires one to synthesize knowledge of the broad events happening in the world with the specifics that are omnipresent at one's specific institution. Through regular reading of scholarly materials and engagement in collegial discussions, mastery of Tier 3 requires an appreciation for the current issues that ubiquitously compete for attention—access, completion, quality assurance, reduced external resources, and global growth being at the top of the list.

I agree with Terenzini's (2013) suggestion that colleges and universities, individually and collectively, must respond and contribute more meaningfully to national and international discussions related to the important issues of higher education. This need positions IR practitioners perfectly. Striving for Tier 3 can lead institutional researchers and planners to provide data-based information that can lead to informed decisions and institutional effectiveness. The future is bright for institutional research and planning in higher education. Institutions in some parts of our world have woven it into the fabric of its daily operations, and in other parts of the world it is growing in visibility and importance. Those practitioners who leverage their previous analytic skills, and knowledge of the institution and the sector with thoughtful consideration of the future of higher education can provide a strong contribution, and thus provide effective decision support.

As we look to the future of IR and planning in higher education across the world, IR practitioners may be inspired by this quote:

Did is a word of achievement,
Won't is a word of retreat,
Might is a word of bereavement,
Can't is a word of defeat,
Ought is a word of duty,
Try is a word of each hour,
Will is a word of beauty,
Can is a word of power.
　　　　　—Unknown Author

References

Brennan, J., Enders, J., Musselin, C., Teichler, U., & Valimaa, J. (2008). *Higher education looking forward: An agenda for future research.* Strasbourg, France: European Science Foundation.

Brennan, J., & Teichler, U. (2008). Special issue: The future of higher education and the future of higher education research. *Higher Education, 56*(3), 259–264.

Gagliardi, J., & Wellman, J. (2014). *Meeting demands for improvements in public system institutional research. Progress Report on the NASH Project in IR.* Washington, DC: National Association of System Heads.

Maasen, P., & Sharma, R. (1985). *What is institutional research? A primer on institutional research in Australasia.* Melbourne, AU: Australasian Association for Institutional Research.

Shin, J. C., & Teichler, U. (2014). *The future of the post-massifed university at the crossroads.* Basel, Switzerland: Springer International Publishing.

Terenzini, P. (2013). "On the nature of institutional research" revisited: Plus ca change? *Research in Higher Education, 54*, 137–148.

Volkwein, J. F. (2008). *The foundations and evolution of institutional research.* In D. G. Terkla (Ed.), *Institutional research: More than just data. New Directions for Higher Education, No. 141* (pp. 5–20). San Francisco, CA: Jossey-Bass/Wiley.

Whitchurch, C. (2009). The rise of the blended professional in higher education: A comparison between the United Kingdom, Australia and the United States. *Higher Education, 58*(3), 407–418.

CONTRIBUTORS

Victor M. H. Borden is professor of educational leadership and policy studies at Indiana University Bloomington and also serves as a senior advisor within University Academic Affairs. Dr. Borden previously led institutional research units at the system and campus levels. He publishes, conducts workshops, and lectures internationally on topics related to developing evidence-informed and inquiry-guided administrative capacities in higher education institutions. He is a past president of the Association for Institutional Research.

Jan Botha taught Hellenistic Greek at different universities in South Africa during the first two decades of his career. He then worked for 15 years in different positions in university administration at Stellenbosch University, initially as director of the Unit for Staff and Curriculum Development and then as Director of Institutional Research and Planning. He participated in the development of the national Quality Assurance system in Higher Education in South Africa during the 2000s and served as president of the Southern African Association for Institutional Research from 2008–2012. In 2014 he became a faculty member again when he joined the Centre for Research of Evaluation, Science and Technology at Stellenbosch University.

Sandra (Sandi) Bramblett is executive director of Institutional Research and Planning/Decision Support Services at the Georgia Institute of Technology. She has served as president of the Association for Institutional Research as well as the Southern Association for Institutional Research. Her areas of interest are enterprise data management and decision support, finance, student success, and higher education policy.

Angel J. Calderon is the principal advisor of Planning and Research at RMIT University. He has over 30 years of professional experience in higher education, journalism, and consulting. He was co-editor of the *Journal of Institutional Research* (1998–2001) and the *Journal of Higher Education Policy and Management* (2001–2007). In 2013, he was co-editor of a special edition of *New Directions for Institutional Research* on global issues in institutional research.

Hamish Coates is a professor of Higher Education at the Centre for the Study of Higher Education (CSHE), University of Melbourne. He was Founding Director of Higher Education Research at the Australian Council for Educational Research (ACER) from 2006 to 2013, and between 2010 and 2013 also program director at the LH Martin Institute for Tertiary Leadership and Management. Hamish completed his PhD in 2005 at the University of Melbourne, and executive training at INSEAD in 2012. His interests include large-scale evaluation, tertiary education policy, institutional strategy, outcomes assessment, learner engagement, academic work and leadership, quality assurance, tertiary admissions, and assessment methodology. He has initiated and led many successful projects, and was Founding International Director of OECD's Assessment of Higher Education Learning Outcomes (AHELO) Feasibility Study.

Amber Douglas works at RMIT University in Melbourne, Australia, in its Policy and Planning Group. She has a discipline background in humanities, law, and public policy and worked in industry and skills policy roles for the Australian and Victorian Governments, and supported performance and governance management for a local authority in the UK.

Peter Hoekstra is Institutional Research Coordinator at the University of Amsterdam. He has been working in the field of IR as head of one of the first Offices of IR in Europe and as leader of a number of projects in this field within the university and in cooperation with other institutions. He currently leads UvAdata, the university's data warehouse project, and UvA Q, a project that is harmonizing and developing the university's course and program evaluations. He was chair of the Dutch Association for IR (DAIR) and is member of the Executive Committee of the European Association for IR (EAIR).

Richard D. Howard directed institutional research offices and taught at West Virginia University, North Carolina State University, the University of Arizona, and the University of Minnesota, and was a professor at Montana State University. He served as president and forum chair of AIR and the Southern Association for Institutional Research, and editor of *Resources in Institutional Research*. His areas of interest include mixed methodologies, student success, and faculty governance.

Jeroen Huisman is professor of Higher Education at the Centre for Higher Education Governance Ghent, Ghent University. Before that, he was professor of Higher Education Management at the University of Bath, UK (2005–2013) and PhD student and senior researcher at the Center for Higher Education Policy Studies, University of Twente, Netherlands (1991–2005). He is editor of *Higher Education Policy* and co-editor of the SRHE Higher Education book series. He is on the editorial board of several higher education journals and chair of the European Association for Institutional Research. His research interests relate to issues of policy and governance of and in higher education.

Manja Klemenčič is Lecturer in Sociology in the Faculty of Arts and Sciences, Harvard University. She is also editor-in-chief of *European Journal of Higher Education* (Routledge). She researches, teaches, and consults in the area of higher education studies, especially on student experience and engagement, institutional research, conditions of academic work and faculty climate, institutional profiling, and internationalization. Manja frequently acts as higher education consultant, and expert to international organizations, governments, universities, and quality assurance and accreditation agencies.

Jang Wan Ko is associate professor in the Department of Education, and director of the Center for Institutional Effectiveness at Sungkyunkwan University in Korea. He served as senior research associate in the Office of Institutional Research and Reporting at George Mason University in the US. He is currently a member of the Advisory Committee for the Ministry of Education in Korea and serves as executive director for the Korean Association for Higher Education.

Janja Komljenovič is a research assistant and Marie Curie PhD Fellow in the EU Marie Curie Research Network 'Universities in the Knowledge Economy.' Her research project is about higher education resectoralization and she is working on mapping higher education industries by using multi-scalar analytics. In the past she researched European higher education, the concept of university autonomy, repurposing of the university, and higher education reforms in the Western Balkans. Before she engaged in academic research, she was a part of European and Slovenian policy making in higher education.

Anand Kulkarni is senior manager, Planning and Research, RMIT University, overseeing strategic planning, policy development and co-ordination, advice to government, and strategic projects. Prior to this he held senior management and executive positions in the Commonwealth and State Government in Australia. His research interests include innovation, industry development, Asian economies, and higher education, and has published in these areas. He holds Honors Bachelor's, Master's, and a PhD in Economics.

Marian Mahat has 15 years of professional and academic experience working in the higher education sector, including several Australian universities, the Australian Tertiary Education Quality and Standards Agency (TEQSA), the LH Martin Institute for Tertiary Leadership and Management, and recently at the Centre for the Study of Higher Education (CSHE). She has made a significant contribution to higher education both at institutional and national levels through developing evidence-based strategic policy, providing advice to institutional leaders and policy makers, as well as conducting analyses of issues affecting the higher education sector. Her research interests include strategic leadership and management in higher education, quality assurance and performance indicators in higher education, university rankings and league tables, and learning outcomes.

Charles Mathies is currently the senior expert (advisor) in the division of strategic planning and development at the University of Jyväskylä, Finland. He has held several university management positions in Europe and the United States. He has published, presented, and taught in Europe and North America on topics of institutional research, student retention and completion, university rankings, university governance, and university research funding. He is also a co-founder and partner in an international higher education consulting firm specializing in data management and assisting universities in linking data to strategic decision making.

Gerald W. McLaughlin worked in institutional research at the US Military Academy and directed IR offices at Virginia Tech and DePaul University. He served as president and forum chair of AIR and the Southern Association for Institutional Research and edited several publications for AIR. He has also published, presented, and been active in SCUP, CSRDE, and EDUCAUSE. His areas of interest include data management, methodology, and student success.

Diane Nauffal is assistant professor in the Department of Education and founding director of the Office of Institutional Research and Assessment at the Lebanese American University. She served as president of the Lebanese Association for Educational Studies and has been active in national research groups on higher education for over a decade. She is currently a member of the National Task Force for University Governance for the Ministry of Education and Higher Education in Lebanon, and an active member of the Association for Institutional Research.

Pablo Opazo studied business and has a Master's in social psychology with emphasis on research methodologies. He is currently a consultant in institutional analysis and professor on the course for business intelligence at the University of Talca, Chile. Mr. Opazo has participated in several institutional research networks in Chile and Latin America and was a visiting researcher at the University of Ottawa, Canada. He has also presented at conferences and special events in Chile, Argentina, Brazil, Nicaragua, and Canada.

María Pita-Carranza has a Master's in politics and administration of education from Universidad Nacional de Tres de Febrero. She is director of institutional quality and researcher of the School of Education at Universidad Austral in Argentina. Her current research topics and concerns are about quality of higher education, rankings, and information management in Latin America—particularly in Argentina—with an "institutional research" approach. Latterly, she has been promoting the creation of a Latin American Association for Institutional Research.

F. Mauricio Saavedra has a PhD in higher education with an emphasis in research methods and institutional research from the Institute of Higher Education at the University of Georgia. He is, currently, the executive director of institutional research at California Polytechnic State University and serves on the board of directors for the Association of Institutional Research (AIR). He was formerly the director of institutional research and research for the social sciences and humanities at Universidad Internacional del Ecuador (UIDE) in Quito. During his time in Ecuador, he taught courses and conducted seminars related to research methods and provided consulting services to the Ministry of Higher Education in Ecuador in relation to the national information system for higher education.

Ninoslav Ščukanec is the founder of the Institute for the Development of Education in Zagreb, Croatia, where he has served as executive director since 1999. His main expertise lies in financing of higher education and in the internationalization and the social dimension of higher education. He currently researches the links between equity and quality assurance in higher education, as well as the development of institutional research in Central and Eastern Europe. He has often served as consultant and education expert in various government bodies and professional organizations working on the reform and development of higher education.

Randy L. Swing is executive director of the Association for Institutional Research (AIR), a nonprofit membership association serving over 4200 members from 1500 postsecondary institutions. AIR provides professional development on institutional research assessment, and conducts a national training program for IPEDS reporters and users. He is a frequent speaker at national and international conferences and author of books and articles on assessment, institutional research, and student success. Prior to joining AIR he held leadership positions at the Policy Center on the First Year of College and also at Appalachian State University. He holds a PhD from the University of Georgia.

John Taylor is professor of Higher Education Management at the University of Liverpool, UK. A historian by origin, he worked for over 20 years in university management before moving into an academic career teaching and researching in the area of higher education management and policy. His main research interests lie in strategy and organization, leadership, performance indicators, the management of research, the role of higher education in developing countries, and the history of higher education. As director of the Higher Education Management Studies Unit, University of Liverpool, he leads management development programs for universities in many different countries around the world.

Karen L. Webber is an associate professor in the Institute of Higher Education at the University of Georgia. Prior to her move to a full-time faculty position in 2003, she was interim associate provost for institutional effectiveness at UGA. She spent over 20 years in the field of institutional research at the University of Delaware and the University of Georgia and remains active in professional associations related to IR. Her publications and areas of research, like IR, span many facets of higher education effectiveness, including IR collaborations on college campuses, faculty productivity, the economic benefits of the doctoral degree, undergraduate programs that contribute to student success, and student financial aid.

Julie Wells is vice-principal, Policy and Projects, at the University of Melbourne, Australia, where she has responsibility within the Chancellery for strategy and planning, governance, risk, policy, and projects. She has worked as a teacher, historian, and in government. Between 1996 and 2002, she headed the policy and research unit within the National Tertiary Education Union, which represents university staff in Australia.

Steve Woodfield is associate professor in Higher Education at Kingston University, London, in the UK. He is a member of the planning group of the UK and Ireland Higher Education Institutional Research Network (HEIR). His research focuses on the policy and institutional management dimensions of the internationalization, funding and regulation, senior management structures, and IR projects for universities on a range of HE policy issues. He also engages in policy development and evaluation projects in his areas of expertise, for both national governments and policy agencies.

Mantz Yorke is visiting professor in the Department of Educational Research, Lancaster University, UK. A varied career in education evolved into a period of six years as a senior manager at Liverpool Polytechnic, followed by two years on secondment as director of Quality Enhancement at the Higher Education Quality Council in the UK. Returning to Liverpool (by now John Moores University), he concentrated on researching aspects of institutional performance, concentrating on "the student experience." He has published widely on higher education and is past president of the European Association for Institutional Research.

Henry Y. Zheng is currently the administrative director for Strategic Analytics at the Ohio State University Medical Center. He is responsible for leading analytics operations and decision analysis in support of enterprise-wide strategic planning, business development, market intelligence, operational improvement, and other academic and clinical operations areas. Previously, he was assistant vice president of Fiscal and Human Resources, director of Strategic Planning, and Business Performance Officer at the Ohio State University. He received both his PhD in Public Policy and Management and MBA from the Ohio State University.

INDEX

Academic Ranking of World Universities (ARWU) 31
accreditation 45
Al-Akhawayn University 149
Altbach, P. 29–30, 253, 175, 232
analytical and technical intelligence *see* technical and analytical intelligence
applied research 25
Association for Institutional Research (AIR) 21
Association of Southeast Asian Nations (ASEAN) 141
Australasian Association for Institutional Research (AAIR) 21

basic research 25
Begg, R. 60, 61
benchmarking 30, 190
bibliometric indicators 191
Bologna Process, see European Higher Education Area
Borden, V. 24, 103, 178, 189
Bradley reforms 104, 105
business intelligence: analytics 159–60, 168; concept 160; maturity models 162–5; technical capabilities 169

Calderon, A. 3, 5, 9–10, 28, 30, 34, 53, 139, 140, 153, 178, 189, 235
Center for Studies of Higher Education (CSHE, UC-Berkeley) 20
Central American University Superior Council (CSUCA) 33

Centre for the Study of Evaluation, Science and Technology (CREST) 120
Charles Sturt University 106–7
Chulalongkorn University 171
Coates, H. 104, 105, 110, 111
Common Educational Data Standards (CEDS) 46
contextual intelligence 4–5, 59, 231
Council for Higher Education Accreditation 45

dashboard 165, 170, 171
data: across national systems 30; and accountability 74, 188, 189; and exchanges 32; and ideology 194; and institutional comparisons 37; and language 35–6; and legitimacy 193–4; and transnational collaborations 32; and transparency 194; culture 35; definitions 35; demand for 71–2; equivalence 34–5; information systems 76, 77, 133–4; intended and unintended uses of 191–2; intentionality of 194–5; making sense of 193; power of, 193; relevance of 195; reporting in Canada 44; reporting in the United States 44; scope of 36; sharing of 33–4; uses of 92–3; 186–7, 193, 195
data analysis 159, 166
data management 36, 134, 142–4, 167, 168, 171
data reliability 136
decision support system 160–2, 215; concept 160; maturity process 217–19

Dialogue between Higher Education Research and Practice 61
Dill, D. D. 7, 187, 202
Dressel, Paul 21, 23

economics of education 47
educational research: and definition 16; difference to IR 18; origins 20
Erasmus+ 33
European Association for Institutional Research (EAIR): forums 62–5; origins 60–1
European Higher Education Area (EHEA) 33, 72
European Union 72
experimental development 25
Extract-Transform-Load (ETL) 162

fact books 188
File, J. 28, 71, 73, 75
Fincher, C. 21, 23
Frascati Manual 24

globalization 175,181
global university 174, 176; and aspirations 182
Goedegebuure, L. 34, 35

Harvey, L. 71,74
Hazelkorn, E. 31, 181, 187, 190, 191, 194
higher education: and accountability 125; and accreditation 129; and consortia 32; and decision making 24; and globalization 28,29; and governance 44; and homogenization 29; and massification 43, 44; and regulation 178,179; and social agenda 47; and strategic actors 193; and systems 129,148; and technology 47, 48; autonomy 71; community engagement 199, 200; drivers of change 7; economic impact of 198, 199; global enrollments 186, 187; impacts of 48, 197, 201; in Argentina 130; in Asia 139, 140; in Australia 102, 176, 189; in Brazil 130; in Canada 44; in Chile 130, 133; in Colombia 131, 133; in Ecuador 128, 131; in Europe 58; in Latin America 128, 133; in MENA region 147–8,150; in Mexico 132–3; in South Africa 116; in the United States 44; international engagement 200; Internationalization 175; legislation 48, 49; massification of 187; meaning of 3; number of institutions 187; political environment 46; self-studies 187–8;

sustainability impact of 200; tensions 7, 177
Higher Education Institutional Research (HEIR) Network 86, 88, 98
Higher Education Management Information System (HEMIS) 117
Howard, R. D. 4, 53, 65, 128, 142;
Huisman, J. 5, 9, 20, 21, 181

information management 188, 215
Institute of Higher Education (UGA) 18
institutional analysis 134
institutional diversity 192
institutional effectiveness 93
institutional mergers 119
institutional mission 177–8
institutional research 4–6; definition 50, 72, 88–9; Europe versus USA 65–6, 67; faces of 8–9, 17–18, 67, 93, 214; global development 230; identity 11–12; in Asia 140, 142, 144, 145; in Australia 103–4; in Canada 49; in Central and Eastern Europe 72–3; in China 141, 144; in Ireland 86–7, 90–1, in Japan 143, 145; in Latin America 129, 135–6; in MENA region 151–3, in South Africa 117–19; in the future 10–11, 26, 51, 125, 233; in the UK 86–90; in the United States 3, 49; measuring success of 7–8; origins 3, 6, 18–19, 213–14; practice of 6, 74, 136; purpose of 76; roles 5, 6, 8, 12, 17, 230–1; use of term 89; value of 97
Integrated Postsecondary Educational Data System (IPEDS) 45, 50, 189
Intellectual Capital Reports 75, 77–8
international students 29
Irish Universities Quality Board (IUQB) 88, 91
issues intelligence 4, 59

Jedamus, Paul 21
Jongbloed, B. 28, 75, 199, 201

King Abdallah University of Science and Technology 149
Klemenčič, M. 4, 71, 74–5
knowledge footprint: challenges 209–10; concept 202–3; framework 203–5; impact of 206; indicators 206–7; uses of 207–9
knowledge resource efficiency 205
knowledge society 232, 233
knowledge transfer 203, 205
knowledge transformation 205

knowledge translation 205
knowledge worker 49

league tables 29
Leslie, L. 28
LH Martin Institute 110

Maasen, P. 5, 10, 234
McLaughlin, G. 4, 53
Mahat, M. 110, 111
Marginson, S. 29, 175, 177–8, 181, 193–4
massification *see* higher education
Mathies, C. 3, 30, 34, 53, 78
MENA Association for Institutional
    Research (MENA-AIR) 151
metapolicy 180
Monash University 108–9
Musselin, C. 29, 187, 189, 232

National Development Plan 121
National Guidelines, *Good Practice for
    Institutional Research in Higher Education* 91
nature of institutional research 25
Neave, G. 20, 60, 67, 214
New Directions for Institutional Research 22
New Public Management (NPM) 29, 189

organizational intelligence 4
Organization of Economic Cooperation
    and Development (OECD) 24

performance indicators 189–90
PEST 203; *see also* SPEEDI analysis
planning office *see* institutional research
Professional File 23
Program for North American mobility in
    higher education 33

QS World University Rankings 31, 153, 175
quality of teaching 191–2

Reichard, D. 3, 19
relational database management systems
    (RDBMS) 162, 163
Research in Higher Education 22

Saavedra, F. M. 128, 133, 136, 151, 153
Saupe, J. 4, 21, 23, 65, 103, 151
Sharma, R. 10, 234
Sharman and Shapiro's typology 32, 33
Shin, J.C. 31, 231–2
Slaughter, S. 28–9, 199
South East Asian Association for
    Institutional Research (SEAAIR) 141

Southern Africa Association for
    Institutional Research (SAAIR) 116,
    121–2; forums 122–3
SPEEDI analysis 203
Standards and Guideline for Quality
    Assurance in the European Higher
    Education Area 73, 74
Statistics Canada (StatsCan) 45, 50
*Statistics of Land-Grant Colleges and
    Universities* 188
Stecklein, John 21
Stensaker, B. 71, 74
strategic actors 177
strategic planning 102; research-driven
    planning 105, 107; research-informed
    documentation 106–7; research-
    supported 107
student debt, United States 47
student equity 104
student feedback 192
student mobility 176
Suslow, S. 21, 23, 43, 46, 51, 54, 103
Swing, R. 5

Taylor, J. 21, 87, 89, 94, 103, 215, 218, 220
technical and analytical intelligence 4, 8,
    59, 230
Teichler, U. 24, 47, 61, 93, 231–2
Terenzini, P. 4–5, 8, 23, 59, 61, 67, 87, 92,
    106, 109, 214, 230, 236
Terenzini's tiers 4
Tertiary Education and Management
    61, 67
*Times Higher Education World University
    Rankings* 31, 175
Toutkoushian, R. 31

U-Multirank 31, 77
University of Melbourne 107
University of the Sunshine Coast 106
university rankings 29, 31, 77, 181, 190,
    192, 201
U.S. News & World Report 153, 190

van Vught, F. A. 20, 34, 35, 60, 187, 201,
    202
Volkwein, J. F. 5–6, 8, 49, 66, 67–8, 94,
    95–6, 123, 142, 151, 214, 229

web analytics 169
Webber, K. 139, 153
Whitchurch, C. 11, 234

Yorke, M. 21, 66, 86–7, 92, 94, 215, 220